In this, the definitive world's greatest stars, not just Garland the legend, but Judy the woman. Drawing on a wealth of previously unavailable material, on the intimate revelations of those who knew Judy Garland, and the memories of friends, contemporaries, and the fans who still revere her, Anne Edwards uncovers the sensational truth behind the Judy Garland legend. Always fascinating and compassionate, and often hauntingly moving, this book is the major biography that Judy Garland's incredible life deserved.

By Anne Edwards

BIOGRAPHY
Sonya: The Life of Countess Tolstoy
Vivien Leigh: A Biography
Judy Garland: A Biography
Road to Tara: The Life of Margaret Mitchell
Matriarch: Queen Mary and the House of Windsor
A Remarkable Woman: A Biography of Katharine Hepburn
(*UK title* Katharine Hepburn: A Biography)
Early Reagan: The Rise to Power
Shirley Temple: American Princess
The DeMilles: An American Family
Royal Sisters: Elizabeth and Margaret
The Grimaldis of Monaco: Centuries of Scandal/Years of Grace
Throne of Gold: The Lives of the Aga Khans
Streisand
Ever After: Diana and the Life She Led
(*UK title* Diana and the Rise of the House of Spencer)
Callas: Her Life, Her Loves, Her Music

NOVELS
The Survivors
Shadow of a Lion
Haunted Summer
Miklos Alexandrovitch is Missing
The Hesitant Heart
Child of the Night (*UK title* Raven Wings)
La Divina
Wallis: The Novel

AUTOBIOGRAPHY
The Inn and Us (with Stephen Citron)

CHILDREN'S BOOKS
P. T. Barnum
The Great Houdini
A Child's Bible

Anne Edwards' many bestsellers include *Judy Garland*; *Vivien Leigh*; *Road to Tara: The Life of Margaret Mitchell*; *Sonya: The Life of Countess Tolstoy*; *Matriarch: Queen Mary and the House of Windsor*; *Royal Sisters: Elizabeth and Margaret*; *Early Reagan: The Rise to Power* (nominated for the Pulitzer Prize); *Throne of Gold: The Lives of the Aga Khans*; *Streisand*; and *Ever After: Diana and the Rise of the House of Spencer*. She is married to the songwriter-author Stephen Citron.

Judy Garland

Anne Edwards

ORION

For Judy and for Steve
in good conscience and with love

An Orion paperback

First published in Great Britain by Constable & Company Ltd in 1975
This paperback edition published in 1996 by Orion Books Ltd,
Orion House, 5 Upper St Martin's Lane, London WC2H 9EA

Third impression
Reissued 2002

A CIP catalogue record for this book
is available from the British Library.

ISBN: 0 75280 404 9

Printed and bound in Great Britain by
Clays Ltd, St Ives plc

Contents

Part One

Somewhere ... somehow ... I want to find a place without any trouble. Do you suppose there is such a place, Toto? There must be. It's not a place you can get to by a boat or a train. It's far, far away—behind the moon, beyond the rainbow ... somewhere over the rainbow ...

–Dorothy, in *The Wizard of Oz*

Part One

CHAPTER ONE

IF Judy Garland's mother had walked for eighteen minutes she would have completely covered the east, west, north, and south of Grand Rapids, Minnesota, where her husband had purchased a small movie house. It was no wonder that a young woman who had dreamed of playing the Palace in New York would not only despair, but would – in order to survive the ordeal of being forced to live in a small, drab town – weave golden dreams of her own.

All of those dreams took her far away from the town's muddied streets, from its lineup of Model T Fords and lumber wagons, from the terror of its winter storms, and from the vulnerability of the small, unprotected white frame house in which she; her husband, Frank; and their two daughters, Virginia (Jimmy) and Sue (Susie) lived. The ugliness did not make her despair; the hopelessness did.

Born Ethel Marion Milne, in Superior, Wisconsin, one of a very large family, she was always petite and feminine, and her mother, Evelyn, favored her, giving her every advantage, transferring her own ambitions to her daughter. By the time Ethel was twelve she played the piano and sang badly, but the fantasy her mother had helped create refused to be crushed inside her small-framed body, and she grew to be a pretty woman with dreams of stardom.

While playing the piano in a local movie theater, she met a good-looking, fun-loving Irishman who hailed from Tennessee and was a tenor. His name was Frank Avent Gumm. They married on January 22, 1914, in Superior, Wisconsin. He was twenty-seven and she was twenty. They formed a vaudeville act, billing themselves as Jack and Virginia Lee,

Sweet Southern Singers, and made the vaudeville circuit in their home territory, meeting with very little success. By the time their first two children had reached school age, Frank had scraped together all he could salvage or borrow and bought the little theater in Grand Rapids, where his mother lived.

Ethel begged Frank to sell the movie house and go back on the road. He refused. Bolstered by her own aggressiveness and her new awareness of the freer role women in cities now had, she threatened to leave on her own.

It was the fall of 1921. Warren Gamaliel Harding had that year taken over the Presidency, succeeding a tired, partially invalided Wilson. Perhaps not a hick, but certainly humble, Warren Harding was redeemed in Ethel's eyes only by his imperious wife, Florence, who had already gained the name of The Duchess. It was Florence who drove her husband on to success against all obstacles. A devotee of astrology and necromancy, she believed her husband's star destined for the highest ascendancy. Ethel, though identifying with the President's lady, felt it was her star, not Frank's, that would bring her into the aureole light. She planned to leave, then discovered she was pregnant.

Frances Ethel Gumm, the future Judy Garland, was born on June 10, 1922, about the same time as Benito Mussolini marched on Rome and took up the reins of dictatorship. Not even Ethel in her greatest moments of fantasy could have imagined that her third baby would someday come to represent to a nation fighting the Fascism of Hitler and Mussolini the ideal American girl.

Ethel and Frank Gumm had actually hoped for a boy so strongly that the evening edition of the *Grand Rapids Independent* carried an announcement of the birth of Francis Gumm, Jr., born to Mr. Francis Gumm, owner and manager of the New Grand Theatre, and Mrs. Gumm. This was corrected on the child's birth certificate, but Frank could not help showing his disappointment.

Soon, however, this third daughter became his favorite, and he called her 'Baby'. She was a snub-nosed, homely baby, who seldom cried and seemed almost unable to contain her great joy at being alive.

Had Ethel not been longing for a glamour that Grand Rapids could not rise to, it is entirely possible that 'Baby' Gumm would have grown up in that small town and married a local boy. That would not have been an unhappy choice in Frank Gumm's opinion. But Ethel's fantasies drew her on, and eventually 'Baby' with her.

As Ethel looked around her, she saw all the young people deserting Grand Rapids for the big cities. Throughout the country a feeling of optimism and prosperity prevailed, and the American Woman appeared to be liberated. At least she could smoke, wiggle the Charleston on a tabletop and travel unchaperoned.

Ethel followed the lives of the famous in magazines and in the tabloid press. She was an avid admirer of the Fitzgeralds, though she never read a line F. Scott wrote. She found Hemingway romantic but she was not sure what sort of books he had written. Hollywood and the films were the only glamorous world she could identify with.

Sitting in her husband's movie-house matinee after matinee while her mother-in-law minded her brood, Ethel studied Chaplin, Lloyd, and Keaton as intently as if she were cramming for a university degree. Her determination was to be admired, and her own realization that she did not have the beauty or genius to make it on her own, to be respected. Her predatory eye had already roved away from Frank. He was good, and hardworking – the least creditable traits Ethel could imagine, especially when out in Hollywood one Rodolfo Alfonzo Raffaeli Pierre Filibert Guglielme di Valentina d'Antonguolla, better known as Rudolph Valentino, had captured the American housewife with an image of dash and daring. Frank Gumm could not be expected to carry any woman off to great adventure. It was, therefore, up to Ethel herself.

Gathering all the ammunition she could, which seemed to be the asset of three daughters, each of whom might grow to be the beauty or great talent she was not, Ethel began her first steps on what was to be her great adventure. She convinced Frank that what his movie house needed was a 'live act' every Saturday afternoon. Using all the knowledge she had picked up from the film comedies she had been studying, she proceeded to work out an act for Susie and Jimmy, then eight and five respectively (Baby remaining in the care of Grandmother Gumm). Child stars were all the rage in Hollywood. Ethel set her hopes high, but after only a few performances of 'The Gumm Sisters' those hopes began to slip. Even at the New Grand Theatre in Grand Rapids, Minnesota, the girls could not be called a smash act. But their mother persevered.

It was on a Saturday night during the Christmas season of 1924 that Baby made her debut. She was two and a half years old and seated on her grandmother's lap watching her sisters perform as her mother accompanied them. She began to cry, wanting to be with her sisters, who were onstage. Her grandmother, hoping to quiet her, carried her to the stage and set her down on the edge. Ethel was furious. 'Get off. Get off!' she called from the pit, where she was playing the piano. Susie and Jimmy froze, not knowing what to do. The audience began to laugh and applaud. Baby laughed and applauded, edging toward her sisters, slipping and tumbling, rising to her feet with Chaplinesque genius, mimicking all the gestures she had watched her mother instruct her sisters to employ in their act. The audience called out for her to sing. Frank Gumm started out onto the stage to carry her off; but before he reached her, she began a chorus of 'Jingle Bells', the only song she knew.

Something happened in that movie house that blizzardy winter day, and both Ethel and Frank were aware of it. The laughter that was always quick to surface in their youngest daughter rose in her voice, and it transmitted itself to the audience.

Nothing could hold Ethel back now. She was convinced her star had just ascended on the stage of the New Grand Theatre. It was impossible for Frank to stop her. She immediately put Baby into the act and sought engagements in nearby towns. The older girls sang at first as a duet, with Baby coming on-stage for a specialty; one of her numbers was a turn as a belly dancer, dressed in a colorful Egyptian costume that Ethel had made.

Ethel's dream flourished, and Hollywood was its ultimate setting. She whittled away at Frank's good nature, and it was not long before house and theater were both up for sale. No sooner had both been sold than the Gumm family piled whatever was left of their possessions, took to the road, and working their act in every town they could grab for a booking, headed West.

Months of continuous travel followed. They lived in rented rooms or slept in the car, and Ethel saw to it that all their bookings brought them closer to Hollywood. Frank drove, handled the business end, and appeared in the act as opener and interlocutor, while Ethel prodded and plotted – her small, pretty, plump hands moving across broken keyboards in her own arrangements; prompting the girls from the pit; and taking a turn as a chanteuse before the end of the act. There were one-night stands and split weeks. Work was scarce and bookings hard to come by. The country might have been experiencing a boom, but vaudeville was already beginning its decline, with vaudeville theaters quickly being transformed into movie houses.

Often they performed before a movie was shown. The audiences were impatient and not always approving. And there was the Gerry Society to contend with, for laws had recently been passed that forced children to attend school. If the Gerry Society caught them, the girls were made to attend a school for a minimum of a week. They minded much less than Ethel, who dreaded the delay in attaining her goal.

The two older girls were very close confidantes. Baby was too young to be a participant in most of their adventures or conversations; and as Ethel was always busy working on the act, she grew extremely attached to her father. She had more in common with that laughing Irishman than the others anyway. They had a similar sense of humor. She loved his

15

stories and his singsong voice and was already resentful of the way her mother could say things to him that would bring a sadness to his face. Sitting on his lap or curled up next to him in the front seat of the old car, she was content and happy. And when she was onstage she always wanted to be sure he would be in the audience and *where* and would direct her glance to that spot.

Prohibition was in, but Frank Gumm always managed to obtain some Irish whiskey. There would be shrill reprimands from Ethel then. Every cent was to get them to Hollywood; at bootleg prices, Frank's whiskey could cost them precious time. The longer the delays, the more difficult Ethel was to live with. Yet Frank was unable to conquer his need at times to blur the edges.

The Gumm Sisters did not play the big cities. They played the cow towns and farm towns and small factory towns. In those places the discontent was a visible, buzzing thing; farmers were hard up, and there was serious unemployment. What Frank saw on the road disturbed him, made him feel uneasy. He wanted to get his girls to safety, to put a picket fence around them and a great many blossoming rosebushes. Unfortunately, the times he felt this the strongest were the times he drank the most.

Frank opened the act singing spirituals and sometimes closed it with a song – 'I Will Come Back'. (Years later this was to become Judy Garland's closing song on her weekly television show.) He was an Irish tenor with a lovely fullbodied voice. Baby would applaud him frantically from the wings. But when Ethel chose to sing a song – 'I've Been Saving for a Rainy Day' – Baby would cry. There was something sad and touching about Ethel when she sang – not because her performance was moving but because it was so terrible and Ethel so untalented, and because the audiences were always hostile to her. Even the small child sensed this hostility and remembered it all her life. A sea of angry people and her mother a sinking ship. It was a haunting image. She wanted the angry buzz to stop, the faces to smile; but she was powerless. At times they even threw food at

16

Ethel. Once a piece of cheese missed its mark and hit Jimmy in the stomach. Jimmy didn't cry, but Baby did.

After three long, tortuous months, the five Gumms arrived in Los Angeles. It had seemed a much longer journey. But for Baby Gumm it had brought her close to the two great loves of her life – her father and a live audience.

CHAPTER TWO

TODAY, except for the signs, it is difficult to know when you enter or leave Hollywood. But when the Gumm family came to the end of their journey and turned onto Hollywood Boulevard, it was bizarre and marvelous. They had traveled all day, part of it through the searing heat of the desert. Frank was exhausted and the three children half asleep, and they had not arranged for rooms; but the brilliant neons were blinding. Ethel wanted first to see the brand-new Grauman's Chinese Theatre, and Ethel always got her way. Holding Baby Frances in her arms, Ethel woke her. Grauman's – the grand and glorious movie cathedral – was the future Judy Garland's first glimpse of Hollywood.

The finishing touches were just being put upon a replica of a Polynesian village in the forecourt of the theater. Sid Grauman, veteran showman, had invited a number of the most distinguished stars to put the imprints of their hands and feet in the wet cement of the forecourt, thus preserving in cement the prints of the immortals. Grauman was also the man who invented the 'premiere' – the initial public showing of a 'super-special' film. Tickets sold for $5; they were purchased by the public to see the stars, and by the stars to be seen by their fans.

The night of a premiere, Hollywood was a carnival. Pulitzer Prize-winning journalist Anne O'Hare McCormick describing the scene in the *New York Times Magazine* in the late twenties wrote:

> The elite of the movies crossed a high bridge erected across the street in front of the Theatre. This 'bridge of stars' was a temporary gangway ablaze with clusters of huge incandescent flowers and raked by Kleig lights like a battery of suns. The stars were announced by megaphones; in ermines, sables and similar equivalents of the imperial purple, like royalty on a balcony, they bowed to the plaudits of the populace.
>
> The throng was so dense that the pedestrian could not fight his way within a block of the place. The parade took place under an awning a block long, lighted like an operating table, between solid walls of gaping people.

Imagine Ethel's excitement at viewing such a scene. Or at having Frank buy a guide to the stars' homes and driving past the giant English manors and Spanish castles with their lineup of foreign cars in the driveways; the stucco sculpture in the forecourts; the swimming pools – some with swans; houses guarded by mastiffs and Russian wolfhounds; and rooftops flying huge American flags. Ethel was mesmerized and at the same time convinced that Baby Frances would transport the Gumms into a world such as she now saw.

Ethel had embarked upon her true career as that great phenomenon, the Movie Mother. Hedda Hopper once said:

> They [the youngsters] arrived in Hollywood like a flock of hungry locusts driven by the gale winds of their prompting, ruthless mothers. One look into the eyes of those women told you what was on their minds: 'If I can get this kid of mine on the screen, we might just hit it big.' They took little creatures scarcely old enough to stand or speak, and like buck sergeants drilled them to shuffle through a dance step or mumble a song. They robbed them of every phase of childhood to keep the waves in

18

their hair, the pleats in the dress, and pink polish on the nails.

Most of the major studios were located on the edges of Hollywood. The Gumms took rooms within walking distance of them and for several days Ethel worked long and hard to prepare Baby Frances for her debut. There were pink organdy frocks to be sewn, a handshake and bow to perfect, reluctant baby hair to tease into curls, and an audition number to rehearse. Sound was not yet a problem in films – though it was just over the horizon. Ethel concentrated, therefore, on the child's ability to put over her personality. She taught her how to use her eyes and her hands; how to look as though she were about to cry – how to quiver her lips and still appear piquant; how to laugh and yet retain her poise. There was the Chaplin walk to be mastered if the role called upon was comedy; the Mary Pickford stance if demure. Feeling sure of their prospects, she left the two older girls with Frank and began the rounds with her youngest child.

Ethel was not prepared for the long queues of mother and child, the rudeness of casting directors, the hopelessness of ever reaching anyone with executive power. But, from the other mothers, she gleaned a bit of knowledge: if she could meet a top agent and persuade him to represent Baby Frances, the child's chances would be estimably better. She proceeded to change her tactics. Baby Frances in tow, Ethel then made the rounds of agents' offices. There were the same endless queues, the same rudeness, the same closed doors.

Her stamina wavered, and Frank managed to talk her into moving the family to Lancaster, a small town eighty miles north of Los Angeles. It was a harsh, inhospitable community, situated in a barren semidesert, unacquainted with show people and with sunbaked prejudices as hard as the rocky cliffs that surrounded it. There was a small movie theater for sale there, however, and Frank took what money he had left and bought it.

One can easily imagine Ethel's state of mind after she

realized the full consequence of his move. Refusing to accept the ramifications, terrified at being trapped in a town and a life even more stultifying than Grand Rapids, and frustrated at the nearness yet distance of the Mecca, of the golden gates, of fame and glamour and fortune, she piled the girls into the old car on weekends and drove into Los Angeles, a trip then taking nearly three hours each way.

Ethel could now see that her chances might be greater if a talent scout caught Baby Frances in action. Her new tactic was to place the child on a stage. Jimmy and Sue had to be included, as Baby Frances could not be expected to sustain an entire act by herself. She signed the girls with the Meglin Kiddies, a booking agency for child acts, and it constituted a large compromise on Ethel's part.

Working from Lancaster, as the older girls had to attend school, Ethel made that grueling trip back and forth every weekend, setting out at five in the morning and driving through dust and sandstorms, desert heat, and torrential rain in a tired car with three sleepy and very irritable children. At times she was rewarded with a booking. Then she had to drive the girls to some small theater not always too close to Los Angeles, rehearse them, and accompany them in their performance.

One weekend while they were playing the Alhambra, just outside Los Angeles, schoolboys who had brought box lunches to the theater, sent the contents whirling toward the three girls with perfect aim. Baby Frances ran from the theater, and it took a half hour to find her and bring her back.

Ethel took bookings for the girls for any price and for any function – luncheons, benefits, fairs. Money appeared to be no object – once, the girls performed for an entire evening for the lamentable sum of 50 cents – the ultimate hope and purpose being that a talent scout or a cousin or sister of some producer or director would catch the act and see the star potential of Baby Frances.

Frank, determined to make Ethel take the girls off the road, concentrated his forces on the business and within a year had expanded and bought two neighboring movie houses. Ethel refused to give in. Aware that the older girls were detracting from, not adding to, Baby Frances' appeal, and deciding the child had gained experience and confidence, Ethel's compromise to Frank was to leave the older girls at home and take Baby Frances out as a solo.

Now it was Baby Frances and Ethel, alone, on the road together – sometimes for a one-night spot; more often for a series of one-nighters that would keep them away from Frank and the girls for a week or more.

In spite of all the waves and manicures and fussy home-made costumes, little Frances Gumm was a chubby, awkward child who was beginning to suffer grievously from an inferiority complex born of comparison with Ethel of the tiny pretty hands and with the thin and pretty children who performed on the same bills with her. She was a quiet, pensive child, who, waiting to rehearse in a theater, would play with modeling clay or talk to her dolls, all of whom she called Peggy. She tried communicating with the other children on the bills, but she was invariably much younger and avoided whenever possible – although she made one friend during those years: Donald O'Connor. She was lonely and sad-eyed, hungry for the companionship of her sisters and the love of her father, confused and hostile toward Ethel whom she felt responsible for these forced separations from the only real contact she had with human love. Ethel was undemonstrative and seemed to consider mothering the same as babying and would have none of it. The 'Baby' was a sales tag only. Ethel expected the child to act mature offstage, well behaved, patient, quick to learn, while onstage she was to appear precocious but winningly babyish.

The youngster began to weave fantasies that Frank would follow them to whatever town she was in and forbid Ethel to take her any farther. In these fantasies, he would buy first-class train tickets and they would travel back to Lancaster, leaving Ethel behind in the strange town.

But when she was home her sisters were in school, and the other children snubbed her because their mothers felt theater children were unwholesome. Most painful were the fights between Ethel and Frank. As she did in the theaters she performed in, she secluded herself in a room with her modeling clay and her doll. At home, another fantasy of the same kind filled her head. Frank would depart Lancaster with her, leaving Ethel behind. Her dream was not that she become a star – but that Frank would become rich and famous and that Ethel and the whole world would have to sit up and take notice of him.

Ethel would never prepare her for a departure. Early in the morning she would come into Baby Frances' room, always aclutter, and order her to get dressed. The child sensed her mother's relief at leaving the scorching, unfriendly heat of Lancaster and the constant reprimands and demands of Frank, but she was always grief-stricken at those leavings and much to Ethel's anger would cry or sulk for most of the journey. If this behavior kept up when they were on tour, Ethel meted out her own form of punishment. No matter how strange the hotel or the city, Ethel would slowly and silently pack her own suitcase and tell Baby Frances she was leaving because Frances was bad. The terrified child would plead with her to remain, the words falling on deaf ears. Then Ethel would take her suitcase and depart, locking the door after herself and leaving the hysterical child alone. After a time she would stop sobbing and just wait and hope; and, as expected, in due course, Ethel would reappear and the frightened child would beg her forgiveness.

Early in her maturity the grown Judy was to say: 'I was always lonesome. The only time I felt accepted or wanted was when I was onstage performing. I guess the stage was my only friend, the only place where I could feel comfortable. It was the one place where I felt equal and safe.'

Of course, that was when she did not need to dodge any flying objects. And so all her lifetime she would struggle to win her audiences, pushing herself to the last measure of her endurance to hold them in her grasp.

CHAPTER THREE

It was called Black Tuesday. The date was October 29, 1929. The stock market had crashed, Brokers and investors were hysterical and the nation in utter disbelief. The ranks of unemployed increased at a dizzying speed. President Hoover blindly refused to provide emergency help. This nation seemed unable to cope with all the destitute families, the jobless, the hungry. Families slept in doorways, on park benches, and in subways. A few lucky ones found shelter in municipal lodging houses.

The Depression had settled in. Across the country there were, as the young novelist Thomas Wolfe wrote. '. . . scenes of suffering violence, oppression, hunger, cold, and filth and poverty going on unheeded in a world in which the rich were still rotten with their wealth . . .'

But Hollywood had found its voice, and millions of people unable to escape from the bleak reality of their own lives sacrificed food and lodging to see the glamour and opulence of a Hollywood film. For movies, with the double feature now in effect, offered four or five hours surcease from despair. The movie moguls poured everything they had into supplying a panacea to a desperate nation. Stars were created, glamourized, lionized: Wallace Beery and Marie Dressler; Joan Crawford; Jean Harlow; Clark Gable; Marlene Dietrich; and such romantic co-stars as Charles Farrell and Janet Gaynor. The industry thrived and was the only one abundant in riches.

By 1934, Ethel had seen the inside of a Hollywood sound stage only once. The girls had performed a bit in a film short called *La Fiesta de Santa Barbara*.* The film was second

---

* *La Fiesta de Santa Barbara* was a two-reel short subject Musical Revue Series, released February 7, 1935, but filmed much earlier, and there remains the possibility that MGM therefore had film footage of Judy previous to her contract. The short, filmed in color,

rate and the girls terrible, but still she was one of the fortunate Movie Mothers. Frank's business prospered. She never knew want for herself or her family. The fact only added to her great discontent. She detested being so squarely middle-class and was determined that the great fortunes and glamour and stardom that only Hollywood could offer would belong to Frances and herself.

What Ethel never took into consideration was what Frances wanted. At that time she was an overweight child with a passion for pistachio ice cream cones and hot dogs. Not athletic, she disliked games and felt terribly inadequate when forced to participate. She was, at ten, still playing with dolls and making doll clothes. What she loved most, next to Frank, was animals, particularly dogs, and to Ethel's chagrin was always dragging in strays, so that there were few times there weren't two dogs to feed. The dogs became a source of joy and an area of torture for the child. On the move, she was throughout her life always attaching herself to an animal and then having to leave it behind. The guilt and the longing would remain with her until she found another dog to lavish even more devotion on. It was a terrible, vicious circle of overwhelming love and attachment, desertion and guilt.

Leaving Susie and Jimmy with Frank, Ethel now took Frances, who was ten, and moved into a small hotel, the Hotel Gates. It was the beginning of many long separations between Ethel and Frank. For two years thereafter they would part for long periods and then come together again. It was difficult for Frances to accept or to understand. She longed to be with her father. She wondered if she had anything to do with her parents' separation.

After six months at the Hotel Gates, Frank sold the

was about a boating party, with glimpses of such stars as Gary Cooper, Harpo Marx, Maria Gambarelli, Warner Baxter, Leo Carrillo, Adrienne Ames, Robert Taylor, Mary Carlisle, Edmund Lowe, Toby Wing, Buster Keaton, Ida Lupino, Irvin S. Cobb, and Ted Healy.

theaters in and around Lancaster and bought another theater in Lomita, a suburb of Los Angeles. He and Ethel reconciled and they rented a house in the Silver Lake district (Frances was in ecstasy about it), which Frank later bought, and the girls were entered in Mrs. Lawlor's School for Professional Students.

There Frances met a sandy-haired, fresh-faced kid named Mickey McGuire (born Joe Yule, Jr.), who was later to become Mickey Rooney. Mickey McGuire was a new experience for Frances. In the era just past when child actors had been starred in short subjects, Mickey had headed the cast of over fifty. Draped in a checkered shirt, a derby slapped on his head, a stogie stuck in his mouth, he re-created the then-well-known cartoon-strip character of Mickey McGuire in a series of the same name. The experience gave him tremendous confidence.

Mickey was just what Frances needed to keep from turning into a morose and totally introspective child, for although she had thought the house in Silver Lake would magically change her life, it had instead made her a closer observer of the violent quarrels between her parents. She overheard accusations made by Ethel to Frank and these had a deep impact on her, for they had something to do with her father's 'immorality', and he seemed to Frances the loser in these altercations. Mickey was able to make her laugh just as Frank, in his carefree days, had been able to do. They hit it off from the start.

Jimmy and Sue had lost interest in being performers and had not performed for a while. But Ethel had a terrible fight with Frank, and putting all three girls into the back seat of the same old touring car, she drove without ever stopping to sleep until she reached Denver, where she found engagements for the girls in a theater and in a nightclub. They remained in Denver for a week. During that time, Ethel followed all the write-ups on the Chicago World's Fair.

It was called the Century of Progress Exposition, and it was the biggest show of its kind. Twenty million tourists were thronging through its gates. Profits were astronomical.

It was a spectacular repudiation of the conditions that existed across the nation with wonders running the gamut from a reconstruction of a Mayan Temple to Miss Sally Rand, stark naked with fans and an outsized bubble. Reading the *Variety* coverage on the tremendous grosses in the theaters on the Midway. Ethel decided to take the girls there.

Although she was never able to really communicate with her sisters, there was one good thing about their presence on this journey – Frances did not experience the loneliness and fear at night that she did when it was just Ethel and herself. Never was she able to cast off the terror at night that she would be deserted, left alone. Many years later she was to say: 'I'm afraid at night. I didn't know how to use the telephone when I was a scared little girl. But now, at the age of forty-one, I *do* know how to use the phone and I make all those nocturnal calls to wake up all my friends about three in the morning. I resent the fact that they're sleeping and they're not around here ... It's almost like everybody were Mama, and everybody went away and I'm left alone.'

Their first booking was at a theater on the Midway. The place was run by gangsters, and acts were seldom paid – and were threatened if they attempted to do something about this. Ethel allowed the girls to work without pay because Frank had given her a sizable amount of money before she had left Los Angeles. And she kept her silence because she felt so sure *someone* would have to see them at such a major entertainment spectacle as the Chicago World's Fair. After three months, however, her money ran out. She was forced to go to the management and ask for their wages. The act was thereupon given immediate notice.

Refusing to wire Frank for help even though they were out of money, she went begging for work for the girls at every nightclub and theater. Finally, they were given a spot on the bill of the Oriental Theatre, where George Jessel was headlined. It was Frances whom the Oriental wanted, having heard her sing 'I Can't Give You Anything But Love'. But Ethel had not prepared a solo act and so the sisters were included, with the proviso that the youngest carry the act.

The night they opened at the Oriental their names went up in lights. All of them ran out to look at this wonder. The last on the bill before ADDITIONAL ATTRACTIONS, their name was misspelled as THE GLUM SISTERS. Ethel was beside herself, haranguing cast and crew to change the name on the marquee. Jessel suggested they change their own, for any review could too easily rhyme Gumm with 'Dumb', 'crumb', and 'bum'. Robert Garland, a newspaper critic, was backstage, and so Jessel suggested they use the name Garland. Ethel, possibly feeling this would set her apart from Frank forever, agreed.

Sue and Jimmy did not want to give up their Christian names, but Frances had an idea that if she changed hers, she would get away from ever being called Baby again. At that time one of her favorite songs was 'Judy', written by Hoagy Carmichael. The lyric began, 'If her voice can bring ev'ry hope of the Spring/That's Judy, my Judy,' and ended, 'If she seems a saint and you find that she ain't/That's Judy/Sure as you're born.'

Reluctant to see her Baby entirely disappear, Ethel fought for the name Babe, but Jessel and the management won the battle. Jessel was master of ceremonies and he introduced the act as 'The Garland Sisters – featuring little Miss Judy Garland with the big voice.'

The act earned enough money at the Oriental to pay for a return to Los Angeles. They arrived at three in the morning. It had been nearly four months since the newly christened Judy Garland had seen her father. Frank, hearing the car pull into the driveway, had run out to greet them. Judy broke away from her sisters and ran into his arms.

'I cried out of happiness,' Judy said of that reunion – 'and that was a first, too. It's hard to explain, but all the times I had to leave him, I pretended he wasn't there; because if I'd thought about him being there, I'd have been too full of longing.'

27

CHAPTER FOUR

EVEN though she had been well received at the Chicago Oriental, the year that followed brought her one studio rebuff after another, Ethel was still in there trying, making the rounds of the studio front offices with her. It was agreed that she had a big talent to match her big voice, but her appearance and her age blocked any further interest.

The experience of being in Chicago without funds had sufficiently clipped Ethel's wings so that she was willing to remain close to home. The family was back together again, and Judy could not have been happier. Bookings were made and kept in theaters around Los Angeles during the school year so that the girls could remain at Mrs. Lawlor's. Two summers were spent at Lake Tahoe at the Cal-Neva Lodge, where the girls had four-week stands. The engagements appeared to be singularly uneventful, but during the second summer they met Al Rosen, a Hollywood agent.

Rosen had come to the Lodge with a friend who was obtaining an unpleasant divorce and needed someone to hold his hand. Rosen was not a big-time agent, but he was a man who knew how to turn a situation to his advantage. According to Rosen, he recognized Judy's potential immediately, as had 'Bones' Remer, who was one of the owners and operators of the Lodge. He also knew she didn't stand a chance as long as Ethel and Jimmy and Sue came as part of the package.

As Rosen tells it, the day the engagement ended, Harry Akst, the songwriter, and Lou Brown, at that time a casting director for Twentieth Century–Fox, arrived at the Lodge. Feeling this was the propitious moment, he maneuvered the cast of characters to Judy's and his advantage.

Rosen's story has Ethel and the girls already in the old car ready to depart when he called Judy back to the Casino on a pretext, Ethel waiting unsuspectingly in the hot sun while inside the large, cool interior of the Casino, 'Bones' Remer, Akst, and Brown played gin rummy. 'Dinah' was Akst's most famous song. Interrupting the game, Rosen insisted Akst play the song while Judy sang, promising Akst he would hear the song as it was meant to be performed.

But another version appeared in *McCall's* magazine twenty years later. In this one, Judy, Ethel, and the girls were in the old flivver ready to return home when Jimmy remembered that they had left behind a box of hats in a closet, and Judy was sent back to retrieve it. On the way, Judy supposedly met 'Bones' Remer, who asked her to accompany him to the Casino, whereupon she met Akst and Brown and Rosen for the first time and in pure innocence requested Akst to play 'Dinah' for her, not knowing he had written the song.

Rosen and the *McCall's* story do agree on what followed.

Judy had never sung without Ethel or her own arrangement. And she was, in her own words, '... scared they'd [the girls and Ethel] all be mad at me – or leave.' Standing in the center of that large, otherwise empty casino, she was not at all sure she had made the right decision.

Never having learned how to read music, Judy did not know what key she sang in. She was advised to begin and Akst would follow. The conditions were different and the youngster was nervous. It gave her voice a distinct tremolo. Her mind was on the anger with which Ethel would greet her when she finally returned to the car. She set a hurried and almost frantic pace. Years later, Bobby Cole, one of her musical directors, was to say: 'We always set the key and pace so that it seemed that Judy would never be able to reach the last note. That way there was always cheering when she did.'

The men were impressed, but Brown was certain, because of her physical awkwardness, that she had no place in films. Rosen had more faith. He gave her a slip of paper with his name and telephone number on it and told her to have her mother call him in Los Angeles in a few days.

They were halfway home before Judy told Ethel about the 'audition' and gave her mother Al Rosen's telephone number. To her wide-eyed and grateful surprise, Ethel was not angry.

Al Rosen became her first agent. This had many ramifications. To begin with, Rosen was interested only in Judy and refused to represent her except as a solo. That was the end of the Gumm/Garland Sister Act. Secondly, Rosen was essentially a film agent and insisted she remain in the Los Angeles area. And thirdly, having formed an immediate and distinct antipathy to Ethel and recognizing the inadequacy of her talent, he tried whenever possible to get Judy another accompanist.

These two – Ethel and Rosen – had swords drawn against each other from the beginning. Both, however, desperately needed the same thing: a star in their stable. No other agent had taken the interest Rosen had. Though Ethel hated the man, she trusted his dedication to Judy's success. She didn't always go along with his decisions, but more often than not she was agreeable.

This insecure youngster was now in the center of a hurricane of hostility, always being pushed, exploited, and disregarded in any human sense. First she had been Ethel's dream; now she was an agent's meal ticket, his chance for the big time. Because of this she suffered severe and irreparable damage as a human being and as a woman. But these same malevolent forces became the prime movers of her career.

Rosen could not afford the time required for formal voice lessons, and yet he felt Judy needed a more intensified and identifiable style to set her apart. A big voice was not enough. He recognized that her delivery was directed to the heart as well as the ear. Employing the help of a cantor in Boyle Heights (the Jewish ghetto of Los Angeles), he had Judy work with him on the famous 'Kol Nidre' and other emotional prayer songs. Then he took her to all the major studios. The answers were always the same. If she had been a toddler or a young woman, they might have signed her.

They all thought her voice was sensational. But she was, at twelve, overweight and not very pretty, and no one knew what to do with her.

Though Rosen could at times cut Ethel out of an audition, he could not control her handling of Judy at home. Ethel was still making those pink ruffled dresses, curling the reluctant thin hair, and painting the bitten nails. The youngster could not have been presented more unbecomingly.

There is a conflict of stories of how Judy first came to the attention of MGM. The most acceptable one is that Al Rosen secured an audition for Judy at the Feist Music Company, which was a subsidiary of Metro, hoping for a recording contract. Someone at Feist, called Roger Edens, was to become Judy's future musical mentor. Edens, a top executive in the MGM music department, was asked to come down and hear this young girl sing. Edens obliged and even agreed to accompany her at the piano.

One cannot help digressing for a moment to conjure up the picture of this youngster – her hair curled atrociously, her clothes ill fitting and in the worst possible taste – accompanied by this sophisticated, handsome young musician – his dress superb, his manners elegant, his speech impeccable. Not yet thirty at the time, Edens had already traveled extensively around the world and was a consummate musician.

Judy asked him if he could play in her key. Years later, she recalled that moment with embarrassment. It was an incredible question to ask a fine musician.

She sang 'Zing! Went the Strings of My Heart'. Edens made her sing it again, this time switching the emphasis on notes, shading the phrasing. By the third time, he was confident his instincts were right. Returning to the studio, he went directly to Ida Koverman, Louis B. Mayer's secretary, to arrange a studio audition. Rosen was contacted.

That day Ethel had gone out on errands and Judy was home alone with Frank. Rosen called to say that he had just won an executive audition for Judy at MGM and for her to get over to the studio right away. Ethel had left instructions

31

that Judy never leave the house for an audition without her knowledge. At the time Rosen called, Judy was playing in the backyard. She was wearing gray slacks and a white blouse, and her hair was brushed back from her face. It was the way Frank Gumm liked his daughter best. He decided he would not wait for Ethel and that he would take Judy to the studio exactly as she was.

With Edens accompanying her, she once again sang 'Zing! Went the Strings of My Heart' – this time for Frank Robbins, the Metro talent chief (later to become a well-known music publisher), and Ida Koverman. Rosen was nervous and excited. The presence of Mrs. Koverman meant Judy might audition for the great mogul, Mayer himself. Judy was told what was about to happen, but she was not in the least overwhelmed.

After Judy sang, Ida Koverman called Mayer down to hear her. Neither Judy nor Frank knew Mayer's power in the studio, and both were rather astounded at the electricity in the room as everyone waited for Mayer to appear. He finally did, secretaries hovering close at his heels, furious at Ida Koverman for interrupting his work, glaring at Judy. She sang, her father close to her for support. The expression on Mayer's face never changed while he listened, and when she was done, he got up without saying a word to her and left, his secretaries once more scurrying behind him.

But though Mayer did not seem to react, he had studied the young girl performing for him: stocky, short, plain, freckled face, big eyes, and pug nose; she was no beauty, but she did look like everyone's kid sister or the kid next door, and Mayer liked to make films with a true-blue-American-family feel to them. He also recognized the strength and talent of her voice and the electricity its emotional power generated.

Never saying a word to Rosen or his client, he left them to speculate. Frank and Judy thought it had been, in her words, 'a big nothing'. Rosen kept calling the studio for word.

Two weeks later it came. Judy Garland was now under contract to MGM.

CHAPTER FIVE

METRO-GOLDWYN-MAYER, the 167-acre movie domain, is not in Hollywood. It is five miles to the southwest in Culver City. In 1934, when Mayer hired Judy, the studio was the busiest; the main lot, with its park, artificial lake, private zoo, schoolhouse, restaurant, hospital, raffish collection of old sets and barnlike buildings, stood quietly in the sunlight like an abandoned city. Whatever was going on inside the big white buildings whose doors were guarded by red lights blinking on and off, warning intruders and interrupters away, was in the power of one man. Louis B. Mayer controlled the life of the studio and was responsible for those blinking red lights.

Mayer was the wealthiest and most influential mogul – just as his company was the wealthiest and the most influential company for over three decades. Upon his decisions or instructions rested the fortune and fate of hundreds of persons. The competition for jobs was fierce and emotional involvement intense. Anyone who had the final word on hiring had in his hand the power of bestowing life or death. And no one in the industry wielded more power during those years in the growth of the American film than Louis B. Mayer.

He was more than a man. He was a demigod to some, a monster to others. He was, according to David O. Selznick, '. . . the greatest single figure in the history of motion picture production.'

Mayer insisted, 'I want to rule by love, not by fear.' He did not recognize how totalitarian that concept – *I want to rule* – was. Hollywood was a jungle in those days, and the matter of survival often rested in Mayer's not-too-lily-white hands, for he was quite capable of using any means to attain his goals. Early in the thirties he was indicted by a Los Angeles grand jury for conspiring to commit usury. He certainly thought very little of working his child performers twelve hours a day, or of starting them off on pep pills to keep them before the cameras.

He had been born in Poland in 1885, son of a poor laborer and a mother of peasant stock. His mother swore he had been born on July 4 – fitting for a future great American. His Polish years were marked by hunger and thirst and great privation. By some miracle, his entire immediate family – father, mother, two sisters and himself – was able to emigrate westward together when he was still a child.

He was brought up in Saint John, a small city in the Canadian province of New Brunswick. His father was a ragpicker, and from the very earliest time the boy had been taught to scuttle along the sidewalks, back lanes and alleys searching the ground for discarded scraps of rusted iron, broken bits of anything, stuffing them in a pack he always wore strapped on his back.

The family fortunes slowly improved. By the time Mayer was a young man, they were salvaging metals from wrecked ships along the coast and were respectable junk dealers. Brothers Ruby and Jake were needed to help their father in the main office, but Mayer was sent to Boston to arrange the sale of their salvage. Louis B. Mayer was on his way. But salvage was not to be his future.

The year was 1907, and a new entertainment phenomenon, the nickelodeon, was sweeping the country. For a nickel, one could see a 'moving picture'. The theaters were, more often than not, vacant stores equipped with folding chairs, and the film was projected on a cotton sheet. There were between 2,500 and 3,000 of these 'movie houses' in the United States. Mayer put up $50 on a three-day option for a theater in the neighboring town of Hoverhill and struggled just under the deadline to raise the remaining cash. Haverhill was a shoe-manufacturing city with a population of 45,000, most of whom were factory workers. The movie house was an instant success.

Keeping his eye to the ground as he had always been trained to do, Mayer extended his interests, and he and his

34

associates became owners of the franchise for distribution in the Boston district. He was now a successful exhibitor. But he wanted more. He wanted to be a movie producer.

Most films were being produced in New York. Mayer, feeling that more sunlight, allowing for longer hours of outdoor shooting, was essential, went to Los Angeles. It was late in 1918. The country had just emerged from a World War.

By 1924, Mayer had managed a merger with Goldwyn on a Culver City site. The studio was to be called Metro-Goldwyn-Mayer. The roster of stars and directors was impressive: Erich von Stroheim, Frank Borzage, Rupert Hughes, Mae Murray, John Gilbert, Will Rogers, and Lon Chaney, to mention a few. Soon afterwards, Goldwyn and Mayer parted company and Goldwyn set up on his own. (Decades later, Samuel Goldwyn was to remark harshly at Mayer's funeral, 'The reason so many people showed up at his funeral was because they wanted to make sure the S.O.B. was dead.')

By the time Judy was signed to an MGM contract, Louis B. was forty-nine years old, and success and power had overtaken his girth, strengthened his haunches, and settled on his face with terrifying implacability. He was no one to oppose.

In a very candid television interview on the David Frost show, Elizabeth Taylor (who, at the time of the following incident, was approximately the same age Judy was at her first meeting with Mayer) revealed what coming face to face with Mayer could be like for a thirteen- to fourteen-year-old girl. Frost asked her impression of Mayer when she was a child star at MGM.

'I thought he was a beast,' she replied. 'He was inhuman. He used his power over people to such a degree that he was no longer a man. He had become an instrument of power and he had no scruples and he didn't care whom he cut down or whom he hurt.'

Miss Taylor had been announced for a film, *Sally in Our Alley*, a musical; and as she was not a singer or a dancer, that meant a lot of work. Her mother was concerned and made an appointment for them to see Mayer.

Relating what occurred next, Miss Taylor explained: 'I am not a singer and dancer, so Mom and I went up to see L.B. because we had been given this big long lecture about "I am your father and whenever you have trouble and whenever you need anything, come to me and I will help you. You are all my children and I am your father and all you have to do is come to me." So I went to his office, which was like Mussolini's ... you had to walk – well, it seemed a mile. And you walked on this white carpet to this white oak desk and all this white kind of carving of leather and the white chair in which this dwarf with a rather large nose peeking over the desk sat and peered at you. It was kind of terrifying because until you sat he'd do – [*a kingly gesture: eyes upon work, hand waving to subject*] – and then he'd say, "Yes, what is it?"

'We said we had read that I was going to do a film called *Sally in Our Alley* and if it were true, then we thought I should start work on it like – dancing lessons and singing lessons. Silence. Dead face. And then he looked at my mother and asked, "What do you have to say?" She said, "We wondered if Elizabeth was going to do the film or not and whether we should start any kind of preparations." And he started like foaming at the mouth and said, "How dare you come into my office and tell me how to run my business? I took you and pulled you out of the gutter and you'd be nowhere if it hadn't been for me."

'Now, I promise you, David, I would have been quite happy in my "gutter" – whatever he thought that was – without him. We said we didn't come up here to ask for anything. We just wanted to know if we were to do anything, and started to walk out. He said, "Get out. Get out of here," and started to foam – literally foam – at the mouth. "Don't you tell me how to run my business! You and your daughter are nothing but guttersnipes. Get out of here."

'And I said (it was the first swear word I had used), "Mr.

36

Mayer, you and your studio can go to hell!" And I ran out of the room in tears.

'I was called about an hour later by the Vice President and the Second Vice President to go in and apologize to L. B. Mayer for telling him and the studio to go to hell. And I said I didn't see why I had to because I thought the way he had treated my mother and me was wrong and not that what we had done was wrong. Anyway, I couldn't because I was so offended by the way he spoke to my mother.'

Frost then asked her if she went back and apologized, and Miss Taylor replied that she never saw or spoke to him again.

At the time of this incident, Elizabeth Taylor had already made *National Velvet* and was a child star. She had had a stable childhood, one much different from Judy's. Born and brought up in her earlier years in England, she had not become a performer until she was ten. Mrs. Taylor had been an actress; Mr. Taylor, a successful antique dealer. Though Elizabeth's mother was ambitious for her, there was never the intense need, the desperate drive for her daughter to be a star. Elizabeth never experienced the same pressures as Judy. Mayer could terrify her all he wished and not destroy her by taking away her stardom. She had family to return to where she was loved and accepted just as she was: Elizabeth – daughter and sister.

From the very beginning, Judy was made to realize how important Mayer's approval of her was and how destructive his disapproval would be. She thought of him at that time, she was later to say, as 'the real grand Wizard of Oz' – and she walked the studio streets with the same mixed emotions of hope and fear that possessed Dorothy on the yellow brick road.

She had actually not spoken to Mayer in their first meeting. Not yet knowing his power over her life, she had not feared him. Ethel immediately delineated his importance. As well, the other employees on the lot were graphic in their fear and their opinion of L.B. Judy began to think of the man as one would of a school principal.

He wanted all of his subjects to regard him as an all-holy father figure, but Judy had Frank to greet her at the end of each day. They would share stories or watch films together in his theater, and Frank would mimic the action on the screen, pretending he was all the players – women and children as well as the men. Judy would join in. They shared more laughter than they had ever been able to share before. The child was happier than she had ever been. Ethel was satisfied and relaxed for the moment, knowing her Baby was signed to the biggest studio of them all; the girls were relieved that they would no longer be expected to perform; and Judy had her dream clutched tightly in her fist. She would never again have to leave her father.

It was decided that she should be given as many chances to perform as possible. That did not mean that Metro was ready to put her before the cameras. Instead, the studio sent her to sing at parties given by Metro stars and executives. Singing at Norma Shearer and Irving Thalberg's home, or at Gable's home, she felt awkward and ill at ease. She was later to say she felt like hired help – singing, eating in the kitchen, and returning to her own modest home at the end of each grand and sumptuous party.

The leading night club at that time was The Trocadero, owned by Billy Wilkerson (who also owned the trade paper *The Hollywood Reporter*). Wilkerson had set up a series of Sunday-afternoon *auditions*. Studios would send over new players and they would test themselves before a professional audience, gratis. Judy's appearance at The Troc, as it was called, one Sunday afternoon, is thought by many to have firmly convinced Mayer and Metro that the awkward little girl might be worth top material.

It was almost three months to the day from the date of that first audition that her world crashed. Frank died suddenly and unexpectedly of spinal meningitis. When she left for the studio in the morning he was taken to the hospital. In the evening she appeared on a radio show with Al Jolson. A call came that her father's condition was very critical. It was a cruel blow that he died before she was able to see him.

Through the years Judy said over and over again, 'My father's death was the most terrible thing that ever happened to me in my life.'

She was never to overcome his loss and sought his image in every man she met, but she was incapable of crying at his funeral. She was so ashamed of this that she feigned it. The following eight days and nights she was inconsolable, melancholy and tearless. Ethel was beside herself, certain that the girl's attitude and listlessness would reach Mayer's ears and be met with great displeasure.

On the ninth day, the dam broke. Locking herself in the bathroom at home, she cried and vomited for fourteen hours. None of Ethel's pleas moved her. When she emerged, she was exhausted, sick, and weak. Ethel demanded she clean up and go straight to the studio, where she was long overdue.

Upon her arrival, they were told that Louis B. Mayer wanted to see them. It was the first time she had an audience with him, but she was never able to discuss that initial confrontation. She did say he gave her some consolation and then went into his now-familiar lecture – 'I am your father and whenever you have trouble and whenever you need anything, come to me and I will help you.'

No substitute for Frank, he did supply the devastated young girl with a figure of authority – half Satan, half God. Ethel regarded him in the same light. For once, her mother's word would not be the last.

CHAPTER SIX

IT must always remain in the area of speculation whether or not Mayer's intentions toward Judy were honorable and paternal, or either. It is a widely accepted fact that he had a penchant for very young girls and that he was possessed of an acute God complex which made the young women he felt he had *created* the most attractive to him. Before, during, and after the time Judy was on the lot, 'belowstairs' gossip linked Mayer with many of the very young female players. Further, such gossip intimated that Mayer never promised stardom if the young girl did comply but that he threatened destruction if she did not. There was no need to doubt his power to do so.

The talk 'belowstairs' involving Judy and Mayer began when she was not yet fifteen. It persisted during most of her MGM contract years. For most of her life Judy denied any such liaison. But certainly Mayer's influence over Judy's life while she was at MGM was more powerful and God-like than over that of any other player. For nearly seventeen years she worked, slept, ate, appeared in public, dated, married, and divorced at his command. He even exerted supreme authority over any medical crisis in her life.

Frank's death made Ethel financially dependent upon Judy's earnings. He had not provided for the years ahead; the estate was small; and she had Jimmy and Sue to feed, clothe, and educate. Judy was earning $150 a week, less Al Rosen's 10 percent. No king's ransom, but in 1934 it was a sizable salary. Ethel now employed a new tactic if Judy misbehaved or threatened any small rebellion: 'I'll tell Mr. Mayer!' she would yell. From the very inception of their three-sided relationship – Judy, Ethel, and Mayer – Judy never doubted that Ethel was on Mayer's side. In her younger years, therefore, she was much too fearful to do anything but comply.

In 1934 there was no provision made by law to protect a child actor's earnings. Legally, these earnings belonged to the parents, but morally one would expect some future protection for the minor. Judy signed her checks over to Ethel without question. She continued to do so for the next five years as the checks and her career rose to stellar heights. But no part of those moneys was ever put aside for Judy.

At the time Judy signed at MGM, Jackie Coogan was a

star on the lot. Though nearing twenty-one, he still commanded $1,300 a week. During his long career as a child star, he had earned over $4 million. Publicly, his parents had declared they were protecting a large slice of those earnings by putting it into a trust fund for him to receive when he reached twenty-one. Arriving at that age, Coogan found there was no trust fund. His father had died and his mother had married their business manager, Arthur L. Bernstein. Claiming disapproval of young Coogan's conduct, they forced him to leave the house his earnings had bought. With the haunting vision of his lost millions, Jackie Coogan went to court to try to salvage what he could. By 1935, his contract had ended at MGM. He was jobless, homeless, and broke.

It was not until May 4, 1939, that a committee of the State Assembly at Sacramento was to recommend passage of 'The Coogan Act' – or the Child Actor's Bill. Through this bill, the court had the power to set aside 50 percent of the child's earnings in a trust fund or other form of savings. For Coogan it was a Pyrrhic victory. He managed to retrieve $126,000 from the Bernsteins, but five years of court battles almost entirely devoured the amount.

During those years (1934–39), Judy never concerned herself about money. Once the cameras began to roll for her, she had no time for anything outside the studio. Her financial needs were small. Ethel had sold the house in Silver Lake, and they moved closer to the studio. She was driven to the lot early in the morning and returned home late at night. Later, when she and Mickey Rooney were making films together, they often slept in the studio hospital rather than return home for the few hours allotted them.

Having Mickey on the lot was Judy's one great compensation after her father's death. Together with Deanna Durbin, they attended the studio school daily from nine to twelve. All three were still waiting for the big chance. Math was Judy's weakest subject, as it was Mickey's. They had much in common. Returning to memories of their days together at Mrs. Lawlor's, Mickey says: 'At Ma Lawlor's, during math lessons, Judy and I swapped mash notes. The notes said such bright and original things as "I love you" and "I'll always love you" and "You look beautiful this morning." The passion was counterfeit and we both knew it. Only our love of fun was real.'

Years later, Rooney's mother was to ask him why he didn't marry Judy, and he was to reply, 'I couldn't do it. It would have been like marrying my sister.'

Mayer had signed her without any role in mind. He also had not insisted on a screen test, which was unusual. He had hired her by instinct; his comment to Ida Koverman had been to the effect that she had a very special charisma that he sensed he could channel to star quality if she did as he said.

His manifesto went out: 'Groom that girl and slim her.'

Orders were issued to the commissary that she was not to be served anything but chicken soup no matter what she ordered, and no matter how hungry or hard-worked she was. After her four-hour session, she attended exercise classes, dance classes, and song-styling sessions with Roger Edens, who was her one studio support. This routine continued for almost a year. Judy – still chubby, but not fat – had learned how to walk gracefully, and talk and sing without distorting her face. It was time, the studio felt, to see how she looked on camera.

The short, *Every Sunday* (also known as *The Sunday Afternoon* and *Every Sunday Afternoon*) was ostensibly made as a screen test for Judy and Deanna. It was a two-reel short subject directed by Felix Feist, and in it Deanna sang a classical song while Judy sang swing. (Judy was later to sing a similar duet – 'I Like Opera and I Like Swing' – in *Babes in Arms* with Betty Jaynes.) Sid Silvers appeared in the film with the two girls.

Mayer was in Europe when the short was finished. Co-incidentally, Deanna's option renewal arose at the same time. Though it has never been determined whose decision it was, Deanna was dropped.

Joe Pasternak was producing for Universal, and he had a script that was written for a young hot or swing singer.

Having heard about Judy, he asked the executives at MGM if Universal could see the short. Studios often lent out players for large fees to other studios. A request of this nature was not unique.

Pasternak could not get over how both the young girls belted out their songs or the tremendous screen presence each had. But the script was for a *swing* singer. Pasternak went back to MGM and asked to borrow Judy for the film to be called *Three Smart Girls*.

By this time Mayer had returned from Europe. According to Arthur Freed (who later produced many of Judy's films), he was responsible for Judy's not being dropped at the same time as Deanna. Ida Koverman claimed there was an edict that no decision regarding July Garland was to be made without Mayer's authorization. Whichever is the truth, or if both are, Pasternak's request revived Mayer's attention. He ran the film, refused to lend Judy – and at the same time was furious that Deanna Durbin had been dropped. But Pasternak never forgot Judy, or his belief in her.

What was MGM's loss was Universal's gain. Rewriting the script to suit a classical girl singer, Universal signed Deanna. The film was to make her an international star overnight and one of her studio's biggest money-makers.

The year that followed was a difficult one for Judy. Mickey had just played in Warner's *A Midsummer Night's Dream*, and having also broken his leg while tobogganing, he had little time to spare. Immediately after the preview of *A Midsummer Night's Dream*, he was put under special wraps. Freddie Bartholomew was the leading child star at Metro, having just made *David Copperfield*. But Mickey was being groomed. He was earning the comfortable salary of $500 a week in mid-Depression. (By the end of the decade he would be making close to $5,000 a week.) Several strong roles were immediately set up for him. He went straight into *Ah, Wilderness!* and then *Riff-Raff* (with Tracy and Harlow), *The Devil Is a Sissy*, and *Little Lord Fauntleroy* (Bartholomew still the star attraction) without much time between. Judy had lost much of her old friend's companionship. The acceleration of his career and Deanna's sudden stardom pointed up the fact that she was marking time. By the end of the year, Darryl Zanuck, now at Fox, asked Mayer to lend Judy for *Pigskin Parade*, which he was producing. Mayer, perhaps remembering that he might have had a star on his hands if he had lent Judy to Pasternak at Universal for *Three Smart Girls*, consented.

Pigskin Parade was a run-of-the-mill film, with a formula plot but *The New York Times* did single out Judy, after noting first the Fox debut of a pretty blonde in the cast – Betty Grable: 'also in the newcomer category is Judy Garland, about twelve or thirteen now, about whom the West Coast has been enthusing as a vocal find ... She's cute, not too pretty, but a pleasingly fetching personality, who certainly knows how to sell a pop.'

CHAPTER SEVEN

ACROSS the nation, while millions were starving, a crime wave machine-gunned itself to an ominous din. G-men were matched against Public Enemies. War was declared, and among others of the criminal elite, Pretty Boy Floyd and Bonnie and Clyde were shot down. It was apparent that Mayer's decision was to let them (film audiences) 'eat cake'. MGM began a twenty-year cycle of what Mayer considered clean and wholesome entertainment.

Films, since their earliest inception, have been a tremendous social force, whose control in the day of the movie moguls gave these men power to mold opinion and attitude. Mayer's intimates were William Randolph Hearst and Herbert Hoover. (Ida Koverman, Mayer's secretary, had once been Hoover's secretary and had brought the two men together.)

44

Mayer's friendship with Hearst went back to 1919, when Paramount had let Marion Davies (Hearst's girlfriend) go as a flop and Mayer, needing money for his new studio, had sold himself to Hearst on the proviso that he make and continue to make films starring Miss Davies. In all the years Marion Davies was at MGM, only one film ever made back its cost – *Little Old New York*. But Mayer held up his end of the bargain. Hearst, for his part, and with his gargantuan power, aligned himself with Mayer whenever called upon.

In 1935, Mayer was known to a wide circle of Hollywood 'society' as 'Trocadero Lou'. His wife, Margaret, was bedridden in their home in Malibu. He was now making $800,000 a year, and his power to sway opinion was second only to that of one man – Hearst.

He was also Hollywood's leading host, throwing Lucullan banquets for his friends and visiting dignitaries that rivalled any kingly affair.

'Troubadors greet the guests as they enter,' Joel Faith reported in a 1935 issue of *Theatre*. 'Splendid food is served. The honor guest is usually surrounded by a bevy of film cuties. Sometimes the ultimate in juxtaposition is reached, as when Miss Harlow is placed next to Bishop Cantwell and Miss Crawford is beside Rabbi Magnin. When George Bernard Shaw toured America he was the guest of Mayer and Hearst. He sat at table beside Miss Marion Davies. When he rose from his chair to view the studio. Miss Davies clung to his arm with a grip of iron. Nor would she let go until news photographers snapped their shutters. Next morning pictures of these intellectuals graced the pages of all the Hearst newspapers.'

It was obvious that Mayer both identified with and envied Hearst. In his office, throughout his life, was a larger-than-life-size portrait of Hearst. It was to be expected that the Hearst philosophies would be the message of Metro films. Bank presidents and politicians always fared well. The true condition of the country was never shown. Young men fought and died in historical wars for Mom, the family

45

back home, and the American flag. Contemporary dramas and comedies had the hero fighting for the same causes.

But as powerful as Hearst was, he was not a match for the gangsterism of Al Capone. From Chicago, Capone viewed the golden rooftops of Hollywood and sent his emissaries out to shake down the film industry for a cut of the take. A man named Willie Bioff arrived in Hollywood along with George E. Browne. Both men immediately took over the IATSE (International Alliance of Theatrical Stage Employees). In this position they could threaten a strike which would stop the cameras from rolling on any lot. For six years they blackmailed the majors in this fashion. MGM was not exempt, and even Hearst could not squash men like Frank 'The Enforcer' Nitti, Paul 'The Waiter' Ricca, Louis 'Little New York' Campagna, Charles 'Cherry Nose' Giou, and Francis 'Frank Diamond' Maritote, who were Capone henchmen.

Bioff demanded $2 million from Mayer, pared it down to $1 million, and settled for $200,000 plus a yearly stipend to guarantee the safe production of Metro films.*

Mayer was forced to listen to Bioff brag how he had everyone in the industry toeing the mark; how men like Mayer, Schenck, the Warner brothers, and Austin C. Keough, the vice-president of Paramount, were at his beck and call; how he blasphemed them when they did not respond quickly enough to his demands; that in five years' time he would be running all the studios in Hollywood; that he was the big power and that Mayer, like the rest, had better play ball.

A man now caught between two awesome powers – Hearst and the Chicago syndicate – Mayer exerted his own form of

* All of the Chicago mobsters mentioned were finally brought to justice in 1941 and convicted and imprisoned on extortion charges. Nitti committed suicide the day the indictments were returned. Bioff was blown to bits after his release from prison by an explosive device wired to his car's ignition system so that it was detonated when he stepped on the starter. Giou and Maritote were shot to death after their release.

46

ego power on his lot. His was 'king' of Metro, and if now not entirely in control of his studio, he held his subjects in an iron fist.*

Each year on July 4, Mayer would throw himself a birthday party that lacked only a twenty-one gun salute in its royal pretensions. For the event he took over the commissary, and all of Metro's star performers, directors, producers, and supporting players were commanded to attend, and those who could sing or dance to perform. Judy's first performance under her Metro contract was at one of these parties, and for many subsequent years she was expected to sing at them.

'We all had to assemble at L. B. Mayer's birthday party in the commissary,' Elizabeth Taylor, giving her impressions on the David Frost show, related, 'and everybody – the writers, the directors, the stars, everyone – and he would sort of stand up and have a "Happy Birthday" sung to him. And the little kid stars like Margaret O'Brien and Butch Jenkins, and one year I was with them and I felt kind of awkward, stiff; for we had to sort of sit around him and pay homage to this man who was obviously slightly crazy. Anyway, at one of these huge things, Perry Como got up and sang, "Happy Birthday, dear L.B. and *fuck you*!" [Bleeped out in final T.V. cut.] It was like a death toll all over the huge commissary, because he had done the unforgivable. He had broken the sacred bond and he had told the old man what everybody else in their own hearts were dying to tell him, and he finally came out and said it; and it was glorious; and

* In 1935 the studio listed the following stars: Lionel Barrymore, Freddie Bartholomew, Wallace Beery, Joan Crawford, Nelson Eddy, Clark Gable, Greta Garbo, Gladys George, Helen Hayes, Charles Laughton, Myrna Loy, Jeanette MacDonald, the Marx Brothers, Robert Montgomery, Eleanor Powell, William Powell, Luise Rainer, Norma Shearer, Robert Taylor, Spencer Tracy, and Warren Williams. Still considered supporting players were, among many others, Melvyn Douglas, Judy, George Murphy, Maureen O'Sullivan, Walter Pidgeon, Mickey Rooney, Rosalind Russell, James Stewart, Franchot Tone, Sophie Tucker, Johnny Weissmuller, and Robert Young.

it was joyous; and it was one of the happiest moments of my life and I was only fourteen.'

Frost asked Miss Taylor how Como's career was affected by this incident.

'He was blackballed from every studio in Hollywood for four or five years – maybe more,' she replied.

Frost pressing on, asking her if she thought it had been worth it.

'Oh, you bet it was worth it! I think that was one of his [Perry Como's] golden moments,' she said.

The one party Judy apparently did not object to appearing at was given for Clark Gable. She was, in fact, very much excited about it, as Gable was her idol. She spent a good deal of time rehearsing with Roger Edens the number she was to sing. Her selection had been 'Drums in My Heart' – a Merman song. Edens insisted she drop it, as it was not for a fourteen-year-old girl. Reluctantly, Judy agreed to sing, in its place, a preface – 'Dear Mr. Gable' – composed by Edens for 'You Made Me Love You'. It told the story of a teen-ager who had a crush on Gable. At the party, Judy was placed inside a huge birthday cake, and as Edens began the song, she popped out. (According to Judy, years later Gable told her, 'Judy, I had a birthday the other day and I hid. I was afraid you'd jump out and sing that song again!')

Mayer liked the song and the way Judy sang it. With Judy, it was included in *Broadway Melody of 1938* (made in 1936 and released in 1937). Before the film was released, Judy was cast in three others – in one, *Thoroughbreds Don't Cry*, opposite Mickey. The studio, feeling certain Judy's star was in the ascendant, wanted to be prepared.

Metro's *Broadway Melody* series had begun several years before and primarily introduced new contract talent. Warners did the same thing with the *Gold Diggers* series and Fox with *George White's Scandals*. Robert Taylor was the star of the '38 *Broadway Melody*, while Eleanor Powell, George Murphy, Binnie Barnes, Buddy Ebsen, Sophie Tucker, Robert Benchley, Billy Gilbert, and Judy supported him.

Bosely Crowther's review of *Broadway Melody of 1938* in *The New York Times* confirmed their confidence:

> There are individual successes in the film .. the amazing precocity of Judy Garland, Metro's answer to Deanna Durbin ... Miss Garland particularly has a long tour de force in which she addresses lyrical apostrophes to a picture of Clark Gable. The idea and words are almost painfully silly – yet Judy ... puts it over – in fact with a bang.

Her best review appeared in *The Hollywood Reporter*, which had as a headline:

NEW 'B'WAY MELODY OF '38' PEAK OF EXTRAVAGANZAS
TUCKER, GARLAND, MURPHY HIGHLIGHTS

The second paragraph of the review carries these accolades for Judy:

> The sensational work of young Judy Garland causes wonder as to why she has been kept under wraps these many months. She sings two numbers that are show stoppers and does a dance with Buddy Ebsen. Hers is a distinctive personality well worth careful promotion.

Judy was a hit, but not yet a star. Nearly two years were to pass before she would be considered one. In the meantime, in Judy's words, 'Metro thought they were raising me. They were just dreadful ... They had a theory that they were all-powerful and they ruled by fear. What better way to make young persons behave than to scare the hell out of them every day? That's the way we worked ... that's the way we got mixed up. And that's the way we lost contact with the world.'

At home she was being called Baby, Monkey, and Pudge. At the studio the image she saw of herself was short, fat, and unglamorous. Even Mayer referred to her as 'my little hunchback'. At the same time, she was surrounded daily by the most beautiful women in the world; this made her painfully self-conscious. Doubts about her ability began to obsess her. Called to Mayer's office, she was told by him that she had to stop cheating on her diet procedure (she would sneak off for a malted or an ice cream cone at the corner drugstore, but studio spies always turned her in); that the studio had a big investment in her; and that without the studio she was nothing. She was, therefore, immediately placed in the hands of a studio doctor and started on a new diet pill. She began slimming down, but as a side effect had trouble sleeping at night. The Metro doctor had a cure for that: Seconals before bedtime.

She was fourteen years old, and her lifetime battle with pills had begun.

CHAPTER EIGHT

'OH, the early days at MGM were a lot of laughs,' Judy once told an interviewer. 'It was all right if you were young and frightened – and we stayed frightened. Look at us – Lana Turner, Elizabeth Taylor, Mickey Rooney, and me – we all came out of there a little ticky and kooky.'

To coin a cliché, the studio was a great place to visit, but not to live. It was very exciting, but no part of life there was real. Consider the impact of being faced with an army of cavalry in full attire upon leaving a schoolroom; and behind the cavalry, the infantry – followed by a circus. Imagine the result of, at the age of thirteen, living daily with truckloads of soap flakes to simulate snow, ketchup for blood, cupboards filled with cardboard food, celluloid swans in front of cellophane waterfalls, buildings with no backs, jungles made of paper, rocks of plaster – and everywhere you looked, the baroque, the outdated, the discarded.

It is quite easy to speculate that Judy, having lost her father and being insecure in this unreal environment and needing acceptance, would do everything in her power in a desperate desire to please Ethel. From this point of her life until the end of her Metro days, she was forced to suppress her own personal needs and desires. For one solid decade she was to eat what others wanted her to eat, wear what they set out for her, see the people they desired. Her day was ruled by the studio, her private life policed. She led a robot existence, controlled by Ethel and by Mayer. Mickey Rooney was an outside force, but he fed her dreams of fame and fortune that seemed to substantiate Mayer's and Ethel's philosophies.

But one person – Roger Edens – was contributive to her growth. A brilliant musician, a sensitive man, Edens was the only one to truly extend compassion during those painful years of her adolescence. And all he wanted from her was for her to be the great artist he believed she was. She trusted him completely, always bowing to his artistic and musical knowledge, confiding the most personal things in her life, confident he would never betray her – and he never did.

He was a genuinely beautiful human being, but he lacked a fighting spirit. He was always in Judy's corner, ready with the towel, the comforting words, the caring; but he did not know how to send her out into the ring with advice on how to win – nor was he able to step in and do battle for her. To the frightened, insecure girl he gave his devotion; he represented all that was good in life.

Another man, Arthur Freed, now came into her life. Freed was a songwriter on contract and had written the lyrics of 'Singin' in the Rain', 'I Cried for You', and 'You Were Meant for Me', among other songs, But songwriting did not satisfy his ambitions. He wanted to produce film musicals. There is no question that Arthur Freed recognized Judy's potential, but first and foremost he saw his own future in that talent. Not powerful enough to get on another star's or director's bandwagon, he concentrated, and indeed chanced Judy's eventually having one of her own.

Freed coauthored songs for most of her early films. By his own admission, no one else, before or since, ever was able to interpret and phrase a lyric of his as Judy did. 'She got into the hearts of her audience,' he said. Freed, however, never won Judy's heart. She trusted him because Edens assured her of his musical know-how.

After her part in *Broadway Melody of 1938*, Judy was cast in a happy, unpretentious racing film – *Thoroughbreds Don't Cry*. The film had been written for Freddie Bartholomew, but Bartholomew was tied up in the unfortunate sequence of custody trials between his parents and his Aunt 'Cissy'* The film was delayed, the studio waiting as long as it could for Bartholomew. Finally, another English boy – Ronald Sinclair – was cast in the role of the son of a lord who brings his horse to America to recoup the family's fortunes.

Mickey Rooney appeared as a jockey (a forerunner of many future roles) and Judy as the teen-age daughter of the woman (Sophie Tucker) who ran a boardinghouse for jockeys. It was the first time Judy and Mickey were onscreen together. The chemistry was unquestionable. The film was appealing, but little more. Judy sang one Arthur Freed–Nacio Herb Brown song – 'A New Pair of Shoes'. She gave it all the heart and all the energy she had. She was above the material, and MGM now knew why they had a *property*. Further, they decided they had a *team*. But Rooney was lined up for another film. There would be a four-to-five-month hiatus before they could appear together again.

Judy was cast in two films without time to breathe between them or after the one she had just completed. Both were strenuous films and the hours grueling, and Judy had

* Aunt Cissy had brought the boy to America with his parents' consent; but when he was earning thousands weekly, his parents and his sisters wanted a whopping percentage of his earnings or custody. The boy chose to remain with his aunt. After several years of costly court appearances, Aunt Cissy won custody—Bartholomew being ordered to pay his parents 20 percent of his weekly earnings and an additional 15 percent to the support of his sisters.

to slim even more for the roles. Surviving on Mayer's dictate of a chicken-soup diet and diet pills, she was to faint several times from hunger. It was suggested that she needed more sleep, but all the pills she took were 'uppers' (pep pills). A new system was inaugurated. Between setups and other performers' scenes (time lags of one to three hours), Judy would be escorted to the studio hospital and given a strong enough dosage of Nembutal to put her immediately to sleep. Fifteen minutes before she was to appear before the cameras, she was awakened, fed a handful of uppers and sent back onto the stage.

CHAPTER NINE

Everybody Sing came next. Harry Rapf produced the film, which co-starred Judy with Allan Jones and Fanny Brice. It was the first time she received stellar billing. Advertising for it stated: 'Here comes the funniest musical comedy of 1938! It's MGM's star-packed swing treat! Funny Fanny Brice brings her famous *Good News* radio character, *Baby Snooks*, to the screen! Allan Jones sings those love songs as only he can! *Adorable Judy Garland zooms to stardom on wings of song!*'

Everybody *did* sing in the film – too often, and with inferior material. But Judy, aided by Roger Edens' arrangements and 'interpolations', displayed her talent as a superb vocal technician. Expert cameraman Joseph Ruttenberg photographed the film and, using extra closeups, captured the essence of Judy's appeal. The trembling lip, the mouth that was fighting despair to laugh, the quivering chin, the dewy about-to-cry eyes filled the screen. Judy was no longer just a prodigy voice. She was a vulnerable young woman who registered pain and past indignities. She was insecure and humble, but never down. She was plain, uneducated, a brown sparrow who had a natural golden voice that made her feathers gleam and the world take note. Audiences walked out of the darkened theaters forgetting both the film and the other cast players; forgetting their own private post-Depression blues. What they remembered was the throb of the small sparrow heart, the quick glad-to-be-alive smile, and the voice that contained both laughter and tears.

Rosen and Ethel were aware of what had happened and that Judy's contract, though providing for semiannual raises, did not pay well enough for her new position. The front office was implacable on the terms. but Rosen did obtain a $200-a-week salary for Ethel as compensation. Supposedly Judy's coach and manager, Ethel was now on the Metro payroll, owing her first allegiance to Mayer.

For Judy, there was little time to think about what was happening to her. *Listen Darling* began shooting within twenty-four hours of the roll-up of *Everybody Sing*. Once again Edens was by her side. Directed, as the last picture had been, by Edwin Marin, *Listen Darling* was superior material in all areas. The script was natural and sensible; the cast excellent (Mary Astor, Freddie Bartholomew, Walter Pidgeon and Alan Hale); and the songs – 'Zing! Went the Strings of My Heart', 'On a Bumpy Road to Love', 'Nobody's Baby', and 'Ten Pins in the Sky' – tailored for Judy, who was also given more of an opportunity to act.

Mickey was now preparing a new Andy Hardy film. He was Metro's leading boy star. The studio had cast him opposite Batholomew in two films – *The Devil Is a Sissy* and *Captains Courageous*. The contrast of personalities served him well. The scrappy, tough kid who also had heart was a crowd pleaser. Metro put him in every film that had a role for him. He was all over the lot – doing impersonations; singing; dancing up a storm; being tough and rough with a heart of pure buttter; being mischievous, moving and merry. In 1938 he won a miniature Oscar as the outstanding boy juvenile (*Boys Town*) that year. It is incredible how fast his star had ascended. In 1937 he had placed 104th in the

Motion Picture Herald's annual popularity poll. By 1938 he was number 3, topped only by Clark Gable and Shirley Temple.

Mickey made the first Andy Hardy film, *A Family Affair*, in 1937. It was a low-budget picture based on an old play, *Skidding*, by Aurania Rouverel that Metro owned and dusted off in its harried efforts to keep Mickey before cameras and public. No matter what the studio anticipated as audience reaction, it did not expect the clamoring for more following the release of the film.

Immediately the studio fed to exhibitors *Judge Hardy's Children* and *Out West with the Hardys*. The series had caught on and was snowballing. It was proving to be, among other things, a great showcase for new young talent. It was natural for Mayer to want Judy to make her second appearance with Mickey in a Hardy film. *Love Finds Andy Hardy* was quickly readied. In this film, Judy, the daughter of a musical-comedy actress, was a young girl visiting the Hardys' next-door neighbors. Andy finds her a nuisance until he discovers she can sing. But even then he is torn by his feelings for his high school sweetheart (Ann Rutherford) and a teen-age vamp (Lana Turner). It was the best of the series to that point, although Judy's role was the least effective. In order to allow her to sing several numbers, the scenario suffered.

In many respects it was a backward step from *Listen Darling*. But once more electricity crackled when Rooney and Garland were onscreen together. Confident that it had found a golden team – double moneymakers like Eddy and Mac-Donald, Beery and Dressler, Rogers and Astaire – the studio sent out its order: line up a series of starring vehicles for these two.

Mickey was Judy's first attraction to a boy of her own age category and her oldest friend and confidant. They had shared much, knew each other well – yet Mickey was squiring other girls to parties and restaurants, all of them more glamorous than Judy. The insecurities, the inferiorities became more ingrown.

At the same time, she was attending the studio school with a select few – Lana Turner, Ann Rutherford, June Preisser, Ava Gardner – and surrounded on the lot by the most beautiful women in the world. Garbo, Lamarr, Colbert, Myrna Loy, Luise Rainer – the list seemed endless, and beauty and glamour appeared endowed upon all but herself. Never in her lifetime did she consider herself a beautiful woman, always very conscious of the absence of two ingredients, she equated with beauty: a good figure and lovely thick, long hair. Forever starving herself and being harrassed about her figure, she also was continually attendant to the 'faults' of her natural hair. It was thin, and onscreen she wore pieces and falls; a naturally mousy brown, it was reluctant to curl or grow. Sitting in the small MGM schoolroom surrounded by the luxurious and lovely tresses of Turner and Gardner – both girls Mickey dated – could not have helped raise her desperately flagging ego.

For over a year Arthur Freed had buttonholed Mayer whenever and wherever he could and spoken to him about the possibility of his producing a film. Freed lacked charm and even a cultural veneer – qualities Mayer admired in men who did not have power or money. Although Mayer thought the young man was capable, he was not swayed to play God in his case or to make it easy for him. 'You find a property, a story – maybe then,' he said in passing.

Freed took the bait. Two things appeared certain. His first film had to be a musical, in which he would be sure of his footing, and it had to have a star role for one of the young contract players. It was natural that he should think of Judy Garland.

Employing the help of readers, secretaries, friends, and family, he scoured the available properties. Nothing. But then, someone mentioned *The Wizard of Oz* by L. Frank Baum. It was owned by Sam Goldwyn and had been for several years, but Goldwyn had shelved the project. To Freed's credit, he saw the tremendous musical potential of the property, which Goldwyn had not. And from the moment he read it, he could visualize Judy as Dorothy.

Working with as much secrecy as possible so that no one else could step in and grab the rights away from him, Freed began negotiations with Goldwyn. During this time Mayer had been on an extensive European trip buying all the foreign talent he could. Greer Garson and Hedy Lamarr were two of the acquisitions from that trip. On his return Freed went to see Mayer and told him he owned *The Wizard of Oz* and that he saw it as a fantasy musical and as a vehicle for Judy.

Sixteen at the time, Judy was full-bosomed and looking very mature. Her Metro image since *Love Finds Andy Hardy* was now of yearning young womanhood. Dorothy, in *The Wizard of Oz*, was a little girl no more than eleven. Mayer thought Judy was wrong for the film and vetoed her inclusion in the package. But he did like the property and agreed with Freed that it would make a good musical. Shirley Temple was under contract to Fox. Mayer set out to borrow her, but first he struck a low blow to Freed.

Quoting Bosley Crowther's *The Hollywood Rajah*:

Mayer himself got great enjoyment from exercise of power and from feeling himself responsible for advancement of someone's career. 'I've taken this boy and I have made a great actor (or director or producer) out of him!' That was one of his favorite and oft-repeated remarks. He felt he needed to make people grateful and beholden to him. He literally bathed in the sunshine of his own esteem.

At the other extreme, Mayer could not stand being wrong about anyone; and the year before he had lured Mervyn LeRoy (Harry Warner's son-in-law) away from Warner's with an astronomical bribe of a $300,000 yearly salary. LeRoy had already proved his competence and genius at Warner's with *Little Caesar*, *I Am a Fugitive from a Chain Gang*, and *Anthony Adverse*. Mayer gave him Luise Rainer (who was then a big star) and a feeble script entitled *Dramatic School* to produce. It was a disaster. Finding this a bitter pill, he was still determined LeRoy would produce great films for him, greater than those he had produced for Harry Warner.

It seemed no one could miss with Shirley Temple. Calling Freed into his office, Mayer let him have the news. The studio was buying the property from him and would give him the grand opportunity of being associate producer. LeRoy was to produce, and Metro was borrowing Shirley Temple. Knowing that if he refused his Metro days would be over and that Mayer would see to it that the other studios wouldn't touch him, Freed had little other recourse than to accept.

Mayer had taken it for granted that Twentieth-Century-Fox – owing him a favor for the future use of Gable in *Gone with the Wind* (to be produced by David Selznick) – would agree. To his amazement, Fox refused to lend La Temple.

Judy and Ethel were brought before the high Rajah and told of their good fortune, being warned at the same time of his ability to replace Judy if she did not buckle down and deliver. While the screenplay was being prepared, she was to go on alternate days of fasting. Dorothy had to look wide-eyed and gaunt.

Judy was delivered into the hands of the trainers. The fasting regime was put into effect, Her teeth were capped; her hair dyed, then bewigged; her body girdled and strapped tight, and hours of supervised practice imposed in how to walk and dance while so restrained. At the same time she attended classes from nine to twelve in the little schoolhouse that was then next to the film library on the lot, struggling to keep up the B's and C's that she was expected to make for credit to graduate from high school.

Publicity releases went out that Metro was sparing no expense in this venture. It was to be one of the top-budget pictures of the year, filmed in both black-and-white and color, with a star supporting cast, directed by the inimitable Victor Fleming, who was one of the greatest directors of that period (*Treasure Island, Captains Courageous, Red Dust, Test Pilot* – and after *The Wizard of Oz, Gone with*

58

the Wind). Harold Arlen and E. Y. 'Yip' Harburg were brought from Broadway to write the score.

Judy was getting the star treatment, but much to Ethel's chagrin, the studio was paying them the combined salaries of $350 a week – and at that, Ethel received the larger amount. Mayer refused to grant Rosen an interview. Before the cameras rolled on *The Wizard of Oz*, Ethel knew Rosen had to be replaced. In one of the most scurrilous sellouts in Hollywood history, Mayer persuaded Ethel to sign with his pal Frank Orsatti. This meant Judy no longer had free representation, for Orsatti was bound by what might be called a 'Devil's pact' with Mayer. Orsatti was famous for introducing beautiful girls to studio executives in exchange for personal favors. Through Mayer's help, he was now a successful film agent. But there was no way he could chance opposing him on any issue or contract. To appease Ethel, Orsatti agreed to a figure of $500 – a raise of $150 a week when at the same time Mickey Rooney, with good representation, was making close to $5,000 a week.

'You can't kill a talent like Judy's,' Yip Harburg said. 'Only bad material can do that.'

Judy was given the best material and surrounded by the best talents in the business. The ad copy announced, 'Dreams Come True! Metro-Goldwyn-Mayer's Technicolor wonder show is the greatest since "Snow White".'

At last Ethel's dream was about to come true.

CHAPTER TEN

WHILE Metro spared no expense constructing the fantasy world of *Oz*, the Munich Peace Pact had been signed; Hitler had paraded through the streets of Asch; the swastika was blazoned on everything; and the world moved toward war.

But the fact that occupied most of Judy's thoughts was that on completion of *Oz* she planned to graduate with a class at Hollywood High School. Customarily, when young contract players had passed all high school requirements, they would be sent to a local high school for graduation and for the few days preceding it. Being well-known performers set them apart, but it did have meaning to the teen-agers.

The filming of *Oz* was Judy's most difficult to date. There was the sheer physical exhaustion of wardrobe and makeup demands, aggravated by the strain of rigorous dieting. It was impossible for her to spend much time in the schoolroom, so a teacher, Rose Carter, was assigned to remain with her for eight hours of the working day. That way, when a stand-in was taking her place while lights and camera were being adjusted, or when she was briefly out of a scene, lessons could be conducted. But imagine the difficulty of such a procedure amid the noise and confusion of forty or more set workers striking and constructing sets; actors rehearsing; sound being adjusted; cables, dollies, and cameras being dragged across the crowded stage, causing anyone in their direct path to jump out of the way, while the lowering of microphones and overhead wires caused the rest of the company to duck for their lives.

Judy's problems were intensified by pressures from the front office, critical of every shot she was in; by Ethel standing constant surveillance like an agent from a foreign country; by the anxiety, the nervousness, and the super-charged energy created by the pills; and by the atmosphere of combat on the set caused by Judy's being cast with a group of seasoned older veterans.

According to Margaret Hamilton (the Wicked Witch of the West), there was little love lost for Judy on the part of the four main male stars (Bert Lahr, Ray Bolger, Jack Haley, and Frank Morgan). Fearful that she might upstage them, Miss Hamilton claims they played against her – not with her. Judy was also much aware that she had been second choice on the film. There was no question that apart from some of the studio technicians; Edens; a young man named Barron Polan, who was Mervyn LeRoy's secretary/assistant; and Maggie Hamilton, she was delivered daily by Ethel into an arena of supermagnified hostility.

Through the years Judy claimed a close friendship with Miss Hamilton, though after *Oz* they saw very little of each other. Meeting Maggie Hamilton clarifies this; for in person, more honestly cast as the mother of us all, she is an irrepressibly warm, demonstrative, chatty lady whose voice soothes, eyes communicate, and easy touch assures. She was and remains symbolically everything Ethel was not. Happily for Judy, she could confide to Miss Hamilton the things that were troubling her.

Maggie, a seasoned performer herself, found her own smaller role exhausting, hardly able at the close of a shooting day to drag herself home. But Judy, coping with much, much more, never seemed at a loss for energy. The older woman, fearing the truth, asked about this; and Judy told her she was being given 'a lot of pills to sleep and a lot of pills to say awake.'

Maggie was horrified. 'Why do you take them? Why don't you refuse?' she demanded.

'Well, I just can't seem to either get up or go to sleep without them anymore,' the young girl replied.

As the end of the film and graduation grew closer and closer, Judy's spirits soared. 'Isn't it marvelous? I'm going to graduate with a class,' she told Maggie excitedly. 'Would you like to see my dress?'

The answer, of course, was Yes, and Judy ran into the dressing room to bring it out. It was nothing like what might have been expected – just a very simple little dress that met all the requirements a graduate must have; but it was the biggest thing in Judy's life, and she was absolutely thrilled about it.

Judy, however, was sent on a tour with Mickey Rooney as soon as the film was complete, meaning she had to forfeit graduation. Maggie was so upset that she called the girl who headed the publicity department and who had organized the tour.

'Do you realize what you have done? This is a terrible thing,' Maggie told her.

'Well, it's only a graduation. It's not so terrible,' the girl responded.

Maggie said, 'It is! It's just really terrible. It's one thing in the world this girl wanted to do and it's just an awful thing! Is there anyone I can call who could be helpful?'

'There's nothing you can do, Miss Hamilton,' she was informed. 'The orders for this tour came directly from Mr. Mayer.'

And of course, there *was* nothing Maggie Hamilton could do. (Subsequently, Judy received her high school diploma from University High School.)

Working along with the scenarist, Harburg and Arlen tried through the musical score to transpose the emotional yearnings that could motivate a young girl leading a drab existence to make a dream come true.

'Here was Dorothy,' Harburg says, 'a little girl from Kansas, a bleak place where there were no flowers, where there was no color of any kind. What does a child like this want? The only thing colorful in her world was a rainbow.'

Arlen got the melody of 'Over the Rainbow' first, but the lyrics did not come easily. When the song was complete, no one was sure about it. It was included in the first rough cut, but during the running of the final it was decided that the song was too cloying and sentimental and should be removed; and it was. Only after the initial sneak preview was it spliced back into the print – and then because it was felt the picture at that point was slow and needed a change of pace and it was too late to shoot a new musical sequence.

Oz was a dream come true, but filming it was a continuous nightmare. Seven assistant directors came and went. Tensions were evident and the emotional temperatures high among cast and crew. The front office pulled out all the stops, and the film was finally brought in for over $2 million – an unprecedented budget for a film in this category. The cast, including a troupe of midgets, grew to over nine thousand. All of Metro's twenty-nine sound stages were ultimately utilized to construct sixty-five spectacular sets. The special-effects department had to produce tricks with actors never before attempted. Cameramen had to film people flying without photographing the telltale ropes. A tornado was to be created, and Dorothy and Toto, her dog, carried off into the sky on it as if it were a giant black bird. Then Maggie Hamilton, as the Wicked Witch of the West, was to be *melted down* to a black pool.

To accomplish the last, the set was constructed about the ground with a platform elevator thirty inches square in the spot where the witch, Miss Hamilton, was to stand. Her dress was nailed all the way around and covering the platform. When she began to melt, the platform descended and the air rose into her dress until finally, nothing was left but the hat.

No one who has seen the film could forget Dorothy's wonder-lit eyes as she wandered through Oz, the innocent child, the little-girl-lost sighing with deep pathos, 'Why, then, oh why can't I?' as she watched the bluebirds fly over the rainbow.

Judy stated later in her life, 'I think the American people put their arms around me when I was a child performer, and they've kept them there – even when I was in trouble.' It was true, and it was because of her characterization of Dorothy. The portrayal was not just wistful or charming, nor did it contain the quality of endearing cuteness that would have been brought to the part by Shirley Temple.

A desperation to believe crept into Judy's performance. She was much more than a young girl in jeopardy as she pursued a dream. Achieving the dream was where the spirit of survival existed. And in the end the dream was one shared by the majority of the American people – that their small, brown lives would be touched with wonder; that there could be a Land of Oz in their own backyards. It was not a children's tale, for it was adult in philosophy; and Judy's eyes and voice mirrored severe human suffering, which they knew and identified with. In Judy's Dorothy, there was a

63

plea for love and protection. It communicated itself with alarming depth.

From the time of the sneak preview of *Oz* the studio was certain the film would be a box-office bonanza, and that Judy was potentially, and next to Mickey, their hottest young property; but they treated her like a poor relation, told her she was only the result of their publicity and that she had a long way to go as a performer. Then the studio sent her by train on that cross-country personal-appearance tour with Mickey (the one Margaret Hamilton attempted to halt), convincing Judy she needed his audience, his charisma to bolster the film. The train ride across the country was the one delight of the trip. Judy loved trains; they took her back to her early childhood and the trip across country with her father, Ethel, and her sisters. She remembered how her father had told her made-up stories of the sleeping towns and the darkened houses as they drove through the strange cities. Train rides allowed her the same fantasies. She would always like them from that date, always take a train before she would drive or fly. She even liked their smell and the rhythm of the wheels on the tracks. On a train, she was herself. There were no pressures; there was no place she had to be.

They arrived at Grand Central Station in New York and went without any time to spare to the theater, where they were billed as America's Sweethearts and did five shows a day (Judy and Mickey, years later, claimed seven, but the theater advertised five). From the moment they arrived at Grand Central, they were mobbed. Police reinforcements were brought in to help protect them at the Capitol where they were appearing, but one can just imagine the bedlam of 15,000 people trying to gain entry to every performance in a house that seated 5,400.

'Come on, toots, we'll knock them dead,' Rooney shouted as they made their first entrance.

Judy Garland was back before a live audience. They stamped their feet, whistled, clapped their hands. Ethel was in the wings along with a long line of studio 'trainers' – ready to reprimand her if she seemed too tired or reluctant; ready with a handful of pep pills and a glass of water whenever the bell sounded and she could step back to her corner.

The Wizard of Oz opened on a Thursday – August 17, 1939 – at the Capitol Theater on Broadway at 51st Street. The advertising proclaimed that Mickey's and Judy's appearances inaugurated the fall season. But Major Edward Bowes, the managing director (later to conduct his famous radio amateur hour), remembered it as one of the hottest days of a long, hot summer and that fall seemed as far away as the other side of the rainbow.

In between performances they went to luncheons, dinners, benefits, broadcasts, and interviews.

One day halfway through their forty-five-minute appearance, Judy collapsed in the wings. Mickey was pushed back onstage. 'Ladies and gentlemen,' he managed, 'my partner has taken ill.'

'She'll be all right! Stall them!' somebody shouted from backstage.

Rooney began a routine about a tennis match and an announcer, interspersing it with comedy sound effects such as *zot, plop, plang,* following it with a similar routine about a Joe Louis fight with crowd noises, bells, et cetera. Becoming nervous, he stole a glance toward the wings. Judy was being helped to her feet by the retinue of handlers. Pushing them aside, she stood alone, and then, catching Rooney's eye, made her way toward him. Back onstage, she continued as though nothing had happened.

CHAPTER ELEVEN

WHILE the rest of the world was beginning to recognize film as an art, Louis B. Mayer discovered the high-gross potential of the film musical. No other studio had the players, personnel, technicians, or space to photograph the grand-scale productions that were part of the prototype called, 'the Metro musical': glossy, Technicolored, dance-packed, song-jammed, star-loaded, chorus-crowded with hundreds of rhythmic robots. Nothing lived, breathed, or contained any semblance of reality. Whatever humanity survived these films did so through the power of star personalities. Rooney and Garland were prime examples.

Oz proved to be blockbuster box-office and sent the story department out on an immediate search for musical properties for Judy. Convinced that two stars meant three times the gross, Mayer sent the department back to look for stories that could co-star Judy with Mickey.

Confident now that Arthur Freed was the man rightly cast as Judy's next producer, Mayer gave him the go-ahead on a Rodgers and Hart show – *Babes in Arms* – that the studio owned. Not the sort of man who did not back up his investment, Mayer insisted Busby Berkeley become a major part of what came to be known as the Freed Unit.

The Freed Unit had as its nucleus Berkeley, Edens, dance director Charles 'Chuck' Walters, music director Georgie Stoll, art director Cedric Gibbons, scriptwriter Fred Finklehoffe, and cameraman Ray June. They worked together (except for Finklehoffe, who did only three) on the four big musicals that co-starred Rooney and Garland (Rooney still retaining star billing in all of them): *Babes in Arms, Strike Up the Band, Babes on Broadway,* and *Girl Crazy.* Except for the third, all were based on hit Broadway shows.

Having foisted Judy as an eleven-year-old Dorothy on the public and won it over, Freed now had to help Judy successfully make the transition to portray a girl her own age (seventeen) in *Babes in Arms* and yet not lose the large audience she had won in *Oz*. This he achieved by establishing Judy's character in the film as a humble Plain Jane (Mary, in this case) who stood back while Rooney took the lead – hoping, praying (always in song) that he would just look at her once as though she were a girl (which he did at the end of the last reel). Ray June, the cameraman, following Joe Ruttenberg's lead, zoomed in – to the desperate need to be accepted in those wide velvet brown eyes, to the fear of always being the loser that caused that lip to tremble; and in the end – though the film *was* Rooney's, and Judy's role a supporting one despite star billing – it was the quality of pathos conveyed by Judy that kept the audience enthralled, and that same searching soulfulness that shot the bright moments so sky-high.

The grind on the film was relentless; the pressures overwhelming. Judy had first suffered the exhausting filming of *Oz*; had been sent on the five-shows-a-day tour; had been cast immediately upon her return in *Babes in Arms*; and then – twelve hours after shooting had ended on that film – stepped into *Andy Hardy Meets a Debutante* (the debutante of the title being played by Diana Lewis). Again with no time between films, she was rushed into the strenuous schedule of the Freed Unit's follow-up to *Babes in Arms – Strike Up the Band*.

'. . . they had us working days and nights on end,' Judy complained in *McCall's*. 'They'd give us pep-up pills to keep us on our feet long after we were exhausted. Then they'd take us to the studio hospital and knock us cold with sleeping pills – Mickey sprawled out on one bed and me on another. Then after four hours they'd wake us up and give us the pep-up pills again as we could work another seventy-two hours in a row. Half of the time we were hanging from the ceiling, but it became a way of life for us.'

This appalling situation caused Edens to go to Freed, who claimed he had his hands tied. Edens did not think Freed was responsible and, in fact, always defended him, but he recognized that neither of them was a match for the man who ran the studio and was their boss. *Babes in Arms* and *Strike Up the Band* had huge budgets for their day (over $600,000). Longer shooting schedules could not be afforded if each film was to have a cast of hundreds; and as Mayer felt not one extra should be cut, the shooting schedule was adhered to, the budget left intact, and

Judy and Rooney expected to continue as the studio demanded.

The people in the front office were still concerned about Judy's weight and kept reminding her that without their vigilance she would be a fat, awkward, unattractive teenager. Judy suffered the indignities of being told she wasn't really a good performer, that they were making her look good, and again and again that there was always someone to step into her shoes.

The premiere of *Babes in Arms* at Grauman's Chinese Theatre on October 10, 1939, was the culmination of Ethel's dream. To all but Ethel the dream might have seemed unreachable. But Baby Frances was a bona fide star – her footsteps in the cement of the forecourt of Grauman's along with threescore of filmdom's greatest, triumphant in *The Wizard of Oz* and acclaimed for her co-starring role with Rooney. Ethel held her hand as Judy stepped onto the wet cement and assisted her as she stepped out again. Then she did a very curious thing.

Judy knelt beside the block of wet cement and with her finger inscribed her name, then planted her hands in the cement for a handprint. As Judy did the last, Ethel leaned over her daughter and with her own finger straightened a letter in Judy's signature.

Stardom changed very little in Judy's life. Ida Koverman had interceded to convince Mayer that Judy's public would accept her in a sophisticated dress, and he had permitted a gown to be designed for her for the premiere. But as she looked around her at the sexy dress Lana wore, her own lost its glamour. It seemed to Judy that Lana was everything she wanted to be. She was not exactly envious of Lana, but she did admire her and constantly put herself down in comparison.

Her inferiority complex was at its apex. Seventeen and a star, she was earning only $500 weekly – $200 of it payable to Ethel. She did not have a bevy of admirers. Her dates – like the ones she had with a young contract player, Robert Stack – were arranged by the studio, not for her benefit, but to place the man's name before the public.

She went to parties given by the young Hollywood set – Rooney, Rutherford, Jackie Cooper, Richard Quine, Sidney Miller, O'Connor, Leonard Sues. She always joined in and performed. On the outside she gave the appearance of a spirited, talented, fun-loving girl. Her sisters were now out of the house. Privately, she was a loner. She had two large German shepherd dogs on which she lavished affection; read a lot – romantic poetry, mostly; drew dress designs – always glamorous in execution; but deep doubts plagued her, sending her into spells of abysmal depression. Much of this could be attributed to the effect the pills were having on her. But other forces were at work. Having now completed her high school studies, she was on her own – her grades not warranting college acceptance; those around her unable to contribute to her intellectual growth. Roger Edens would discuss music and musicians and books and authors with her, but she was too embarrassed to tell him she had never heard the names before; and her schedule was such that there was never any time to go to libraries to find out for herself. She was beginning to look for the meaning of things, but it was a lot like stumbling about in a heavy fog.

Waking dreams haunted her – thoughts that would not remain buried. There were men in closets peering lasciviously through solid wood doors. She dressed in the bathroom, locking herself in. She insisted on wearing a slip under everything, even if Wardrobe felt it was unnecessary. From the very beginning her studio biography revealed the truth about her background, while other players were given glamorous pasts. She hated interviews. 'There's nothing to say about *me*,' she would confess. The story she would repeat was about her father's death. 'He was a gay, handsome Irishman and we loved each other madly,' she confided to one and all.

As Christmas, 1939, approached, she decided (though she did not tell Ethel) that when her contract was over, she would become a writer. She spoke to her close friend Barron Polan about this, telling him, 'There are just so many things locked up in my head. I feel that if there was a can opener that could open my brain, all these thinkings and feelings would gush out like some unstoppable water tap.' She was encouraged to write some of them down.

In whatever few moments came to her, she composed fragments of verse. Soon she had enough to fill a small book. In perhaps one of her first totally private acts, she hand-copied the poetry, giving the copy to a printer to bind in tan leather. Polan had many of the same qualities as Edens – the polish, the charm, the intelligence, the gentle understanding. They had become good friends during *The Wizard of Oz*, and when his birthday came around she presented him with her book of poems which Polan has held on to throughout the years.

The poems do not unveil Judy as another Emily Dickinson. However, they do indeed reveal a great deal about Judy. They reflect all the Rupert Brooke, Shelley, Keats, and Browning she had been reading (later she was to admire Edna St. Vincent Millay), and a deeply sensitive romantic nature is exposed.

Whatever the critical assessment, the need to compose and publish the poetry screamed out for attention to be paid to that need. But there seemed no one close enough to hear her.

CHAPTER TWELVE

As 1940 rolled into high gear, Judy and Mickey were propelled from *Andy Hardy Meets a Debutante* directly into *Strike Up the Band*. Neither had very much free time, but what there was seemed provident to spend together. 'Somehow,' as Mickey declares about that period, 'it was easier to withstand public pressure when we were together. Wherever either of us went we were recognized.'

They would frequent the nearby amusement piers –

Venice, Ocean Park, Santa Monica – riding the roller coasters, wandering through the fun house. Rooney threw big parties at his new, fairly palatial house on Densmore Drive, playing the drums and doing impersonations; or the two of them would sing duets like 'Manhattan' or 'How About You?' As Rooney says, 'Work and fun were inextricably interwoven. It was impossible to tell just where one ended and the other began. Our work was our fun, and our fun was our work.'

On Sunday mornings he would drive to Judy's house in Hollywood and they would have breakfast together, followed by long talks. 'I was going to write a musical comedy for her,' Rooney recalls in his autobiography. 'She was going to sing the songs I wrote. We'd do our own play. We'd capture Broadway. We'd be the most successful team in history.'

It was, ironically, as their scriptwriters had divined. They would dream together, and in a crowd Judy would encourage him to go on, standing back, performing with him but seldom alone. But that was where it ended. His dates were tall, gorgeous, and always by his side when Judy stepped away from the piano.

Playing opposite Judy, though, he stood in constant admiration. 'Her timing was like that of a chronometer,' he continues in his autobiography. 'She could deliver a comic line with just the right comic touch or say a poignant line slowly enough for the poignancy to hit hard but still stay short of schmaltz. She could turn on intensity, as I could turn on intensity, memorize great chunks of script, as I could, ad-lib, as I. Alone she could take an ordinary scene and by sheer strength of talent make it a scene that people everywhere remembered.'

And later he says, 'We were a couple of teen-age kids, proud of our talent and our poise ... I couldn't rattle Judy and she couldn't rattle me. God, we had fun.'

Actually, those early months of 1940 were halcyon ones for Judy. The work was as grinding, but she had Rooney and Barron Polan and Roger Edens to talk to; and her home situation was the happiest it had been since her father's death. Ethel had met a man named Bill Gilmore and had fallen in love.

William Gilmore was no replacement for Frank Gumm. He lacked the warmth, charm, and communication that came from mutual talents and interests. Broad, weathered, and masculine, he looked as if he might have wandered off a Western set. A 'dress' extra perhaps – because he was not of the stuff of real cowboys. For that matter, his background was unclear, and so was his occupation. He possessed very little knowledge of films and the industry; stocks, mines, and investments punctuated his conversation. It was obvious he had bummed around the country, had held a variety of different jobs, and had come to California in search of a golden dream.

Judy did not take to him, but so relieved was she that Ethel's attention was diverted that she welcomed him into the family. Yet from the day Bill Gilmore married Ethel and moved into the house, Judy planned her own departure. Being only seventeen made that difficult. It was a waiting game – but a short one. In six months she would be eighteen, an age when it seemed plausible for her to have an apartment of her own.

And a place of her own had become imperative – for those early months of Ethel's marriage to Gilmore reopened doors that had been sealed shut for a long time. For a number of years the pressures of Judy's career had been so intense and Ethel's vigilance so consuming that sex had played only a small part in either of their lives. At the same time that she wanted to appear glamorous, to attract the young men she fancied, and to be thought of as the belle of the ball, Judy had desperately tried to bury all thoughts of sex, choosing a more romantic attitude. Ethel's seducing, touching Gilmore was difficult for a young daughter to observe – and, as Ethel had not been as affectionate with her own father, impossible for Judy to accept.

On the screen Judy was being confronted with an image of herself as America's sweetheart – Andy Hardy's next-door neighbor, the girl one eventually marries but with whom one never has premarital sex. Rooney ran off with all those sex bombshells, but Judy and the audience were convinced – because Judy represented what she did – that he would eventually come home to her.

But offscreen there was Ethel being unfaithful to her father's memory; and there was Mayer, who, with his wife ill, with his power and money at its zenith, and with the encroachment of middle age, had – after a number of years spent in the pursuit of his ideal of the American woman – let loose the satyr in him. There was a great deal of lecherous humor about the libidinous forays conducted at the beach house taken by a friend and much talk referring to the place as Metro's Casting Couch.

Judy was, therefore, affronted and confronted daily by a man who had set himself up as a father image and who was, at the same time, an outspoken moralist and a dirty old man.

Mayer was famed for saying, 'A son can hate his father but he *must* respect him.' In view of Mayer's behaviour, this was damned near impossible for the 'children' on his payroll.

CHAPTER THIRTEEN

NINETEEN hundred and forty was a leap year; and on February 29, both Judy and Rooney were in the audience of the ballroom at the Ambassador Hotel as nominees for an Academy Award. Bob Hope emceed the second half of the program, which was broadcast live on radio. The Awards to be given were for films released in 1939. It is the height of incongruity that Rooney had been nominated for his performance in *Babes in Arms* as Best Actor of the Year, whereas Judy's nomination for the same year was as Best Juvenile Performer (totally sexless, therefore).

Nineteen hundred and thirty-nine was the year *Gone with the Wind* had been released. (Judy had attended the premiere at the Cathay Circle Theatre with Barron Polan.) The majority of awards – Best Film Director, Script, Supporting Actress, Supporting Actor, etc. – went to that film. However, Rooney lost out not to Gable, but to Robert Donat for *Goodbye, Mr. Chips.*

The award for Best Juvenile Performer was won by Judy, who had also sung the winning song, 'Over the Rainbow.' Publicity pictures of Judy standing with winners David O. Selznick, Vivien Leigh, Robert Donat, Leslie Howard, and Hattie McDaniel reveal a piquant young lady, badly dressed and poorly coiffed, looking like a youngster dressed in her mother's clothes.

Although Judy was escorted by Rooney to the Awards, another girl stood by as his date for the party immediately following. It was fate, because at that party Judy met the man who was to be her first *grown-up* romance – Tyrone Power. Not only was Power young and beautiful, he was the most popular rising star in Hollywood, having made *In Old Chicago* and *Alexander's Ragtime Band* the previous year. Power told her she had a woman's body and had to dress accordingly. He recognized that rather than a child in adult clothing, Judy was a restless, searching young woman. He found that 'nervousness' exciting, her need for masculine attention compelling.

There were stars in Judy's eyes, and Mayer saw them immediately. Word went out to Louella Parsons that no mention of Power and Garland must be made in her column. Louella, who was answerable to only one god – Mayer's friend Hearst – obeyed. Judy was called into Mayer's office. She was never to see Power again. Mayer's main reason was the sophistication factor. Films portraying Judy in the same All-American Girl role were being prepared. *Babes in Arms* was doing extremely well, and *Strike Up the Band* would soon be released. Judy was under eighteen; Power had dated all the worldly young starlets in Hollywood. There were accepted codes, laws to be respected. This was a period when girls under eighteen were called 'San Quentin Quail', implying that a man could be sent to prison if the girl claimed he had molested her. It was a time in which Errol Flynn and Charlie Chaplin had been loudly and openly condemned for relationships with young women. It was the height of hypocrisy for Mayer to cast the first stone, and it was incredibly insensitive of him not to realize how important this first affair was to Judy – making her for the first, and perhaps the only time in her life feel beautiful and loved. Mayer, in pursuit of winning his case through Ethel, now began to talk about her great future and a new contract making her a very rich young lady.

Only a few days had passed when on March 9 an anonymous telephone call was made to the West Los Angeles police about a plot to kidnap Judy. A nineteen-year-old youth was taken into custody, and he confessed that he and an older man had planned to kidnap Judy, take her into the mountains, and hold her for $50,000 ransom. The older man, identified as a 'Frank Foster', was at large, and the police had organized a search for him and placed a guard around Judy's house.

Terrified, Judy called on Power, who immediately took things into his own hands. Believing Judy should be away from the area of danger, he drove her down to Tijuana, leaving himself open to the scandal of a possible arrest on charges of the Mann Act (transporting a minor across a state line for immoral purposes). Ethel was told. Within hours, Judy and Power were forced to return to Hollywood. It was the last time they were to see each other as young lovers. Upon his return, Power began to date Lana Turner. It was the ultimate blow to Judy's ego. Power offered no explanation; but of course, studio pressure could very well have been responsible for his breaking off the affair so coldly and so sharply.

The kidnap scare faded into the past and Frank Foster was never found, but the episode and the disappointment in Power had unsettled Judy. The pressures and work schedule at the studio had increased to an even more frenetic pace.

She was suffering extreme insomnia, and no quantity of pills seemed to help her sleep. No longer was she able to be 'knocked out' for an hour or two between scenes. Nights were intolerable, sleepless; and the presence of Ethel and her stepfather troublesome. The house was too small and privacy impossible. She was a harassed, desperate young woman who did not know where to turn to find her own happiness and maturity.

On Tuesday night following the Power fiasco, she appeared with Bob Hope on his radio show (she was making weekly appearances at the time). There she met David Rose, who conducted the orchestra. He was thirty years old, married to but separated from comedienne Martha Raye, and he had a quiet, intelligent, and mature manner. Born in London and educated at the Chicago College of Music, he also was a fine musician and a cultured, knowledgeable man. He was an established orchestra leader who specialized in symphonic arrangements of popular songs. He spoke to Judy about her musical phrasing, her cadence, her vibrato. She was certain she had fallen in love.

They began to see each other in any free time she had, and on June 10, her eighteenth birthday, he presented her with a ring and they announced their engagement. Earlier that day she had posed with Ethel and Mayer in Mayer's office for reporters to announce her birthday and had given no indication to Mayer or the studio of the news release she was to issue later on her own. As soon as the press was informed, Mayer was contacted. She was called back to Mayer's office. He was beside himself. Rose had two strikes against him: one, he was not yet legally divorced; and two, he had once dated Jeanette MacDonald (whom Mayer had courted). This time Judy resisted, but she did agree that they would see each other on a more private basis until Rose was free and they would postpone marrying until a suitable new film image could be devised for her. In the meantime, she announced that she wanted to move out of her mother's house and into an apartment of her own. Mayer said he would condone this only if she had a 'chaperone'. There was a

76

young woman employed on the lot with whom Judy had been friendly. Mayer suggested the girl, whom he thought to be of good character and fine reputation. Judy agreed.

Moving into an apartment of her own filled her with new-found self-assurance. She was overworked, overmedicated, and underfed; but she was eighteen, in love, and on her own. More happiness did not seem deserved, but it was to come. Barron Polan had left MGM and was now an agent with Leland Hayward. Convincing Ethel that Judy was being 'had' in the Mayer-Orsatti arrangement, he persuaded her to sign with Hayward, thereby representing Judy himself. It was not as simple as that would seem. After long and angry negotiation with Orsatti, Hayward bought Judy's contract from the Orsatti agency for $25,000. Judy, at that time, was still getting $500 a week and as a 'bonus' being permitted to retain the money she would earn from guest radio appearances. By this time she had already made millions for Metro.

However, on September 26, Mayer presented her with a new contract that Hayward and Polan had fought for vociferously. It was for seven years, and she was to receive $2,000 a week for three years, $2,500 for the two years following, $3,000 for the last two years, with a guarantee of forty weeks' work each year. A total of $680,000 over seven years.

Ethel went with her to get the contract approved in Los Angeles Superior Court (Ethel receiving a sizable percentage of Judy's salary until Judy reached twenty-one). That evening the blond, deeply tanned Rose and Judy, celebrating in Judy's apartment, planned an early and secret elopement.

The next day, Judy was commanded back to Mayer's office with Rose. The girl with whom she had been sharing her apartment turned out to have been a studio spy and had betrayed the lovers' plans.

Under threat of his being blacklisted from every radio station and film lot, Rose agreed that they would wait the year Mayer, as stern patriarch of the studio, had originally demanded.

77

Part Two

MAGGIE: You'd think someone would come to me and say: Look, Maggie, you made us all this money. Now we want you to develop yourself. What can we do for you?

QUENTIN: Darling, they'd be selling frankfurters if there were more money in it; how can you look to them for love?

—After the Fall,
by Arthur Miller

CHAPTER FOURTEEN

'Love,' in the words of Victor Hugo, 'is the greatest thing in the world because it makes an angel or a god out of a grocery clerk.' But as a film star already has godlike stature, what height remains for ascension? Judy, with blind faith in David and herself, wanted nothing more than to be eighteen and in love. But the studio would not permit that.

With *Little Nellie Kelly, Life Begins for Andy Hardy, Ziegfeld Girl,* and *Babes on Broadway* set for the year to follow, she was not being given much time for her private life. When the two lovers were together, Judy was exhausted. In his quiet way, David tried to exert what pressure he could to get Judy to fight the studio on the rigors of her schedule and on their insistence that she remain on a regimen of pills and dieting.

David worked hard. He was musical director of the Tony Martin radio show, and also was in demand as a musical arranger. But watching Judy's backbreaking daily routine shocked him. There were 6 A.M. makeup sessions, wardrobe fittings, exhausting work before the cameras, dance rehearsals, new songs to memorize, dialogue to learn, sittings for the still photographer, interviews, and a shooting schedule that had her putting in (with almost no rest) sixteen- to eighteen-hour days. It was logical he would believe she should have at least one square meal a day for her own survival. She began to gain a little weight. As soon as this happened, a dress form of a fat woman appeared beside the mirror where she stood to have her wardrobe fittings. *'Do you want to look like this dummy or a star?'* an attached note reminded her.

The studio became more exacting. In its hands eighteen

hours a day, she was forced to adhere to the soup diet Mayer had decreed. Chicken soup, black coffee and cigarettes (she was smoking four packs a day to fight her appetite), and pills every four hours became a way of life.

She later told Jinx Falkenburg and Tex McCrary in an interview, 'I swear there must have been a vat full of chicken soup at the MGM commissary with my name engraved on it. If I sneaked in for a chocolate sundae with pecan nuts and bogs of whipped cream on top – I used to dream about those things – I would always get the same story: "Sorry, Mr. Mayer has left instructions about what you are to eat today – chicken soup." '

The lovers' favorite song was 'Our Love', which Rose had composed for her and which he interpolated into his radio program as often as possible; but as it stood, their love was not enough to sustain them. All Judy dreamed about was getting married. Marriage and love seemed interchangeable to her. Once she was married to David, her life would be totally different. She convinced herself of this. It got her through the majority of nightmare days. The rest of the time she relied on the pep-up pills the studio dispensed.

The rigid dieting kept her five-foot-two-inch frame down to ninety-eight pounds, but often, when she was near collapse, she would plead to Chuck Walters, the dance director, 'I'm too hungry to continue.' Walters would reply 'Get on with it and you won't be hungry.' Judy called him 'the man with the bullwhip'.

The making of the films churned relentlessly like clouds in a hurricane sky. In *Little Nellie Kelly* (with George Murphy and Douglas MacPhail) she was allowed to grow up and have her first real screen kiss. *Ziegfeld Girl* found her with star billing – above that of Hedy Lamarr and Lana Turner – and a role that gave her a more glamorous image. Judy Garland had matured before the public's eyes.

Strike Up the Band was released to general acclaim and top grosses. It underscored Mayer's philosophies and was overripe with such doggerel as momism, the kind banker, the reaping of fair reward, just deserts for good and evil; and once again an American flag proudly waved over a cast of thousands as they all marched in musical step to their happy endings.

Judy was to pay her last visit to Carvel in *Life Begins for Andy Hardy*. In this one Judy had also been allowed to grow up. Perhaps the most amusing fact about this film was that the Legion of Decency branded it 'unobjectionable for adults' – which was another way of saying it was objectionable for children. This occurred because of a scene in which a telephone operator seperated from her husband invites Andy up to her apartment for an evening of unspecified 'fun'. However, Andy's father – Judge Hardy – prevails in the nick of time, giving his son a lecture on the importance of fidelity to the girl he will one day marry (Judy).

In her own life, marriage was constantly on Judy's mind. It was not difficult to understand why. Driven by fantasies having their roots in frustration, rejection, and deprivation, she believed marriage would sweep away the past and purge the memory of those lonely hotel nights and of dismal one-night stands, as well as the patina of despair caused by her father's death, and remedy her ravaged ego. But most of all, it seemed logical to her that the circle of David's arms would be an amulet against sleeplessness. Perhaps this last was the most powerful incentive, for her nights were harrowing bouts with insomnia. Alone, she would fill each room with a blasting radio; take as many Nembutals as she dared; then, terrified she had taken too many, counteract their effect with enough 'uppers' to keep her awake.

Not only the studio but also Leland Hayward was concerned about the advisability of her marrying David Rose. Hayward's reasons, however, were not the same. He was to all intents and purposes worried about the true depth of Judy's feelings toward David Rose and her motivations for wanting to marry him. At the same time, having now obtained a star client and knowing how unstable she was, he did not want to chance her ability to maintain stardom if the marriage failed. He tried to talk Judy into living with Rose but not marrying him. She was reduced to anguished tears and then anger at this suggestion. A violent argument with Hayward followed, and she never again felt the same toward him; and though he had more power and influence at the studio than his fledgling agent, Barron Polan, she demanded that Polan alone represent her.

The night shooting ended on the Hardy film, Judy and David had dinner with Ethel and Gilmore. There was to be only a few days' hiatus before rehearsals for *Babes on Broadway* were to begin. Forgetting any dream of a big church wedding, Judy pressed for an immediate elopement. For the first time in their lives, Ethel conceded to a move that might be difficult in terms of her daughter's career but seemed paramount for her happiness. Being content herself, Ethel was tasting a bitter dose of guilt for the past. And also, as we know the intensity of Ethel's need and ability to dream, one can imagine how this dream of Judy's would appeal to her and block out all else. It was first agreed that the elopement would be kept secret. Then Ethel and Bill Gilmore hopped on a plane headed for Las Vegas with the young lovers, and at 1 A.M. on July 26, 1941, in a simple ceremony, Judy became Mrs. David Rose. A wedding picture survives: a radiant, painfully young Judy smiles up at the golden-tanned older man who is now her husband; and they are flanked by a stern, riveted Bill Gilmore, a smiling Betty Asher, and an exceptionally nervous-looking mother-of-the-bride.

Twenty-four hours later the studio had found out about the marriage and angrily demanded Judy report immediately for work on *Babes on Broadway.*

Fantasy, that grand comforter, enabled Judy to return to the harsh demands of a musical-filming schedule. The newly-weds had found a house they had fallen in love with and were preparing to move in. They bought the house from Shirley and Archie Preissman, but it had once been the mansion of Jean Harlow. Redecorated for the Preissmans by Tom Douglas, the house was done in what might be called Marie Antoinette by Courtesy of Metro-Goldwyn-Mayer. It abounded in superrealistic copies of French antiques, satins, and brocades, and the details were carried out in 'true' eighteenth-century style to the quill pen on the baroque library desk. Judy was in ecstasy. The house represented the fruition of all her childhood fantasies. The years she had dreamed of her father's sharing such a house with her! She was not yet worldly enough to recognize the pseudo antiquity of the decor; the house gave her a sense of history, of permanence, of roots. Years of ill-heated hotel rooms and small suburban stuccoed houses in ice cream pinks and vanillas that seemed too common, too small to be a real home made the new house a dream come true. That its real history had begun less than twenty years before, that it had been originally built and designed for another Metro star, that Harlow had lived nights of anguish within its walls – died there – had no reality for Judy. She loved the thick white, wall-to-wall carpeting, the gracefully curved legs of the furniture, the delicacy of the wallpapers and lush richness of the fabrics; and that quill pen actually thrilled her.

To add a touch of the whimsical, the preposterous, David was a devotee of miniature trains, early American variety. His collection was (and is) vast, and of museum quality. His bachelor house had been small and in the San Fernando Valley, but the grounds had been able to accommodate his 'railroads' (the trains, though miniature replicas, were large enough to ride in). Through the elegant glass doors of her small 'chateau' Judy glanced out at one thousand feet of track that circled the house and a splendid, new, perfect replica of a train depot of Western origin and nineteenth-century vintage.

She was nineteen and had never run a house in her life. Ethel hired a couple to care for it. They treated Judy like a child and took their instructions from Ethel. Searching for dignity and an area of capability was not easy. Then she discovered she was pregnant. She was right in the midst of shooting *Babes on Broadway*. She kept it to herself for several weeks, finally sharing the news with David. Not so young as Judy, he saw the problems a pregnancy and a child represented. His lack of all-out enthusiasm dismayed and shook her. She went to Ethel carrying the 'good news'. Ethel was upset and tried to explain what a baby *now* would mean. Yes, of course, Judy could complete *Babes on Broadway* before any physical signs would be detected, but the studio had another film – *For Me and My Gal* – lined up directly to follow. More of a consideration was her film image in all the pictures in release, about to be released, and planned for in the future. Motherhood did not suit Mickey Rooney's or Andy Hardy's girlfriend. Judy was distraught, but Ethel told her to go home to her husband and not worry about the problem for the present.

A Machiavellian sequence of events followed. Ethel immediately went to see Arthur Freed, who was producing *Babes on Broadway* and would be producing *For Me and My Gal*. They met with studio executives. There is no way of knowing whose suggestion it was, but they all agreed that the best thing for Judy's career and for the studio would be for Judy to have an abortion. Ethel seemed assured that though abortion was illegal in the State of California and Judy, therefore, would be forced to have the operation sub rosa, it would still be performed under the best of all circumstances. She went back to Judy who was both shocked and shaken by the proposal.

David appeared to be unable to talk with her sisters, or to broach such a delicate subject to Roger Edens, embarrassed to do so with Rooney, and estranged from Leland Hayward, Judy consulted Barron Polan. Very young then himself (early twenties) and not knowledgeable in the ways of women, Polan did not recognize the full portent of the situation except in terms of his friend/client's career and his own. He took a placatory, yet noncommittal stand.

She had the abortion at a Hollywood hospital. Ethel accompanied her; the studio doctor performed it. Press notices went out that she had suffered a small tonsil flare-up. In forty-eight hours she was home, and forty-eight hours after that she was back in the Metro recording studio, working on the synchronization of some of the big musical numbers in *Babes on Broadway*.

CHAPTER FIFTEEN

PERHAPS if she could have forgiven herself, she could also have forgiven David. If she had loved herself more and her need for approval had been less, she might have fought the studio and Ethel on the abortion. No one had drugged or kidnapped her. She had finally just weakened and agreed and, with Ethel leading the way, had followed obediently in step to the hospital room. She had signed fraudulent papers, betrayed her own needs and desires, and then, terrified of the ordeal before her, had not even taken a last, desperate stand. She could not forgive herself, so how was it possible for her to forgive the others?

Early training had not taught her how to fight on her own or for herself. Never allowed to court the idea that she owed any fidelity to her own needs, she considered herself a chattel to her 'career'; and she never once came to understand that it was *her* career, her bandwagon, and all the others were on for a free ride. That explains a great deal in terms off the various repeats of her submission to power pressures during her lifetime. She fell back on what seemed her only recourse – her vulnerability, her terrifying need for compassion, time, and help. She had no experience at infighting and had no one really in her corner. And she was only nineteen years old.

For one year after the abortion she tried to keep the marriage together, but for all the wrong reasons. No longer trusting David, her own love shriveling and dying in her as though it were the fetus of their aborted child, nonetheless she feared divorce and what it would mean in terms of Ethel

87

and the studio. The dream house, dream husband, dream marriage had no substantive meaning. It was like living inside the boundaries of one of her own films. But she did at least have temporary asylum.

To add to the fears, the insecurities, the United States had entered the war. On a private level she was aware that their marriage afforded some protection against David's being drafted. Divorcing him at such a time seemed disloyal. Then so many of her male friends faced induction or enlisted. Barron Polan was the first to go, and it was difficult for her to cope with the enormity of this 'desertion' – for in a way, she thought about his leaving in that manner.

She tried very hard to take a patriotic, romantic, Mayer-oriented position in seeing friends and loved ones off to the wars, but it was pretty much a sham and very difficult for her to come to terms with.

So the work continued, and that was good. It was familiar, and though it was increasingly painful, the pain was her own and one of the very few things she could set such claims on. But suddenly her loss of weight had gone too far. The diet pills were stopped. She was stick-thin and pale-faced, and her nights were torturous, frightening bouts with insomnia. She would at last fall into an exhausted sleep at four in the morning – only to have to be awakened at five to go to the studio. As soon as the diet pills stopped, however, she had severe withdrawal symptoms. The pains were constant, and she suffered fits of nausea.

She was doing radio and camp shows in every spare minute and was preparing *For Me and My Gal* – once again to be filmed with 'the Freed Unit.' It was to be her first big starring musical apart from Rooney. There were endless meetings and conferences as to the casting of her male partner in the film. Casting was not easy. The role was extremely avant-garde. Harry Palmer, the ambitious, extortionist anti-hero, the vaudevillian who would sacrifice his partner (Judy) for his career and maim his hand rather than face military service was not the sort of role any of the MGM male contract players thought would carry them on to stardom. Also, Harry Palmer had to sing and dance well enough to believably end up playing the Palace.

A young man named Gene Kelly had been brought out to the Coast from Broadway, where he had made unmemorable supporting appearances, and had been signed by David O. Selznick. He made an extremely bad test and Selznick dropped him, deciding he had no film potential. Judy had met him previously in New York on one of her personal-appearance tours. He was, at the time, appearing in a supporting role in a Broadway show, and she had spent an evening with the cast. Judy was pleased to see him again.

She was still married to David, but they were quickly becoming strangers – the hostilities growing between them. Kelly was sympathetic. He was married to Betsy Blair, and the union appeared sound. He gave Judy no real indication that he would ever offer her more than friendship, but she did continue to fantasize that he *might*. Instinctively, and apart from all personal considerations, she felt Kelly was the right person to play Harry Palmer.

She went to Freed and to Buzz Berkeley, who was to be the film's director, and insisted they cast Kelly. The test was rerun. It did not improve upon a reshowing; but personal interview and further tests, and the well-being of the film's star, Judy, convinced them they should gamble. Kelly was signed to a Metro contract, his first film bringing him star status in a major musical. In a forerunner of his *Pal Joey* role, he portrayed the heel with more naiveté than villainy. Set in the First World War, it represented MGM's early bid for a patriotic war-film ending: Kelly proves himself to really be a hero and by the final fadeout is reunited with Judy while the Armistice is signed; peace once more reigns in Leadville, and they appear as headliners at the Palace Theatre.

Seeing the film today is a moving experience. Never did Judy look so vulnerable. There are several moments in close-ups when there is a striking likeness to Monroe. The eyes widen in unguarded pain; the mouth trembles, quivers;

the skin has that luminous, third-dimension, touch-or-feel quality to it; and the voice is a quiet sigh of anguish.

The combination was a good one, though at the premiere Kelly got laughs in all the wrong places. But Judy proved she no longer needed Rooney. Her dancing with Kelly was the best she had done, and in the blending of their voices a special tone was created, the flatness of Kelly's voice somehow causing Judy's voice to sound fuller-bodied. But the rendition of one song – 'After You've Gone' – should make the film now a classic. It was one of the first times an 'up,' fast song had been slowed and sung torchily. Edens' arrangement is brilliant and contemporary even today, and Judy, her face in a close-up that filled the screen, her voice clear – never missing or failing – rose to her greatest film presence.

The reviews made note of her growth and her frailty (she was thin and pale in this one – her own frailness aiding and abetting the role). Kate Cameron in the New York *Daily News* said, 'Judy looks thin and frail throughout the picture, but she seems to have developed enormously as an actress and entertainer since her last screen assignment (*Babes on Broadway*).' And *Time* observed, 'Boney-faced Judy Garland is already well graduated from a sort of female Mickey Rooney into one of the more reliable song pluggers in the business.'

Judy was now one of the top ten box-office stars in America. She was earning a tremendous salary. She had made it. But pressure and exhaustion plagued her. There was no rest at home – only a growing hostility; and Ethel and Bill Gilmore, now taking over as Judy's managers, were constantly at her about the property and mining investments they were making with her money to enable her to someday be very rich as well as famous. All these investments unfortunately turned out to be poor risks and cost Judy eventually more than she had originally invested. In fact, since Ethel and her husband received a fee for their services, they ended up the only beneficiaries.

She was ill and she knew it and was aware that it was not

just a physical thing, nor was it caused by her pill addiction. She felt her whole world was falling apart. She went to Joe Mankiewicz, who had recently become her friend and for whom she had great admiration. Mankiewicz was an excellent writer, a witty raconteur, and in Judy's eyes, at least, the first true intellectual she had ever known who would talk with her on an equal level. Somehow she was afraid of Edens' disapproval, but that was not the case with Mankiewicz.

Mankiewicz was a sensitive and perceptive man. He recognized the depth of her mental anguish and the extent of her confusion. He contacted the eminent psychiatrist Karl Menninger for her, and Menninger, in turn, recommended an early associate of his, Dr. Ernst Simmel, who practiced in Los Angeles. He was an elderly man, a distinguished German refugee, and a psychoanalyst.

Mayer was more outraged at Mankiewicz for usurping his authority and giving a Metro star advice than he was concerned about Judy. He called Mankiewicz into his office and proceeded to viciously berate him. The younger man grew not only indignant but also deeply angry that Mayer would value his own ego above the possible help that could be given a deeply disturbed and unhappy young woman. He handed in his resignation, but Mayer refused to accept it. Finally, though, after keeping him inactive for a very long time, Mayer released him, and Mankiewicz went to Twentieth Century-Fox.

Secretly Judy began forty-five-minute sessions with Dr. Simmel prior to her reporting before the cameras. The doctor spoke with a heavy accent that was difficult for Judy to understand, and he was also slightly hard of hearing. The sessions were strained, but the important factor was that she recognized her need for outside professional help and at great physical expense sought it out and kept after it. Analysis was a painful experience for her. It brought things to the surface that she had consciously forgotten years before; and having chosen an older man as an analyst, she found 'confession' impossible. Now she had these rumblings

91

in her head, these lurching anxieties in her chest, the twisting in her stomach to contend with, added to all the other problems. And there were many.

There was no way Mayer could understand that Judy was suffering severe psychological disorders. He regarded his stars as children, and his brand of discipline was to arrange for Judy's film schedule to be *toughened* – reasoning that if she worked harder, she wouldn't think so much.

In February 1943, she divorced David. A step toward her own independence, it still was like a woman who had walked on crutches all her life throwing them away when she was not yet sufficiently rehabilitated to walk alone. Having sought psychiatric aid in secrecy and feeling the need to discuss her frustrating sessions with someone, she turned to her mother. Ethel was alarmed and went immediately to Mayer to discuss this turn of events. The psychiatric sessions were thus ended for the time being.

It had been eight years since Joe Pasternak had tried to get Judy over to Universal and had hired Deanna Durbin in her place. Now he was on the Metro lot, preparing to shoot *Presenting Lily Mars*, the Booth Tarkington novel bought orignally as a straight dramatic vehicle for Lana Turner. Pasternak preferred the concept of doing it as a musical to star Judy, whom he had never been able to forget. Mayer agreed, and the film was set into motion. Pasternak and his wife, Dorothy, warmed immediately to the film's star. 'She had,' according to Pasternak, 'a small-child quality, pathetic, making you want to hug and cuddle her. She admired Lana and no convincing could make her believe she was anything but second choice – a replacement. It took her a long time to appear from makeup. She thought she was ugly. Mario Lanza had some of the same problems.'

Pasternak again comments: 'Musicians are the biggest critics in the world. If they don't think a singer is doing justice to an orchestration, they feel sad. But not with her. When she did a song for me, she would go over it once or twice with Roger Edens at the piano and then Take One –

finished. Perfect. She was the same way with her lines in action – very quick.'

Unfortunately, his effusive Hungarian enthusiasm and peppery personality was not a combination Judy could relate to. She was fond of him – enough to spend the few spare hours she might have at his house playing tennis with him and Dorothy – but she was unable to take them into her confidence. The rumblings were growing louder.

'I prayed for her,' Pasternak confesses. 'I saw what might happen and prayed. You know? Such a great talent. She deserved God's personal attention.'

And then about her film appearances: 'She was not too glamorous for the girls to dislike her or be jealous of her, and she was beautiful enough for the men to fall in love with her. Those eyes – when she looked at you! She sold herself to everybody individually and collectively. You believed everything she did.'

Judy was maturing and reading, and she began a new campaign at the studio: would MGM consider giving her a leave of absence to try the stage? Mayer laughed at her and came back through Ethel with a 'Don't-put-your-daughter-on-the-stage, – Mrs. Worthington' philosophy. But it was all unnecessary. Judy could fantasize herself as Lynn Fontanne as much as she wished; it hardly mattered. The day after *Lily Mars* had stopped rolling, she was cast once again opposite Mickey – this time in *Girl Crazy*.

But Judy no longer had faith in her film image. And she was now less amused or exhilarated by the kind of immature ribbing Rooney gave her on the set. It no longer seemed funny when Rooney would mug out of sight of the director – like a 'tic-ravaged chimpanzee' – trying to make Judy ruin a take. Nor could she get into the spirit for practical jokes such as the one Rooney played, when she was taking a nap between takes, by planting a smoke pot at her door; screaming, 'Fire!'; and dashing a glass of cold water in her face. These 'gags' continued throughout *Girl Crazy*. When Judy appeared on the set in white calfskin boots, he quipped, 'You look like a vanilla ice cream cone.' Judy, retaliating that once, replied, after measuring Rooney's scarlet cowboy clothes, 'You look like a rationed bottle of ketchup.'

A fan magazine ran an article at that time. 'Doesn't Judy do anything but work?' it questioned. Indeed, she worried, fretted, fantasized, dramatized and traumatized; but she had very little personal life. There were men she saw on the lot and had crushes on – there was still Kelly; there were Oscar Levant and Johnny Mercer; but there was no time for any relationship to grow. *Girl Crazy*, the George and Ira Gershwin show which reunited her with Rooney, was a backbreaker filled with large production numbers. Busby Berkeley, who had directed the team three previous times and had also been at the helm in *For Me and My Gal* and *Ziegfeld Girl*, began the film. For the first time Judy had a personality clash with a director. (It was the beginning of a series of such clashes.) Berkeley was a task-master, and the precision he demanded for his grand-scale production numbers meant Judy had to reshoot scenes over and over. He did return to the film to handle the spectacular finale, which deployed one hundred dancing boys and girls and a complex of rodeo routines – but Norman Taurog replaced him otherwise.

She sang fine songs like 'Embraceable You', 'Bidin' My Time', 'But Not for Me', 'Treat Me Rough', and 'I Got Rhythm'. Her presence was open and warming, while Rooney was beginning to acquire the detachment of a veteran vaudevillian, and her popularity was gradually overtaking Rooney's; but her concern for her future was growing out of all perspective. *Time* said, 'If she were not so profitably good at her own game, she could obviously be a dramatic cinema actress with profit to all.' She was becoming convinced that if she did not make the transition, her bubble would burst. But she had more fear that the strenuous work involved in a musical would destroy her physically than that her voice would leave her. She was suffering nightly bouts with what she called 'the terrors'. Alone, in her 'dream house', the bills piling up (she was soon to lose it because of nonpayment of the mortgage) as

Ethel and Bill invested more and more heavily in 'sure things' for her; taking uppers now – not because she needed to lose weight but because she could not bear the withdrawal agony not taking them caused; able to sleep only with the aid of Nembutals; so terrified of silence that she was never anywhere without radios or music or live conversation or telephone calls – she was actually already experiencing a nervous breakdown.

She begged Ethel to intercede with Mayer and to send her down to the Menninger Clinic for six months. Ethel went to Mayer, but the edict came back: she was to do a guest spot in a star-studded wartime musical, *As Thousands Cheer*. When she completed that assignment (perhaps her weakest film appearance, in which she sang the ill-suited 'Things Are Really Jumping Down at Carnegie Hall' to José Iturbi's pretentious piano), she expected time off. Instead, Mayer sent her on a personal-appearance tour to promote *As Thousands Cheer*.

In July, 1943, she walked out on the stage of Philadelphia's Robin Hood Dell Theater to make her first concert appearance. She was backed by the ninety-piece Philadelphia Orchestra under the baton of André Kostelanetz. Her hair was dyed a startling red-blond, and she opened with a quartet of Gershwin songs. She looked, was dressed, and acted like a girl at her first formal party who was scared stiff no one would dance with her. It was incongruous considering the 36,000 fans seated on benches, in aisles, on rooftops, in trees, on steps, and on the hillside of the outdoor arena.

Afterward she said, 'I thought to myself that they were probably thinking what was I doing there anyway, so I just sang louder.'

By intermission she had loosened up and was singing songs from her own movies. The crowd roared, stamped, clapped, and whistled. Kostelanetz had imported six hot saxophonists, a jazz trumpet, and a boogie-woogie pianist for 'The Joint is Really Jumping Down at Carnegie Hall' and the concert was a huge success. Talk was that Judy might do another concert the following winter; but shortly after her return to Hollywood, simply keeping in front of the cameras was more than she could cope with.

The sleeplessness set in ruthlessly. She wandered the house at night, terrified at every sound. The long years of ringing people in the middle of the night began. There were late calls to Dr. Simmel, her analyst. She was desperate to level with him, to correct some of the lies that she had told him. One night she couldn't reach anyone. Taking vodka along with her Nembutals to speed their action, she lost count of her intake. Near collapse, she finally reached Dr. Simmel. He came right away.

Those 'in the know' at the studio called it 'her first phony suicide attempt'. It was, of course, more a scream – a desperate plea for help. For five years thereafter, she saw Dr. Simmel for fifty minutes morning and night, and yet all that time she found the elderly man difficult to talk with and actually walked the floors at night rehearsing what she would say to him.

She needed a lot – but mostly a man who could love her unfailingly: a heroic man who at the same time could accept without question and with loving balm the tarnished days and nights of her youth; an alter ego who matched her sensitivity, who had fears of his own but had overcome them and would help her, who knew or feared no other allegiance or threats; but finally, a man with whom she could have a fulfilled sexual experience.

Not unobservant, Mayer now considered the possibility of a 'made marriage' for Judy – a marriage to a man of sensitivity and talent, certain strength, and above all, loyalty to Mayer and MGM. He cast a searing eye about the available men on the lot. No one was exempt; every man was vulnerable.

But in the meantime, he was making plans for Judy's next film.

CHAPTER SIXTEEN

HE was born in Chicago, the son of Vincente and Nina Lebeau Minnelli, stars of Minnelli Brothers Dramatic and Tent Shows. At three he was pushed onto the stage to play Little Willie in *East Lynne*. Until he was eight, he had no real home. Life was a temporary dwelling – a tent, a hotel room, a theater. Then his family moved to Delaware, Ohio. All his youth was spent in yearning. His own world seemed small and shabby to him. He knew not only that he must rise above it but that he would. Strong-willed, self-opinionated, he had two talents: an ability to fantasize a world of elegance and beauty, and the capability to sketch those images, pinning them like rare butterflies on his drawing pad. It was not enough to satisfy his compelling needs. The world he fantasized must become the real world, his own non-existent.

He envisioned drawing rooms Coward and Gertie Lawrence would feel at home in; ballrooms elegant enough for the suave Astaires. His walk, his voice, his dress became Upper Park Avenue or Lower Belgravia; but his eyes – those large, soulful, dark Italian eyes that one always felt looked into, not at, you – never fitted the role. With dizzying speed he went from designer of costumes and sets for Balaban and Katz Theatres to Broadway.

The year was 1931, and he was still in his early twenties. He designed a three-hundred foot curtain for Earl Carroll's 1931 *Vanities*. It was spectacular, in a style one might call 'sumptuous gorgeousness'. One degree more fabulous and it would have been either camp or kitsch, but young Vincente Minnelli had the good fortune to possess an instinct that knew exactly how far one could stretch extravagant taste to keep it within the bounds of acceptability.

Grace Moore grabbed him to design costumes and sets for her operetta *DuBarry*. It was such a lavish cornucopia of luxury and richness that there seemed only one place the designer could have more room for growth. Happily, he was hired by the Radio City Music Hall, the world's largest theater, as art director – a post he held for three and a half years. He was, therefore, rather handsomely paid to work out all his most opulent fantasies.

During the next five years, he was able to hone his talent to a finer edge. In speedy procession he marched as art director from such splashy musical productions as *Ziegfeld Follies* to *At Home Abroad*, *Cabin in the Sky*, *Hooray for What?*, *Very Warm for May*, and *The Show Is On*. But the world of theater was now also beginning to feel small and shabby to him. He rightly believed his was a pictorial imagination; and when the chance came for him to go to Hollywood, he grabbed it.

He arrived in 1940 and became a new member of 'the Freed Unit' on the Metro lot. He was forced to 'apprentice', and that nettled him; but as his aspirations were directorial and his ambition an educated though calculated thing, he reined in his leaning toward arrogance and managed to check his vanity. Freed and Mayer both recognized his uniqueness; and Freed, who so desperately felt his own artlessness, turned almost immediately to Minnelli for confirmation and inspiration.

By 1942 he had graduated from his apprenticeship and been given his first film directorial assignment – *Cabin in the Sky*. He had set the mood in the original stage version; he did so again in the film. Minnelli's art was not personal but visual, not meaningful but decorative. The cinéastes, however, were wooed by his stylistic flourishes. He had already entered his name in the history of the film musical.

His acquaintanceship with Judy had been minimal. They had met on the lot, but he had not been involved in the making of any of her Freed films. Now it was suggested that they work together on *Meet Me in St. Louis*, a screenplay based on a series of *New Yorker* articles by Sally Benson, which Mayer had scheduled as her next film; but for openers, Judy did not want to make the picture, feeling it would be impossible for her at this time to appear in another musical with a lot of production, costuming, and rehearsal as well, she was not drawn to Minnelli. He made her feel uneasy, unsure of herself. She was also not that convinced that he was the great director Freed said he was. *Cabin in the Sky* was skillful and pictorial, but only Ethel Waters' singing had moved her. After that he had done a stylistic but less-than-great musical, *I Dood It*, with Red Skelton.

Mayer threatened suspensions if she did not agree to the film. It seemed incredible to her, but she was broke. The Gilmores had not put aside any of her money for taxes; they had tied up what she did have in poor investments with no current resale value; and her dream house was being repossessed for default on the mortgage payments. It hardly mattered that she weighed only ninety-two pounds (the studio liked her to maintain a weight of ninety-eight pounds) and that each morning when she entered the East Gate of the studio, she would get so violently ill that she would have to go immediately to her dressing room to rid herself of her breakfast.

She reported for work on *Meet Me in St. Louis*.

CHAPTER SEVENTEEN

IT was the highest-budget film Judy had starred in, and she was carrying the weight of the film squarely on her own frail shoulders. She was surrounded by supporting players such as Tom Drake, Mary Astor, Lucille Bremer, and Leon Ames; but only little Margaret O'Brien had any meaning at all at the box office. Having failed with *I Dood It*, Minnelli was out to prove himself on this one. Always a perfectionist, he was, with each day of shooting, more difficult and demanding, sometimes making Judy go through a scene twenty-five times. This did not increase the rapport between star and director at the beginning of the picture.

But the more Judy saw of herself on film, the less hostile she became toward Minnelli. She was not just good: she was the best she had ever been as an adult performer. There were no Garland mannerisms; even the tremor in the voice was controlled. Esther Smith was a real, a sensitive, an interesting young woman. She lived on film and apart from Judy.

Perhaps the most moving and beautiful moments in the film occur when Judy is onscreen with little five-year-old Margaret O'Brien, who portrays her baby sister – a tenderness, a communion of spirit transfers itself so completely from one to the other. There is one especially poignant scene in which the child has had a fit of hysteria and runs out into the snow. Esther (Judy) follows. She is the older sister who, in the absence of her mother, at that moment becomes maternal. The father is home and, crossing the hallway to his study to bring himself to a momentous family decision, does not see the two girls entering the hallway after him – Esther protecting the child with her coat, gently leading her upstairs, soothing her.

For a musical, the film had a distinctive and very special style. It was apparent Minnelli, much in the fashion of Cukor and Wyler, had a phenomenal ability in presenting women onscreen. Halfway through the picture, Judy decided she could trust him. As always happened with her, this meant she turned to him for advice and for support. He helped her with the selection of her personal wardrobe, her makeup, her hairstyles. He agreed with her that she should be given the chance to prove herself in a straight dramatic role. He even had in mind a Paul and Pauline Gallico story – *The Clock* – that Robert Nathan, the same fine writer who had authored *A Portrait of Jenny*, had scripted. Before she had finished shooting *Meet Me in St. Louis*, she had gone to Arthur Freed and asked him to schedule *The Clock* as her next film. Freed was very negative toward this suggestion. He believed that the public wanted to hear her sing. Judy did not let it go at that.

Meet Me in St. Louis, a sentimental film that was carried along on a wisp of a story about the trials and tribulations of a family in St. Louis at the turn of the century, was declared by *Time* to be 'a musical even the deaf should enjoy. They will miss some attractive tunes ... but they can watch one of the year's prettiest pictures'. The review went on to call it 'very near first-rate'. The picture was to become one of MGM's alltime grossers, second only to *Gone with the Wind*; but when shooting ended, it was nearly Christmas, 1944, and the only thing Judy was sure of was that she could not possibly go on much longer alone – nor could she cope with another musical.

The studio, with the additional success of the film's score ('The Trolley Song', 'Have Yourself a Merry Little Christmas', and 'The Boy Next Door'), did not immediately agree to Judy's appearing in *The Clock*. Freed, recognizing her fast-failing stamina, convinced Mayer, Thau, and Mannix that Judy should be allowed to do a straight dramatic role. They vetoed Minnelli's directing the film, however, as they did not think it was a vehicle that would be right for him. This was a poignant, narrow-canvased love story; there was no opportunity – except in the use of Grand Central Station and other Manhattan locales – for Minnelli's broad-stroked genius. They assigned Fred Zinnemann to the film, and the film did indeed get under way with him as director.

Zinnemann was a gentle man and easy with Judy, but she had a native instinct that they were wrong together, that as star and director they struck no sparks that would help her ignite the screen. She also had her mind set on Minnelli's directing her in her first straight dramatic role. She went to Freed. Early rushes proved that she was right – that Zinnemann did not have the feel for her personality. He was taken off the picture and Minnelli brought in to direct.

The Clock was a love story about two young people meeting, falling in love, and marrying during a two-day period in World War II. For the first time Judy truly liked her image on the screen. It is understandable, for in the film she was presented as a love object. Her hair was groomed in a glamorous fashion; her clothes were tasteful. When one sees all her films in chronological sequence, this one stands out – and not simply because Judy does not sing in it, but because it is the film that caught her true beauty. She is breathtakingly lovely – the girl who has blossomed into a beauty overnight, transformed by love, by her first sexual awakening.

Never before or after *The Clock* did Judy ever reach such a cinematic moment of transcendence, turning fantasy into reality, as in the moment when she rushes into Robert Walker's arms in Grand Central Station after believing they had lost each other for good. Or the scene in which she tries to seek help to find him from a U.S.O. service officer and cannot explain how, having known the soldier only twenty-four hours and not even knowing his last name, nor he knowing hers, her life will be meaningless unless they are reunited. The film is filled with haunting images: the brutal civil wedding service in which the words are lost in the roar of the subway trains underneath; the wedding 'dinner' in the Automat when Judy begins to cry – 'It was so ugly – so ugly!'; the delicious banter between Jimmy and Lucile Gleason, playing a milkman and his wife, who befriend the young couple; and the incredible high-angle shot at the end of the film in which, having seen her new husband off to the wars, Judy is totally and completely lost, swallowed up by the mass of crowds in Grand Central Station.

Without lavish costuming, recording, dance rehearsals, and production numbers, the work was not physically taxing, but no other film had asked as much of her emotions. Minnelli seemed to understand this – protecting her all he could on the set, keeping intruders away, spending evenings with her, going over her next day's scenes for interpretation and understanding. She was experiencing a great new happiness. And a unique thing was occurring: the sense of womanliness, of sexual awakening, of being beautiful and loved transferred itself from her role to her personal life. The door of the world was open again. She could make plans. The future was a thing she might not have to fear.

There was someone she could love who she thought loved her. If there were sharp pangs of doubt, some small cavil of reservation, she managed to override these outbreaks and placate her own hesitation.

It was far too difficult to separate the real from the unreal. All she could hope to do was keep one guess ahead. She knew she could not survive alone. She trusted this man with the big eyes and the promise of soul buried there. She believed his own talent and value to the studio was great enough so that he could not be blackmailed or driven to forfeit her on his own altar of ambition.

Later she was to doubt that, to question if Mayer's approval and Ethel's enthusiasm for the match had not been founded on the fact that he was a studio, a company man – and that they could control Judy through him. Very soon after they were married, Judy did begin to feel that Minnelli had never had any intention, as she had hoped he might, of assisting her in breaking away from the torture of making film musicals exclusively, of helping her become a dramatic and comedy actress of the stature of Katherine Hepburn, whom she greatly admired.

But in the beginning and with all the force of a desperation to believe, she convinced herself that if she did not want to work, he would not want her to work; and that if she *could* not work he would fight to make the studio understand. And so, on June 15, 1945, just a few days after her twenty-third birthday and the end of shooting on *The Clock*, they were wed – she for the second time, he for the first.

She had wanted a church wedding, but decided that perhaps she was not strong enough to cope with ritual; so in Ethel's living room, with Ira Gershwin as best man and with the ceremony performed by Dr. William E. Roberts of the Beverly Hills Community Presbyterian Church (which she had never attended), she was wed to Ben Vincente Minnelli. She wore a pearl-gray jersey gown. Louis B. Mayer took Frank Gumm's place by her side, giving her in marriage. He also helped them purchase an extravagant hilltop house –

not only in setup like some cinematic Valhalla, high on a panoramic hill with a sweeping three-hundred-and-sixty-degree view of Hollywood, Beverly Hills, and the Valley, but also set back and approached by a winding, almost inaccessible road. The theory was one Mayer believed in: stars and directors were children who needed expensive toys; and maintaining those toys would force them to behave, would guarantee that they could not afford suspension.

This house was built for great theatrical moments, as though its courts and estuaries hid secret audiences. Vincente decorated it in impeccable taste with rare antiques and a collection of fine eighteenth-century porcelain. Judy's first home had been baroque but comfortably ersatz, none of the elegance ever seeming more imposing than that of a studio set. She knew that by Vincente's standards she was wanting in matters of taste and style; although she felt uncomfortable in the house – as if she were a trespasser – she held her silence. But a new inadequacy set in.

In the meantime, *The Clock* was released. *Time* said: '[Minnelli's] semi-surrealist juxtapositions, accidental or no, help turn *The Clock* into a rich image of a great city. His love of camera booms and dollies makes *The Clock*, largely boomshot, one of the most satisfactory flexible movies since Frederick Murnau's epoch-making *The Last Laugh*.'

Minnelli had directed Judy in her first all-dramatic role with success, but he had also succeeded in making his camera and his art the star, and that star was now very much in the ascendant at Metro. However, Mayer wanted him to return to the area the studio knew would be the most financially rewarding – the Metro musical.

The Harvey Girls was scheduled for Minnelli and Judy, with *The Ziegfeld Follies* and *Till the Clouds Roll By* after that. Three vigorous, expensive, backbreaking musicals. Judy turned to Minnelli for help, expecting him to fight the studio's decision for her. She thought she had the winning trick up her sleeve, that Vincente would now *insist* she be given time away from the cameras – for almost immediately after her marriage she discovered she was pregnant.

CHAPTER EIGHTEEN

HER daughter Liza was to describe Judy years later as 'a beautiful chameleon, whom you knew best when you knew you didn't know her.' Judy, through her entire life, tried to be what everyone wanted her to be and thought she should be something other than what she was. When she married Vincente Minnelli, she had made eighteen films in eight years; she was in poor health, addicted to pills; and appearing before the cameras did not come as easily as it once had. Her marriage to Minnelli, in spite of whatever attraction existed, was a plea for attention and understanding. There was a quiet sureness about Minnelli that gave her a sense of well-being. He was an older man and in a work situation was decisive about what was best for her. He had taste and talent and held Mayer's respect, which was a good deal like gaining parental approval. He was also solvent. For Judy, therefore, marriage was to be an escape from debts, anxiety, and fears. It was supposed to be like coming home for the first time. But it was none of these things.

The self-assurance Minnelli projected was merely one face of ambition. For him films represented a special glamorous world, and stars a special, glamorous race. True, there was a flashiness to films, but still their satellites were fairly acceptable in all societies. It was a partial guarantee of a social passport. Appearing to be a shy man, possessing a cargesse of style, he lived greatly on externals. He needed the admiration of his peers far more than the affection of a young wife, and acceptance in the social world more strongly than the bond Judy expected in their union.

There was no question that left to her own devices at that time, Judy could be an embarrassing figure. She was self-indulgent, self-deceiving, needing constant attention. She was also very ill. Mickey Rooney refers to the period of time just previous to her years with Minnelli as 'the time before the illness set in'. It was obvious to her co-workers and early friends that Judy was not the same girl they had known. She was fighting pill addiction and struggling to avoid a complete nervous collapse. With the strength only the weak can possess, she managed to survive the rigors of three full-scale musicals and the birth of Liza during the first two years of marriage to Minnelli.

Liza was born on March 12, 1946, by caesarean section. The pregnancy and the delivery had been painfully traumatic, and following the birth Judy suffered a severe depression, accompanied by a fear of having sexual relations that lasted a very long time. But, as well, she was weakened by the birth and on her feet and back at work too soon. One day she fainted on the street. Upon Dr. Simmel's advice, a family conference including Minnelli, Ethel, and Gilmore was held at which retirement was discussed. But Judy was committed to several films that had been written and/or purchased specifically for her. The idea was vetoed, and after only a few weeks' rest the work grind resumed.

The films Judy made during these early years with Minnelli and after *Meet Me in St. Louis* and the *The Clock* were the least inspired of her career, but they were entertaining and, in the case of *The Harvey Girls* and *Ziegfeld Follies of 1946*, all-time box office champions. *Till the Clouds Roll By*, a film biography of Jerome Kern with Judy playing Marilyn Miller, was a failure, the few highlights of the film being Judy's singing of 'Who' and 'Look for the Silver Lining'. To quote Norman Zierold in *The Child Stars*:

Unfortunately, the star of these joyous extravaganzas was ill, plagued by nervousness brought on by the tensions at the studio, the competition, the staggering work load, the desperate attempts to gain weight, to lose weight, and sleeplessness. A jumpy, irritable Judy dragged herself to work with tears in her eyes and muted resistance deep in her heart. As the relentless drain on her energies continued, that resistance occasionally turned on the director. And the director, unfortunately, was sometimes her husband.

'I was employed by the studio and Judy was now against the studio,' Minnelli was later quoted as saying. 'Judy was full of fears. I urged her to enjoy being the great star she was and is, but she didn't know how to do that and still doesn't.'

Minnelli was always concerned with film budgets and production schedules. Viewing Judy as his star, he tried to immerse her in these discussions, to make her aware of her responsibilities. This left little time for him to be a husband. Judy increased her pill taking. What a difficult swallowing of ego and pride she must have suffered with each pill – what a frightening loss of self. And at the same time how much anger and hostility was she suppressing in order to present the tender but joyous and exuberant image she had created on the screen? Even with Minnelli's presence on their huge estate, she was utterly lonely and yet afraid to be alone. Thinking kept her awake, and the nights were long. She began to take more sleeping pills than she had ever taken before. Doors were now shut between husband and wife, and each of them was living a separate and single life; both were protecting what they cherished most, and in both cases, it was not each other.

Minnelli – tired and overworked himself, and having great difficulty on his own part in coping with his marriage and his position in it – knew only one thing: his life existed on film. What life he could not stir inside himself he would transport to the film he was directing. Judy, in attempting to protect her sensitivity, her womanliness, in trying to hold herself together while outwardly working to be what Ethel and Mayer and Minnelli and her fans wanted her to be, leaned heavily upon her pills for support, courting sleep and, unconsciously, death.

There were times when she thought she was losing her mind and others when she feared she would suffer a nervous breakdown. She seemed to be just far enough off center of the collapse to cope with day-to-day living; but she was, in fact, *dead* center, already suffering a breakdown but fighting the totality of one. This had been the case for two years – would continue to be for several years more; but by hanging on to whatever hope or outstretched branch was in her path she was able to keep from being carried away and under.

At this time there was the baby, who was christened, at the Episcopal church on Santa Monica Boulevard and Camden Drive in Beverly Hills, Liza May Minnelli. Under her father's direction, her mother was starring in *The Pirate* and had managed one day away from the cameras for the baptism of her firstborn. Afterward, all the guests returned to the huge pink Regency house for refreshments. It was one of the only pleasant breaks in the filming of the picture. The other was when Liza May made her screen debut in the film, sharing a close-up with her mother, sitting on her lap. 'This was just for fun,' Judy told the press, 'and there'll be no more roles for Liza until she's able to pick them for herself.' She beamed; she held Liza close to her.

The Pirate was the most sophisticated vehicle Judy had starred in up to that date. The original costume play by S. N. Behrman had been written for Alfred Lunt and Lynn Fontanne. Changes were made to suit it to the talents of Judy and Gene Kelly, and to advantage. It was also the most strenuous role Judy had undertaken. It required virtuoso acting; dancing like a dervish in an attempt to keep up with Kelly; changing character at the drop of a hat; being volatile, lusty, and comedic; and socking over a Cole Porter score, including the exhausting 'Be a Clown'. She played the role with a highly polished sense of comedy that was unique and striking. She looked gaunt, more mature, and troubled. Her fighting spirit was beginning to flag.

She was securing as many pills as she wanted from a studio masseuse and still smoking four packs of cigarettes a day. Her weight was now so low that the studio was doing what it could to force her to gain, but eating nauseated her. Her physical condition was weak and growing weaker.

It was the beginning of her working problems. Unable

much of the time to bring herself out of drugged sleep, she would appear on the set late, tense, supercharged by the huge quantity of uppers she had taken to counteract the Nembutals. No matter how strenuous and exhausting her day was, she was unable to eat. Suffering from fatigue and malnutrition, she was destroying her health, and she was short with the film's crew and cast. In the end it was Kelly's film, his triumph, for he dominated the footage in no uncertain terms.

The film was dazzling, full of vitality, flamboyant; the roughhouse session of clowning set to the tune of 'Be a Clown', spectacular. It was the last number in the film to be shot, and Judy rehearsed with exhausting rigor four solid hours before the final take.

She preceded Minnelli home that night. He remained to tie up ends and prepare for the long chore of post-production: cutting, editing, fine-edging his product for its final polish.

Walking the floors sleeplessly for hours waiting for his homecoming, she was conscious something was happening to her. When he arrived, she begged for enough time away from the cameras to be a mother. That was, of course, the problem – she *begged*, not demanded. She wanted a happy world and everyone in it happy, but she was at a loss as to how to accomplish this. With all her wit and ability to laugh at herself, she had a melancholy heart. And because she felt such a failure as a person, even Liza caused her deepening loneliness. More and more the small child was being entrusted into the care of her nurse, Miss MacFarlane. The branch had been taken away and seemed out of her grasp.

Dr. Simmel was aging quite badly and had been ill. A serious block had occurred in their therapy sessions. Judy was no longer able to hide the truth from the old gentleman. He had broken through to her, and rather than freeing her, it seemed to make communication more difficult; a deep and lacerating wound was opened. In an unguarded moment at one of her sessions she had revealed the growing doubts she had about her father. It is much easier to speak about those who earn your anger than those who claim your love. Judy had hung on to the image of her father that she had molded out of truth and fantasy. But she had witnessed something in her childhood that had never let her be at complete peace with that fantasy. Some shadowy memory, some overheard conversation when she was still a very little girl intimated that Frank Gumm might have had homosexual relationships. That possibility had enforced her anger toward Ethel; believing her mother must have been responsible built her own guilts and her need to make up to whoever the father substitute was in her life for Ethel's 'destruction' of Frank.

Having exposed herself so openly to Dr. Simmel, she now seemed unable to face him. Therapy was halted temporarily, though the old analyst was never far away. In the meantime, he was wise enough to know that perhaps this was a time when his patient might do better with another doctor. He suggested several, but Judy would not accept his recommendations.

Then one morning she could not wake up.

On July 12, 1947, Louella O. Parsons reported:

> Judy Garland is a very sick girl and has suffered a complete nervous collapse.
>
> For weeks there have been rumors that all was not well with Judy and Vincente Minnelli, her director husband...
>
> Yesterday, Minnelli said, 'Judy is a very sick girl, and the only thing that is important now is to get her well. She is under a doctor's care and in a highly nervous state.'

Minnelli went on to say he was sure that if Judy could only recover her health, they could work out their domestic problems.

She was moved to a private sanitarium that Dr. Simmel recommended. An attempt was made to keep this secret, but the word was out – the world knew. Judy Garland had cracked up. She was twenty-five years old.

110

CHAPTER NINETEEN

'I DON'T want realism. I want magic! Yes, yes, magic! I try to give that to people. I misrepresent things to them. I don't tell the truth. And if that is sinful, then let me be damned for it!' So said Blanche Dubois in *A Streetcar Named Desire*. The Tennessee Williams play was the smash hit of the 1947 theater season. Blanche Dubois' now-famous speech was relevant to the times. The country was suffering the postwar blues. The economy was slack, unemployment high, wartime marriages falling asunder. The people of the nation wanted a panacea for their fears and insecurities. They wanted 'magic', and they found it in the new world of television and the golden world of films.

For years Judy had been grinding out 'magic'. Her daily chore was to misrepresent the truth, and like Blanche she no longer was able to tell the truth. Instead she presented what everyone wanted to hear. She was now being damned for it.

She sank into a severe depression, and she was so incapable of coping with day-to-day living that even Minnelli and the studio agreed she had to be temporarily hospitalized. A private sanitarium for rich patients with mental disorders was chosen. It was to be the first of many such institutions that Judy would go to in the next few years. Her career was like stale air around her. She was being plagued by frightening visions. There was no doubt in her mind that the pills had affected her sanity.

Outside her small bungalow hospital room, she viewed through iron bars the charred California desert. Inside there were constant surveillance, hushed voices, and great loneliness. She was being treated for severe melancholia, addiction, and malnutrition. She was placed next to Ward Ten, the 'violent' ward, and the sounds that emanated through the thick stucco walls frightened her.

111

'About the second day,' Judy says in *McCall's*, 'I noticed that [the patients] all used to gather on the lawn near my bungalow. I finally wandered out on the lawn one day and joined the group ... As far as I could gather, not one of them was demented in the common sense. Most of them were just too highly strung and too sensitive for reality ... I realized that I had a great deal in common with them, in the sense that they had been concentrating on themselves too strongly, the same as I.'

At five in the morning she would lie wide-eyed while it was supposed she was asleep and a nurse would search her room.

'Every bottle, every drawer, every stitch of clothing, every corner,' Judy reports. 'It took me about five mornings to get up enough courage to ask her what she was looking for. The first time I asked her, she didn't even answer me. She just kept looking.'

They were constantly on surveillance for pills that Judy might have smuggled in. She was managing to obtain them from somewhere. Probably the other patients. They confined her to her room. The loneliness became more than she could bear, and she begged to see Minnelli, wanting to persuade him to bring Liza to visit her. Minnelli, however, was hard at work on a major film; and anyway, it seemed more sensible for him not to visit her often, for she slipped into deeper fits of depression after each departure.

The cost of the treatment – and it was coming out of her own funds – was astronomical: $300 a day. At the same time, the Federal Government had slapped a lien on her earnings and bank accounts for back taxes that Ethel and Gilmore had not paid, and the studio had put her on suspension, which meant she did not receive her salary until she returned to work. The staff feared she was growing dangerously suicidal. After consultation, and at Judy's insistence, it was decided Minnelli should bring Liza to see her mother.

'She toddled into my bungalow and into my arms,' Judy told *McCall's*. 'I didn't know what to say to her. She wasn't two years old. I just held her, and she just kept kissing me and looking at me with those huge, helpless brown eyes of hers. I jabbered a little but mostly held her. But we laughed, too. After a short while they took her away. I lay down on the bed and started to cry. There have been many blue moments in my life, but I never remember having such a feeling.'

Her hospital bills were presented directly to her. She was overwhelmed at the cost and began to suffer severe anxiety. But something more frightening occurred. A pattern was forming in her life, and as ill as she was, she recognized it. She would from this time say over and over again, 'I'd trade a shopping cart for the stage any day,' and deeply mean it. 'I'll try to put them both together someday,' she would add.

Recalling sessions with Dr. Simmel, there was a re-awakening of her great and desperate need for the man in her life to take over her financial support, to be manly, protect her from the outside world, cleave together with her. What she wanted was all the paternal security she believed Ethel had stolen. And what she was doing was punishing herself because she felt she had no right to the refuge she sought. If she didn't perform, she was a naughty girl. Ethel had repeated that refrain so often that it was indelible. And Ethel must have been right, because her father had sanctioned those road trips; and she would rather believe Ethel right than that her father might want Ethel and the girls away for other, more carnal motives. She rationalized this by convincing herself that Mayer, Rose, and now Minnelli all had been reproving – their attitudes toward her objurgatory, their disappointment grudging and reproachful when she was unable to perform.

For the second time a husband had taken the studio's stand against her. Thinking to get her back on her feet, Minnelli had already begun the drumbeat – 'back-to-work-back-to-work'. They had lived on a grand scale befitting a movie star and her director husband. There was no money put aside for hospitalization or back taxes. Minnelli earned a good salary, but it had not been of such long duration for any savings to have accumulated, and their life-style was above his means and included, and was dependent upon, her ability as a big-income earner.

There were scenes to be reshot on *The Pirate*, and the studio had purchased a script from Albert and Frances Hackett (who later scripted *The Diary of Anne Frank*), tailored for Judy and Gene Kelly. The thinking was that Judy and Kelly could become an adult team as Judy and Rooney had once been a juvenile duo. It was apparent that the studio executives had never seriously concerned themselves with her illness, that they expected a few weeks' 'rest' in a sanitarium would get her back on her feet and able to appear before the cameras. And it was also quite clear that Minnelli agreed wholeheartedly with their theory.

By this time her marriage was irreparably damaged. Too many hostilities, too many doors closed between husband and wife existed. But there was no place else to go but to the home they had shared. And there was Liza. Judy refused, however, to work under Minnelli's direction; and though they remained legally married several years longer, *The Pirate* was the last film they were to do together.

Also, there were the mounting hospital bills, the pressuring of the Internal Revenue officers, and the terror of an insolvent future. Against all medical and psychiatric advice, and without consulting Dr. Simmel, Judy returned to Beverly Hills and notified the studio that she was ready to begin work on *Easter Parade*.

Charles 'Chuck' Walters – former dancer, the dance director of the Freed Unit, and the man whom Judy had called 'the man with the whip' – was the studio's directorial choice. Walters had been given his first film, *Good News*, to direct that same year, and the studio was pleased with the end product. Judy and Walters were to be involved professionally for the next three years. It was to be a stormy, difficult association.

Judy agreed to Walters as director and was elated at the

thought of being reunited with Gene Kelly, who was also to star in the film. But shortly before the cameras began to roll, Kelly broke an ankle during a dance rehearsal, and Fred Astaire stepped out of so-called 'retirement' to replace him.

Once more the image Judy had created for the screen was reinforced in this film. She was the Plain Jane, the wallflower, the awkward girl who appears to be without hope of winning the leading man. Always she had to prove herself, to show him that the other women who clustered around him might be far more attractive but that she alone could help him achieve his true goals. She had to work harder than anyone else, take more abuse, swallow her ego and pride; but in the end she was noticed and accepted for just those reasons. Insecure as Judy was in private life, one can just imagine how each of these film roles tore at her own confidence – while conversely, her tremendous 'believability' in them, no matter how unreal the situation and script, was what made each film a winner and Judy a greater star.

The score was written by Irving Berlin and contained the great 'A Couple of Swells', 'Better Luck Next Time', and 'When the Midnight Choo-Choo Leaves for Alabam'' (a tremendous song-and-dance duet). Judy received top billing over Astaire, and as the small-time chorus girl chosen by Astaire on a bet as an experiment to prove he could make even this awkward, unattractive, untalented girl a star under his tutelage, she rose once again 'like a phoenix' and in *Easter Parade* gave one of her best performances.

Memorable is the scene on a city street in which Astaire tells her she has no sex appeal. Hurt to the bone, suppressing tears while displaying a game and fighting spirit, she walks ahead of him down the street, undulating, hands on hips, to show him men will turn and look at her. But they don't, and desperate and out of Astaire's sight she grimaces in a grotesque and hysterically funny manner; and of course, passing men do turn and look at her, and Astaire is puzzled but impressed. A funny, winning scene – but for Judy a Pyrrhic victory.

Wan, pale, exhausted, her marriage a sham, attempting to fight the extremes with which the pills tortured her body, 'putting on a face' for Liza, for the camera, for the public, Judy was in worse shape than she had been when *The Pirate* had been completed. *Easter Parade* called upon her to dance strenuous routines with Astaire, and there had been some reshooting on *The Pirate* at the same time. Internal Revenue had claimed most of that hard-earned salary. She was not very far ahead of where she had been when she collapsed.

A guest shot in *Words and Music*, the Rodgers-and-Hart biography, was next. She played herself and sang 'Johnny One-Note', and with Rooney outrageously cast as lyricist Lorenz Hart, she sang, 'I Wish I Were in Love Again', which had originally been cut from the film *Babes in Arms* because of the sophistication of the lyrics. *Words and Music* was a lame film based on a weak plot line. Metro had thrown in all the stars it could as guest performers to salvage it, but only Lena Horne singing 'The Lady Is a Tramp' and Judy singing 'Johnny One-Note' ever succeeded in bringing the film to its peak.

This was to be the last appearance Judy was to make on film with Rooney. On the set, none of the old camaraderie could be struck. Rooney was struggling with his own loose footing. Approaching thirty and a skeptical third marriage, with Andy Hardy dead and parts for a thirty-year-old perennial juvenile difficult to come by, Rooney was nearly broke himself and being labeled 'washed up'. He was not much in the mood for his old mugging, the practical jokes; his life had run down like a watered watch. Being reunited with Rooney did not help to buoy Judy's flagging spirit.

Migraine headaches were now plaguing her. Minnelli had taken an unsympathetic stand with regard to her 'illness'. He felt she could control the pill intake; he was embarrassed by her behaviour; he withdrew more and more, so that more and more she was alone. The studio had promised her a six months' rest with pay if she did *Words and Music*. She counted on it. She tried to occupy her mind in order to fight the pills.

It was a shattering time in Hollywood, and throughout the nation – the time of the beginning of McCarthyism. Many of the top writers whom Judy knew had been attacked. Ten writers, known thereafter as 'The Hollywood Ten', were black-listed and faced jail sentences for standing up for principles Judy believed in. She was asked for help, and she gave it. Standing up to be counted along with many other stars (her admired Katharine Hepburn for one), Judy released the following statement:

Before every free conscience in America is subpoenaed, please speak up! Say your piece. Write your congressman a letter! Let the Congress know what you think of its 'Un-American Committee'. Tell them how much you resent the way Mr. [Parnell] Thomas is kicking the living daylights out of the Bill of Rights!

Mayer was furious. He did not like to have his 'children' soiling their hands with politics even if the freedom of the land was at stake. His position – due a great deal to his association with Hearst – was also pro-McCarthy. He reprimanded Judy severely.

One night, suffering a sleeplessness that had lasted through thirteen days and nights, she took what could have been a tragic overdose of sleeping pills. Luckier than Marilyn Monroe, who a dozen years later – suffering the studio's wrath, suspended, alone at night, and plagued by the same pill addiction and sleeplessness – was to die from such an overdose, Judy was 'saved' – which, of course, caused the press to label it 'another phony suicide attempt'.

Refusing to see Dr. Simmel, Judy turned to a younger man – attractive and charming: Dr. Herbert Kupper.

CHAPTER TWENTY

DURING Judy's hospital stays, Liza remained at home with her father. For the child, those days were idyllic. He treated her like a princess, gave in to her every whim, took her to the studio and let her ride the boom that raised and lowered the cameras, and even had pint-sized replicas of the costumes in his films made for her and for her friends.

Now Liza recalls: 'He really understood me. He treated me like such a lady. Even then, he dealt with me on a feminine level. To do that to a little girl is probably the most valuable thing that can happen.'

Liza also remembers her friends and herself (Dean's daughter Gayle Martin and James's daughter Portland Mason) dressing up in the costumes her father had brought home and giving a show for her parents on the back lawn. She would strut and sing, and Judy would shout from the 'audience', 'Sing out! Kick higher!'

In a sense this, Judy's second serious suicide attempt, was a way of singing out, of kicking higher – for no one except Dr. Simmel had taken the first attempt seriously. Dr. Kupper, who was now in charge, felt strongly that she needed clinical help. Consulting with Dr. Simmel, Dr. Kupper recommended Anna Fromm Reichman's sanitarium. Hostile now to anything Dr. Simmel suggested and because the last clinic he had sent her to had been a bad experience, Judy refused to go there. Alternatives were sought.

The Austh Riggs Center in Stockbridge, Massachusetts, was finally agreed upon. An eminent psychoanalyst, Dr. Edward Knight, was just joining the staff directly from the Menninger Clinic, where he had been trained. In an unusual move, it was decided Dr. Kupper would accompany her. That choice was to badly influence any benefit to Judy that Riggs could have effected. Dr. Knight was not to arrive in

Stockbridge until the eighth of August (1947); Judy, the fourth of August; and Judy had obviously convinced Dr. Kupper that she could not be without private and personal psychoanalytical help for these four days.

The Main Street of Stockbridge has been immortalized by Norman Rockwell in one of his most famous paintings. Rockwell has lived there for many years and is a familiar sight riding his bicycle down Main Street. Weekly covers of *The Saturday Evening Post* reveal the townsfolk in just about every aspect of their daily lives during that period. Stockbridge appeared to represent small-town U.S.A. more than any other single town in the country. But it was a one-sided portrait. Years later, Arthur Penn in the film *Alice's Restaurant* was to capture another aspect. Yet there was, and is, more to Stockbridge; for the truth is that far from typifying small-town U.S.A., it was, and still remains, one of the most unique communities in the nation. Like the man with a thousand faces, it has a mask for every taste; but under each is the same liberal, fighting, rebellious spirit that could in 1776 make the area (Lee, Lenox, Stockbridge) the toughest battleground of the Revolution, while in 1972 it could count up more votes per capita for George McGovern than any other voting precinct in the country.

There was a fair share of the Daughters of the American Revolution when Judy was in Stockbridge, but the town has always attracted the young, has always been a gathering place for artisans and artists. Nestled in the rolling Berkshire Hills, its Indian trails lure hikers in spring and fall, its ski runs skiers in the winter. Even then it was a glorious outdoor salon of sorts for writers (today Norman Mailer, William Shirer, William Gibson, and Stefan Lorant live there, to name just a few of the town's current writers-in-residence).

But what has, since the twenties, given the town and its Main Street a singular and very special ambience has been the gracious, lovely, large facade of Austen Riggs. It was once one of the area's grandest private homes; its green lawns, wide driveways, and elegant buildings welcome. Set back only fifty feet or so from the sidewalk, it remains in appearance more a stately home or a luxury inn than a psychiatric clinic. One building is, in fact, called The Inn. Patients are not placed behind barred windows or bolted doors. A sense of freedom prevails, and patients between therapy sessions mingle with the townspeople. Often after therapy has ended they remain, as William Inge did, to live in the town – Riggs having a community spirit within that binds patients for years thereafter.

There is also a tremendous theatrical atmosphere at Riggs. It certainly must be one of the few psychiatric centers to have a successful little-theater workshop. This all must have been considered in the decision that Judy should go to Riggs. It made good sense to believe that Judy would be able to adjust to the atmosphere of this clinic, whereas she had not at the previous institution.

Riggs is expensive, and as a general rule no one is taken on short tenure. (Judy was expected to remain several months.) Most of the patients have affluent backgrounds and are well educated, sensitive, and intelligent. Some are alcoholics, some addicts, others desperately insecure. Most are young, and many who have walked up that driveway are famous (the aforementioned William Inge, for one).

The first error to be made regarding Judy's journey to Riggs was allowing Dr. Kupper to accompany her. And the second surely was the decision for her not to go directly to Riggs and become oriented before Dr. Knight's arrival but to remain at The Red Lion Inn (down the main street from Riggs) until that time. It was August 4, and the height of the Tanglewood summer concert season (Tanglewood, which is in the adjoining town of Lenox, is the summer home of the Boston Symphony Orchestra). The Inn was packed, and every time Judy went through the lobby she was not only approached but often physically stopped by admiring fans. Judy could not bear being touched by strangers and, therefore, was forced to remain secluded in her rooms for most of the time. She had several rooms, for beside Dr. Kupper she was accompanied by a maid and a secretary. There were many reasons why in the past therapy had not been successful with Judy. Her public acclaim, for one thing, preconditioned her relationship with her analyst. Whenever the analyst pointed out a failure in the handling of her private life, she could match it with a success in her professional career. And for another, there was always someone on the outside who was willing to keep her supplied with pills.

A pattern formed the first four days that Judy spent at The Red Lion Inn previous to her sessions with Dr. Knight (who arrived on August 8, with intensive therapy scheduled to begin with Judy on the fifteenth). She became overly dependent upon Dr. Kupper, consulting him three or four times a day. When Dr. Knight arrived on the eighth, angry words passed between the two men. Dr. Knight issued an ultimatum that Dr. Kupper leave before he began sessions with the patient and that the patient move to the Center. Judy fought this decree, remaining on the side of Dr. Kupper. Dr. Kupper finally gave in and on August 14 returned to California.

Left alone, Judy now refused to move to Riggs from the Red Lion Inn, and Dr. Knight relaxed his ultimatum. Sessions began the morning after Dr. Kupper's departure. It was the most intensive therapy Judy had experienced. For four days her relationship to her father was almost surgically exposed. It was very clear that she believed her father had been homosexual, that she had overheard something of a homosexual nature, and that she bitterly blamed all this on Ethel. She also discussed his death and brought up an incident that she had not revealed before. When her father had been taken to the hospital, just before his death, fluid had been emanating from his ear. A childhood blanket of Judy's that she had never been able to cast away was taken by Frank from the house to protect his ear. Upon his death Judy reclaimed it and kept it close to her for a very long time. Then one day it was gone, Ethel apparently having disposed of it. Judy could not forgive her for this.

At the end of each day she would return to the Red Lion Inn devastated, exhausted, and without professional nursing care. Her maid gave her massages, but Judy would end each evening in an enervating fit of tears, finally having to take a generous dose of barbiturates to fall asleep. She was still having easy access to pills, even though Dr. Knight had spoken to all those close to her.

By August 19, he once again issued an ultimatum: she would have to move into Riggs. But by now other pressures existed for Judy. Able at The Red Lion Inn to take all the calls that came in and to make all the calls she wanted, she was constantly, in her free time, on the telephone to California – to her agent, her manager, Minnelli, and Dr. Kupper. During her short absence the studio decided she should be cast in *The Barkleys of Broadway*, again opposite Astaire. Her agent managed to convince her that financially and professionally she desperately needed to accept this offer and to return to Hollywood right away. The press had been brutal in its recent treatment of Judy. The fear seemed to be that her audience might defect unless she could prove that she had simply been a victim of bad publicity.

The next morning, August 20, without discussing the move with Dr. Knight, she left Stockbridge with her maid and secretary, flying out that same day for the Coast.

Charles Walters was once again to be her director. She had gained back some weight in Stockbridge and was immediately placed on a crash diet at the same time as she began dance rehearsals. 'By now,' she says of that period, 'I was just a mechanical hoop that they were rolling around.' Her migraines returned worse than ever. She would go days without sleep, the Nembutals she took not seeming to affect her any longer except to throw her into deep depression. 'I just wanted to go somewhere to lie down and stop,' she confesses. But Walters wouldn't hear of it, and Minnelli remained on the side of the studio. First, she was late to rehearsals; then she began missing entire days.

Gathering what courage she had left, she called a meeting with the front office. Freed and Mayer were there. It was an emotional and disturbing confrontation, and Judy left Mayer's executive office in tears after being chastised for

122

being ungrateful after the studio had made her a star, and reprimanded severely for not being able to put a halt to her bad habits, pills and drinking (she was now drinking heavily when the pills did not seem to work). Her absenteeism from the set grew worse. One morning when she did not appear as scheduled, she was sent a telegram. She had been fired from the film.

Neither she nor her agent could reach anyone. Freed was 'not on the lot' and Mayer 'out of town'. All other executives were 'in conference'. Within twenty-four hours no more calls were necessary. It was already in the newspapers. Ginger Rogers had replaced her. And she was made the 'heavy'. She had been fired because she was 'unreliable, temperamental, and ungrateful'. No one also mentioned that she might be ill.

She turned back to analysis and then, growing increasingly despondent, she confessed that she thought analysis was of no avail to her.

The doctor replied that if she did not continue she would be dead in six months – because she was definitely suicidal.

It seemed to her a cold, cruel analysis, but now she began to fear herself.

CHAPTER TWENTY-ONE

THE studio had a change of heart. It had purchased Irving Berlin's smash New York hit *Annie Get Your Gun*, and under pressure from Berlin, Judy was called back to the studio to play Annie Oakley. It was the one role Judy truly had been longing to play; and although she was in no physical condition to even consider the gargantuan challenge Annie presented, she hastened to accept. Shortly thereafter, she was horrified to discover that her hair was falling out because of her heavy narcotic intake. It shook whatever small confidence she had.

Her first assignment for the role was to learn how to shoot a gun. Terrified of firearms all her life, she seemed unable to do this. Next came the accent. Always able before to mimic any language, she found that Annie's backwoods drawl escaped her. The front office was buzzing. There were meetings on the set, in the commissary, at the homes of Freed and George Sidney (the director). Replacement was discussed, but Freed wanted to give Judy every possible chance. They decided to record the music first. The records (a collector's item now) were completed with a sense of relief. Judy's voice was better than ever. Her accent was not good, but the power and delivery were so brilliant that it seemed it could be overlooked. Filming began again. Judy knew she wasn't any good. Her performance was bad, and she looked haggard and strained.

One day, while she was rehearsing the 'I'm An Indian Too' number in full Indian costume, a note was delivered to her by a stooge. It read, 'Your services are no longer required.'

Judy recalled that her anger was such that she could only stand and stare at this stranger, finally saying, 'You can't do this to me. With this makeup on, I don't even know what tribe I belong to. What reservation do I go to?'

Betty Hutton was called in to replace her.

Judy went home where her marriage was now a sham. Depression enveloped her. Retreating to her own room, she regressed to the kind of self-imposed isolation she had suffered as a child – communicating only with baby Liza, as she had once done with her dolls. Suicide was constantly on her mind. She felt the press was against her, her audience lost, and her career over. Then she received a call from her old friend Joe Pasternak.

There was a saying in Hollywood that you didn't have to have talent – you just had to be Hungarian. Pasternak possessed a Hungarian heritage; spoke with an accent 'seasoned well with paprika'; was ebullient, lively; and had the ability to infuse his spirit into his cast and crew. What distinctive talent he personally lacked he was able to recognize instantly in others. Having known Judy as a young woman and produced two of her previous films – *As Thousands Cheer* and *Presenting Lily Mars* – he wanted her now to replace June Allyson, who was pregnant, in his current production, *In the Good Old Summertime*. It meant Judy had to report to work immediately.

Perhaps the quality that Pasternak admired most was great talent. He believed Judy was a genius in her field, and respected her wholeheartedly for this. More courtly than any of his predecessors, Pasternak treated her with humor and gentle persuasion and was able to get her through the making of the film without serious time delays while at the same time extracting a top-notch performance from her.

One can pick up the mood on a Garland–Pasternak film by some of Pasternak's remarks:

'Sometimes there was friction between her [Judy] and the other actors because she was cute. I could understand. But they couldn't. It's like a family of five or six children where one is the most talented and it's difficult to hold back your admiration and give everybody the same amount of love.' ... 'You couldn't stay angry at her [Judy] very long. She'd come in after doing some foolish things that she couldn't help doing and look at you with those sad, beautiful eyes and start singing, and you'd forget you wanted to bawl her out.' ... 'I've made a hundred and five pictures – only four of them with Judy. But I never ceased to wonder how God had given so much talent to one little person!'

She had been on suspension after *Annie Get Your Gun* when Pasternak asked the studio for her services. The front office was violently against this, but Pasternak persisted and won. He saved Judy's life, but he was not aware of this.

His faith in her rekindled her spirit. She accepted the role immediately. The film was a remake of an early James Stewart–Margaret Sullavan vehicle called *Shop Around the Corner*. Originally, it had been a contemporary story set in

Hungary; Pasternak placed it in turn-of-the-century Chicago. Judy had gained back some weight and was feeling sturdier. Pasternak decided she should not be forced onto a crash diet and that period costuming could help to conceal her weight gain. It was both a humane and a sensible decision, and the story, which only nine years before had seemed so moving, now also had vitality, charm, and a lovely comedic quality. The plot revolved around two antagonistic co-workers in a music shop who unknowingly carry on a correspondence love affair. Van Johnson was her co-star, and they were supported by the talent of Buster Keaton, Spring Byington, and S. Z. 'Cuddles' Sakall.

According to Pasternak, Judy hardly flubbed a line in the entire production, seldom had to have more than two takes for any scene, and learned her musical numbers in no time at all. Her voice was clear and brilliant and warm. She sang 'Play That Barbershop Chord', Eva Tanguay's old hit 'I Don't Care' (giving it a very unique and new arrangement), and 'Meet Me Tonight in Dreamland'.

Life with Minnelli, however, reached an impasse only short weeks after the completion of *In the Good Old Summertime*; and on March 31, 1949, Judy and Vincente made their announcements to the press. 'It's true – we're happier apart,' Judy admitted. 'Yes, we have separated' was all Minnelli would say.

Within the next few weeks, the small amount of emotional security Judy had been able to muster through the making of the Pasternak film went to pieces. She was back on the treadmill – pills, sleeplessness, and suicidal tendencies. For the first time, she accepted the truth: that without professional help she was not going to survive. She felt she had to get far, far away from Hollywood. This time Dr. Kupper recommended Peter Bent Brigham Hospital in Boston.

On May 28, 1949, accompanied by her new manager, Pasadena socialite Carlton Alsop (married then to Sylvia Sidney), Judy arrived in Boston. (Pictures survive of Judy on the steps of the hospital with a nurse by her side. She

126

bears the look of a woman who is recuperating from a severe and debilitating illness – one who has been in the hospital for a long time). 'She feels better already,' Alsop confided to the press. 'Maybe all she needed was to get away from Hollywood for a while. After all, she has spent almost her entire life on a movie lot. She has made twenty-seven pictures in thirteen years. She's a little tired and she's under suspension.' He did not add that after all that productivity, and in spite of the fact that she had been one of the top ten box-office attractions for 1940, 1941, and 1945, Judy Garland was broke. There was not, for that matter, money to finance the Boston trip and the hospitalization. Alsop appealed to Mayer; and Mayer, playing the 'indulgent father', agreed to pay her bill.

Judy was at Peter Bent Brigham Hospital for thirteen weeks (Alsop remaining close by with his wife to make sure 'all remained well'). She was placed on a rigid schedule. Pills and liquor were withdrawn, and lights went out in her room at 9 P.M. and remained off whether she slept or not. She was fed three generous meals a day. After four weeks, the first agony of withdrawal ended. Since Judy was weak and despondent and yearning for Liza, the doctors at the hospital decided she was ready for some kind of 'active therapy'.

Peter Bent Brigham has an annex for retarded children. It was suggested to Judy that she 'give' an hour or two a day to the entertainment (storytelling, singing simple songs, etc.) of these children, many of whom had been there for twelve or thirteen years. The experience was a traumatic one for Judy, remaining with her for years after and influencing her decision thirteen years later to star in *A Child Is Waiting* – a nonsinging role in which she portrayed the music teacher in a school for the retarded.

'All I can remember is their eyes,' Judy recalled later.

In her childhood she had imagined men staring at her through closed doors. Before live audiences she was aware of 'all those eyes upon you'. She was drawn to men with soulful eyes, liked to play sad-eyed clowns, and was haunted in her lonely hours by the memory of Liza's wide brown eyes. These retarded children – some in their late teens and early twenties but still mentally no more than seven or eight – were unguarded in the desperate need to be loved that their eyes revealed. Most retarded 'children' live out their lives in institutions, and after the first year parents' visits become farther and farther apart. Other family members seldom visit – so that when a parent dies or leaves the area, the 'child' is always 'waiting' for that representative of outside love.

The 'children' at Peter Bent Brigham Hospital responded immediately to Judy. They had seen *The Wizard of Oz.* Her voice was familiar to them. From the very first moment she entered the ward they waved and called 'Hi' to her, thinking she was someone they knew well; for unable to retain the memory of a book or story or film for more than a few hours, they did store familiarity. That inimitable Garland voice could not be misplaced, and its warmth assured them they had not been mistaken. Judy was someone they knew. Judy represented outside love.

One child – a small, dark-haired little girl not much older than Liza and with those same wide brown eyes – resisted. Her gaze fixed and followed Judy over the entire ward; but she remained huddled, totally withdrawn, her body wrapped about itself in a fetal position. She had not spoken a word in the two years she had been on the ward, communicating with neither the other children nor the staff. Rejected completely by her family, she had no visitors.

It became the major point of each day for Judy to spend time with this little girl. She talked to her conversationally, expecting no reply and moving on to another story or confidence without stopping. She told her all about herself and Liza and about California. She sang nursery songs to her. Braver after a time, she reached out and touched the child. The little girl listened to her but never returned an emotion, a word, or a touch. The staff was hopeful, and Judy continued. Being needed in this direct situation took Judy away from her former destructive self-concentration. She improved slowly but steadily. The migraines lessened; the

128

depression lifted greatly; and she was able to sleep. After three months Mayer, who was still paying the astronomical bills at the hospital, insisted that she should be able to return to work or be released from her contract, thereby acquitting Metro of any financial obligation to her.

Once more Joe Pasternak appeared as her savior. He was set to produce a film entitled *Summer Stock*. Hearing about Mayer's ultimatum, he went to Mayer and requested Judy for the lead. Mayer agreed. Pasternak rang Judy personally at the hospital.

This time, returning to work was to be a big mistake. The hospital felt Judy needed another three months to fully recuperate; but feeling more alive than she had in years, Judy disagreed. She accepted Pasternak's offer and prepared to leave Peter Bent Brigham. The last thing she did was go to the ward to say goodbye to the retarded children.

The staff had prepared them for Judy's departure. The older ones were dressed for the occasion, and each one presented her with some flowers from the hospital garden. But the little girl was not present. Judy went in search of her and found her on the last bed of the last ward. Judy walked over to the child and sat down on the edge of the bed. The child huddled there, staring at her with wide, sad, dark eyes.

It was a moment that obviously held great meaning for Judy. The child might well have been retarded, but she was sensitive enough to realize she had been rejected and deserted. Her muteness was a defense, a wall against further rejection. The staff had fully briefed Judy on this problem. They had felt Judy could break through to the child. Now Judy was in terror that if she did – and *leave* – the little girl would retreat even deeper into her own solitary confinement. Still, she could not do anything but reach out to the child and try to draw her into an embrace, for Judy was by instinct a maternal woman.

The child broke out of the embrace, screaming and shouting Judy's name at the top of her lungs. The sound was blood-curdling, and all the other children and the staff came running. Then throwing herself prostrate into Judy's arms,

129

she clung to her fiercely and words, mostly unintelligible, poured from her between sobs. But Judy understood that the child did not want her to leave; and though she missed the train, she remained with the child for several hours until the storm had spent itself. She sat there by her side until she had fallen asleep. 'I love you, I love you,' the exhausted child said before she closed her eyes. 'If you love me, you must promise me you'll talk to the nurses, because they love you very much too,' Judy replied. The child nodded her head.

There is no question of the impact this episode had on Judy's life. It harked back to those terrible hours she had spent in strange hotel rooms when she had been no bigger than this little girl; the fear that she would be deserted by Ethel and everyone she knew. It brought to the surface her own guilt at leaving Liza in California, guilt that was reaffirmed by her holding and loving this strange child when Liza needed her love and might be feeling frightened and rejected. So, though the children had helped her get well and she was on her way to physical rehabilitation if she could sustain it, her state of mind was still not stable; and at Peter Bent Brigham no psychoanalytic help had been initiated to enable her to understand any of her emotional reactions.

Returning to California fifteen pounds heavier than when she had left, she existed without pills and for limited hours slept without them; but she was in many ways even more insecure, even more confused at the role she wanted to play in her own life, than she had been before going to the hospital.

Upon reporting to the studio an ultimatum was issued: *lose fifteen pounds before cameras roll.* Judy began the diet-and-pill regimen, but was able to shed only seven pounds in eleven days. The studio was upset. Louella Parsons came out with an article chastizing Judy: 'I could spank Judy,' Louella said, 'for not doing as the studio asks.'

The ball went back to Pasternak. Judy was still overweight. What was to be done? Pasternak's decision was to let her play her film role (a New England farm owner who allows a summer stock company to use her barn for the summer and ends up as star of the show) at the weight she was. It gave her a truer farm-girl look, and Pasternak hoped that by Judy's not having to concern herself with diet, her health would be assured. Such was not to be the case.

With Judy once again having to face many of the same problems she had before Peter Bent Brigham, often alone – Minnelli having moved out, Liza being shifted back and forth, her friends occupied elsewhere – the sleeplessness set in again; and the pill pattern was set into motion and with it the alternating fits of highs and lows. Cut off from supply at the hospital, in the studio she could obtain through her masseur any amount that she needed. Pasternak was helpless to save her now. She was riding roughshod for destruction. Her performance was just as good as ever, but her working habits were impossible. She was constantly late, not appearing for retakes, refusing to come to rehearsals, and being short-tempered with everyone. Charles Walters was the director; Gene Kelly, her co-star. Neither ever worked with her again.

Two weeks after shooting ended, it was found that an additional song-and-dance sequence was needed. The 'Get Happy' number was developed and Judy called back to the studio. Everyone was shocked to see her. She had lost over twenty pounds in two weeks and looked frail and quite ill. No one knew how she would get through the strenuous added takes, nor how they would ever match the plump Judy in the rest of the footage. The decision was to proceed anyway.

The 'Get Happy' finale was without question the best footage in the film. Judy's weight loss was glaring. Every reviewer was to pick it up, but her performance in the sequence was so exciting that no one truly seemed to care.

Judy went home; she was the weakest she had been in years, and those closest to her (at that time Kay Thompson, the doctor, the Pasternaks, Roger Edens, and her agent and manager) feared she would break completely. She was sent to the seaside resort of Carmel for a rest.

CHAPTER TWENTY-TWO

'IT was a childhood,' Liza says, 'to be reckoned with.' At three to four years of age it meant moving back and forth from her father to her mother; being exposed to Judy's fits of depression, her suicide attempts, a hushed house one day, a madhouse the next. There were visits to the sets to watch her mother tensely perform. Hours spent waiting in silence on huge sound stages for her father to take her to lunch. There were enormous birthday parties, all with the same hired clown. And often there was her mother performing for her alone at home. She was a shy child. She liked to play games and pretend she was someone else, and even at three her eyes were wide and inquiring, dark and sad, and wise beyond their years.

She went to Carmel with her mother. Judy might not have been able to make it without her. The two of them played together in the strange, rented house, filling it with familiar games and stories and scents and sounds. It might have been difficult to discern who was playing mother, who the child. The roles were to be confused throughout their lives. Judy was bruised and hurting badly, and Liza was helping her soothe her wounds.

This strange idyll lasted less than three weeks of the proposed six months. A call came from the studio. June Allyson was pregnant again and had to be replaced in the film she was preparing to do with Fred Astaire – *Royal Wedding*.

It was incredible that Mayer should even consider recalling Judy so soon after *Summer Stock* and all the production problems of that film. More so since *Royal Wedding* was to be a splashy musical with no fewer than seven lavish dance numbers in which the female star would have to participate. He had had an expensive lesson with Judy in *Annie Get Your Gun* and had been responsible for most of Judy's bad press. It was possible that the move was made because he assumed she would refuse to return so soon, thereby 'forcing' the studio to place her on suspension and saving it a large sum of money. (Her contract then had one more year to run at a salary double the salary of the President of the United States.) Actually, if one wanted to examine more closely Mayer's 'generosity' in picking up Judy's bills at Peter Bent Brigham, one would have to place it in its proper perspective. He had been the one to place her on suspension. That meant that though the studio paid her hospital bills for three months, it did not pay her salary.

There was, of course, the possibility that Mayer still did not take her illness seriously, that he considered her – as he was quoted by the press – 'a spoiled, bad girl having a temper tantrum.' In that case, work could seem a logical curative or punitive measure; and two and a half weeks might appear a sufficient duration of time for her to be self-indulgent. Another factor was the success of the Garland-Astaire pairing in *Easter Parade*. Mayer was convinced that a successful team *more* than doubled the gross of a film, and very little meant more to the man than the figures he had to present to his stockholders. With Mayer still the highest-salaried man in America, Metro profits had to be substantial to ensure such a large salary.

As in the past with Thalberg, LeRoy, and Minnelli, Mayer had once more found a personable and talented young man, Stanley Donen, who with Gene Kelly had just directed his first film – *On the Town*. Thinking Donen might be capable of the same stylistic flourishes as Minnelli, it was natural that Mayer would believe that working together, Donen and Garland could create an exciting film chemistry. And he must have convinced Judy of this, for she – to everyone's amazement and her doctor's horror – accepted, returning with Liza immediately to Hollywood.

Her reasoning had been that the press, seeing the studio's faith in her so reinstated, would have a change of heart and that the past might be forgotten if the present included a successful film. Rehearsals began immediately upon her

133

return. There were those seven dance routines to learn, as many songs, costumes to be fitted, weight to be maintained. The masseur started on her 'fitness treatments', and pills were again easily accessible. The migraines returned. Sleeplessness plagued her; she was nervous, tense, ill. One morning she thought she might have had a stroke. She was unable to get out of bed.

For the second time she was fired through Western Union. The telegram was delivered to her house. She was not only off the film, but 'refusing' to work on a film in progress was a breach of contract. She was fired from the lot.

Minnelli and Carlton Alsop were at the house moments later. Judy was in a hysterical state. Minnelli was trying to do what he could to protect Liza from seeing her mother so distraught. It was only a short time before the press was at the door and on the telephone. Insinuating headlines came before the day was ended. There were strong hints that Judy was both a drug addict and an alcoholic.

No one kept the papers from her. She read them alone in her bedroom. She could hear the men's voices downstairs but Liza was apparently asleep. Dragging herself off the bed, she went into her bathroom, locking the door after herself. She was very conscious of what she planned to do and very frightened. It seemed to her that the humiliation was just too much. She thought she wanted to die. But it is obvious that if this had been the case, she would simply have emptied the bottle of Nembutals that was on her bedside. Instead, she broke a drinking glass and cut her throat – 'lightly' (her own word), 'so that it wouldn't hurt too much.' As soon as she saw the blood spurt, panicking with the sudden realization of what she had done, she had unlocked the door of the bathroom and stumbled back to her bed screaming and crying hysterically. Minnelli and Alsop were at her side in a matter of seconds.

On June 21, 1950 – eleven days after her twenty-eighth birthday – United Press issued this release:

Judy Garland may not make any more pictures

for Metro-Goldwyn-Mayer, a studio spokesman said today.

Miss Garland rested at home with a bandage on her neck while Jane Powell tried out for the part in *Royal Wedding* over which Miss Garland cut her throat slightly with the edge of a drinking glass Monday night. The action took place after she found out she had been taken off the picture.

'Jane Powell is the number one candidate to replace Judy,' said Arthur Freed, producer of the movie. 'Jane is trying out the songs right now on a rehearsal stage. We hope Judy does come back to make movies, but we can't say positively.'

An MGM spokesman added that whether 'the now nervous singer will ever face a camera again remains to be seen.'

After sixteen years, it was 'all over' between Judy and Metro. Mayer did not even send condolences. There was no severance pay, no retirement, no residuals for the twenty-eight films she had appeared in which had made about $80 million for the studio and would make that again in replay and in television sales.

Mayer issued this statement to the press: 'I couldn't have done more for her if she had been my own daughter.' Judy had been released from her contract 'in her own best interest.'

In desperate financial straits until she could figure out what to do with the huge house and with her future, Judy asked Mayer for a loan. Mayer called Nicholas Schenck, Chairman of Loew's, Incorporated. Schenck refused. As he replaced the receiver, Mayer's words to Judy were 'If they'd do this to you, they'll do this to me too.' (It was a prophecy that was to come true a few years later.)

She got up to leave his office. There was that long walk across the thick carpet, and she was not yet steady on her feet. He came quickly from behind his massive white, carved desk and took her by the arm. He had bought her her first

135

wrist-watch; masterminded her career; controlled her love life, weight, and appearance; arranged her abortion and her divorce. He offered her a 'personal' loan. She could not do other than accept. They grasped hands tightly at the door to his outer office. Later she confessed to feeling a great terror come over her. She was saying goodbye to her Hollywood years.

She walked out of the MGM Administration Building into the blinding California sun. Her eyes teared and she adjusted her sunglasses as she hurried to her waiting car, never glancing up at the people she passed. A floppy hat was pulled down around her face as she settled far back in the rear seat. Then she closed her eyes as the driver headed out the front gate of the studio.

Part Three

I played the stage, the Capitol,
And people said, "Don't stop";
Until you've played the Palace
You haven't played the top.

For years I had it preached to me,
And drummed into my head;
Unless you played the Palace,
You might as well be dead.

... it became the Hall of Fame—
The mecca of the trade;
When you had played the Palace,
You knew that you were made.

So I hope you'll understand
My wondrous thrill;
'Cause Vaudeville's back at the Palace,
And I'm on the bill.

—Roger Edens

CHAPTER TWENTY-THREE

AT the beginning of her severance from Mayer and the studio, Judy felt like a displaced refugee. There seemed no place for her to go. Her film career appeared to be behind her. *Summer Stock* was yet to be released, and she knew her performance had been creditable; but word had passed from studio to studio; rumor spread by mouth to press – Garland was an untouchable. At her own studio she had been replaced by Leslie Caron, Jane Powell, and Debbie Reynolds. At Twentieth Century-Fox, Marilyn Monroe had startled audiences and awakened studio executives in *The Asphalt Jungle* and *All About Eve*.

Mayer's loan was little more than what recently had constituted a week's salary. Admittedly, that amount was above the national yearly income for a family of four, but that had to be placed in its proper perspective. Judy had never handled her own money – had no conception of the cost of things. Since achieving stardom at MGM, she had lived in the manner of royalty. Houses were showcases; clothes were specially designed, cars and chauffeurs ordered on demand; secretaries answered mail; maids cleaned; cooks commanded kitchens; children were in the hands of nursemaids; bills were paid by accountants; and you never saw the money you earned. What she knew was that in order to keep all these things in running order, she must perform nonstop. Now the mechanism had ground to a heavy halt.

Panic set in. She was broke. In a similar situation average people would, perhaps, move to a small apartment, tend house themselves, take any kind of job to tide them over. But Judy had no idea how to accomplish such a foreign way of living.

Instead, she moved into the Beverly Hills Hotel – possibly one of the most luxurious hotels in the world, but the one she was accustomed to visiting when close friends and business associates came to California. Her suite (she had Liza and a nursemaid with her) cost over $150 a day. She never thought to ask, however, how much it was costing her; and had she, it is doubtful that she would have known what else to do. One thing was obvious, though: Mayer's loan would not last long with such a high standard of living.

Louella Parsons (in her book *Tell It to Louella*) stated: 'I have heard it said that much that happened to Judy was the fault of Hollywood. I can't agree. I can only say, however, that it could only have happened in Hollywood.'

Hollywood citizenry is not notable for a sense of loyalty. Riven, at the time, by mushrooming clouds of McCarthyism, Hollywood trembled in fear. Pink subpoenae were being received at the most famous houses, commanding their occupants to appear before The Committee. But those who did not receive subpoenae were not free and clear; they could be guilty by association. It was an economic condition that the Hollywood elite had always had to survive. To be connected with a film that failed, a falling star, a has-been director could mean the taint would rub off on anyone too close. That is why there were during those years so many 'comebacks' in Hollywood. One bad film and you were reduced to the status of 'has-been'.

With that fear always hanging over their heads, members of the industry who had a free choice, could not afford the risk of hiring a star who might crack up at any moment and throw their budget or film into chaos. Judy was fully aware of her position. In some ways, she accepted this harsh truth with a sense of relief. Appearing before the cameras was unthinkable. She was sick and exhausted. For days she never got out of her hotel room. Then she was presented with her first weekly bill. The same anxieties and terrors as when she had seen her hospital bills grasped her, and Mayer's loan was running out.

To further complicate her situation, she was without representation. She had, the last few years, been represented by the Berg-Allenberg Agency, but Phil Berg and Burt Allenberg had split. Berg, whose private client she was, no longer had an association with the office. Had she been a winner at that time, there is no question that Allenberg would have held tenaciously on to her agency commitment. It would seem, however, that no matter how reluctant he was in moral attitude to walk away from her, his business acumen won out.

Most plaudits have gone to Sid Luft, who was to be her future husband, and Abe Lastfogel, of the William Morris Agency, who would finally come to represent her, for starting Judy out on a new career – the concert stage. But in fact, it was Ethel who was responsible for the second phenomenon of stardom in her daughter's life.

Now divorced from Gilmore, Ethel rushed to Judy's side. Whatever her motive, whatever enmity had been between them, however complex Ethel's reappearance in Judy's life and Judy's acceptance of that presence – each now desperately needed the other, and neither had anyone else to turn to. True, Ethel had two other daughters, but they had gone their own ways: Sue marrying bandleader Jack Cathcart and living in Las Vegas; Jimmy now married to Thomas Thompson and residing in Dallas. One of Ethel's sisters, Norma, did live in Hollywood and was, in fact, struggling to make a career for herself as a singer. Married to a stunt man and fighting Judy's image (her voice had a distinct Garland ring to it), Norma did not seem to Ethel to have a real future. Except for one brother, Frank Milne, the other close members of her large family were not part of the entertainment world, and as Frank was a gambler, Ethel did not approve of him and was always angry when Judy advanced him money. Ethel, not prepared yet to go it alone, turned to Judy.

It seemed perfectly clear to Ethel that since Judy had started on a stage with a live audience, she could begin again there. Convincing Judy that cabaret or theatre exposure would not be as demanding as films, Ethel then had to set about, as she once had, to find an engagement. She never had to persuade Judy of the financial necessity of her working. Judy was almost too much aware of the fact, and it pained her gravely.

Having been out of the business for years, Ethel could only hope to tap familiar and old haunts. She went to the Cal-Neva Lodge; and though the terms of that contract aren't known, the fee Ethel was to receive was reported as fair and satisfactory. The two women then went to Roger Edens, who helped them put together an act. (This was fundamentally the same act that Judy later took to the Palladium.)

By the time Judy arrived at Cal-Neva Lodge, *Summer Stock* had previewed. After viewing it at a private showing, Billy Rose was prompted to write her an open letter in his syndicated column, *Pitching Horseshoes*, titling the letter 'Love Letter to a National Asset' and addressing it to Judy at the Cal-Neva Lodge, Lake Tahoe, California. Rose (who had once been married to Fanny Brice) wrote in part:

> I found your portrayal of a farm girl in 'Summer Stock' as convincing as a twenty-dollar gold piece, and when you leveled on Harold Arlen's old song, 'Get Happy' – well, it was Al Jolson in lace panties, Maurice Chevalier in opera pumps! ... Naturally you're wondering why I'm taking heart in ball-pen and writing you this love-and-kudos letter right out in the open. Well, like everyone else, I read the front-page stories about you a couple of months back, and from the lines between the lines I sensed that you had been having a bout with the jim-jams yourself, and that you no longer cared much whether school kept or not ...
>
> This letter – and I know it's plenty presumptuous – is to point out, in case you haven't thought of it yourself, how important it is to millions of people in this country that school continue to keep for Judy Garland ... It gets down to this, Judy: In an oblique and daffy sort of way, you are

as much a national asset as our coal reserves – both of you help warm up our insides.

The letter was signed 'Your devoted fan, Billy Rose.'

All the principals in the Cal-Neva plan to present Judy Garland for the first time in a supper club are now dead, and with them died the explanation of why Judy never did honor that contract. She remained at the Lodge for several weeks at their expense and worked on musical arrangements with Roger Edens. But then she abruptly left and returned to the Beverly Hills Hotel, now checking into a seven-room suite, which included connecting rooms for Ethel; for a secretary, Myrtle Tully; and for Liza and her nursemaid. Judy then proceeded to indulge herself in an eating binge that within a very short time added an additional thirty pounds to her five-foot-two-inch frame.

Now, answerable only to herself, she was flaunting Hollywood and all the demands and restrictions being a film star had imposed. When her hair once again began to fall out, she clipped it short and wore it in a boyish style; and taking what little money remained, she bought an air ticket to New York, moving Liza and the nursemaid back to Minnelli's care and sending Ethel to stay with Norma. The hotel was told to send the bill to her agents. Berg and Allenberg, although they no longer represented her.

In New York she checked into a luxury hotel, devoured almost every dish on the Room Service menu, walked all over Manhattan, and cheered New York to win over Philadelphia in the 1950 World Series. Friends extended her loans which enabled her to survive, but it was her exposure to the crowds of people who grasped her hands, the contact with the fans who appeared to love and care for her that kept her alive.

She became exceptionally heavy. The joy, the ecstasy of her new personal freedom faded fast. The hotel bill was ballooning as quickly as she was. Anxiety riddled her body, stirring her into constant wakefulness; and there was not the pill availability she had had in California.

Plump, matronly-looking, on edge, she attended a cocktail party and at it met Michael Sidney Luft. Later she claimed it was love at first sight. Perhaps, but it is more likely that she simply responded to his flattering male attention, which had not been coming her way for a long time. Always a romantic, Judy needed romance in her life now more than ever before to help her reestablish her sense of 'womanliness'; it is therefore, not difficult to understand Luft's appeal for her.

He did not stand in judgment of anything she did. He was a rebellious spirit, rootless, and without any specific talent or trade. Born in New Rochelle, Luft had grown up in Bronxville, New York, and had attended the Hun School in Princeton, the University of Pennsylvania, and the University of Miami. Athletically inclined as a young man, he had always been a glib talker and a bit of a show-off. He came from a small middle-class Jewish family, and he seemed able to break ties quite early. At the age of nineteen he was living on his own in Ottawa, Canada, where he was involved in the production of an Aquacade. It was his first taste of professional show business, and it made a strong impression on him. On future records he claimed that in 1940 he had joined the Royal Canadian Air Force and that once discharged, he had traveled to Hollywood. In Hollywood he looked up an old schoolmate from Bronxville, dancer Eleanor Powell, who was then a star, and for a time was her secretary.

After that, records state he was a Douglas test pilot and a technical adviser on the flying sequences of a low-budget film called *Charter Pilot*. The film was what was then called a 'programmer' – meaning it was to be booked as the bottom half of a double feature. In it was actress Lynn Bari, known at the time as the Queen of the 'GI's.' Luft married her and immediately stepped in to take over her career. His intention was to promote an independent film with himself as producer and Miss Bari as star. A lovely-looking lady, a reliable performer, and a popular supporting player, Miss Bari, unfortunately, did not have the charisma on which stars and independent films are banked, and so for eight years Luft floundered through a marriage in which his wife was the bigger wage earner.

Broad-shouldered, easy-mannered, Luft had a free-wheeling, unrestrained attitude that had a special charm for Judy. It was new; it was exciting; and there was a sense of surprise at her own attraction to him. He was not at all like her previous husbands.

She returned to Los Angeles, and Luft followed. Neither had a job, and both were involved in divorce actions. They saw each other constantly, and what he said, coupled with Ethel's initial push, nagged at her. In essence, it was 'The hell with films – why not the stage?' And if the stage – why not the Palace? He also suggested he manage her career. But Judy still had too much respect for the Hollywood 'system' and was inclined to believe she needed a strong and well-established Hollywood agency. She went to Phil Berg, who was now with Abe Lastfogel at William Morris. Berg discussed it with Abe and they met with Judy. The next day the new alliance was announced in *Variety:*

Hollywood, October 10 [1950]:
Judy Garland signed an agency deal with the William Morris office, which will function hereafter as her representatives [*sic*] in all phases of show business. First move will be to set up guest shots on radio, but the star will not be available for TV work 'for the time being'.

In the same issue of *Variety* was the announcement that 'finally free' from her Metro contract, Judy Garland was 'back in harness'. There was mention of the possibility of her replacing Mary Martin in *South Pacific*, recording two Decca albums, and/or doing a film or stage musical version of Booth Tarkington's *Alice Adams* for Jerry Wald and Norman Krasna at RKO. But the most significant item in the short article mentioned talk of a late-January European trip.

Judy discussed the idea of her giving a concert at the

Palace with Abe Lastfogel. Lastfogel did not laugh at her – which she was afraid he might. He did, however, discuss the advisability of trying out the act first before reaching New York. He asked, 'Why not the Palladium in London?' Judy replied, 'Why not?' but she never gave it serious consideration.

All talk of film and stage activity soon faded. She did record an album and appear on eight radio shows with Bing Crosby and in a *Lux Radio Theatre* adaptation of *Easter Parade*. It was just enough work to keep the wolves away from their door – 'their' implying Luft and herself. Luft was now acting as her business manager and handling all incoming revenue. It could not have been an easy task, for Judy still had a mountain of debts, including moneys owed the Government for back taxes.

During her CBS radio performance of *Easter Parade*, there was an incident that on the surface might have seemed rather unspectacular in the life of a famous person. She met a devoted fan, a man named Wayne Martin who for fourteen years had submerged his own personal life into a total and vicarious absorption in Judy's life and career. A thoughtful, quiet, semi-scholarly man, he had been a loner much of his life, living in a Hollywood apartment that was a jumble of Garland 'artifacts'; records; clippings; pictures; a few letters from Judy, signed to him in 'her left-handed longhand'. Wayne Martin was no teen-ager, romantic boy, or shy Romeo. Asked to define his fanatic dedication, which persisted and was constant through the years that followed that first meeting, Martin was quoted as saying, 'As soon as the overture starts, a feeling comes over the whole audience – the anticipation and the love. When she sings, there's a cry from her being. People want to help her.'

The Garland Cult had surfaced.

CHAPTER TWENTY-FOUR

LIZA, speaking to a *Time* interviewer from the floor of her apartment as she hugged her dog and smoked cigarettes, talked about the years with Luft and her mother. 'We started moving around a lot from one house to another. Usually we moved in the night. That was probably because Mama was so broke and maybe she owed money to landlords. Anyway, every time we moved, I'd find myself in a different school. Private, if we could afford it; public, if we couldn't. As a result, I hated school.'

And speaking to Stephen K. Oberbeck of *Good Housekeeping* magazine, she recalls, 'When Mama was down in the dumps, I'd say, "Come on, Mama, let's go to the park and ride the roller coaster."'

This wasn't the life Judy had wanted for Liza. She would have had it another way if it were possible. Money always seemed the key. She had worked all her life, and there wasn't anything there for Liza's security and future. Luft promised her he could change all this, and she believed him because she wanted desperately to do so.

On March 23, 1951, she went into court to obtain her divorce from Minnelli, charging mental cruelty and telling Judge McKay from the witness stand in a slow, deliberate voice, 'He [Minnelli] secluded himself and he wouldn't explain why he left me alone so much.'

Even for Hollywood, the provisions for Liza were most unusual. Judy was to have legal custody, but the child would spend six months each year with each parent. However, in the words of the pact, '... The child will be given utmost "freedom of locomotion" and changes from one home to the other will be irregular to avoid the child developing a feeling of regimentation.'

Whatever differences Judy and Minnelli had had in the past, it seems he knew that Judy adored Liza and that Liza loved her mother, and that the bond between them was far more important than the rigors Liza might suffer or the circumstances she could possibly be exposed to in spending six months with Judy.

Certainly there was little chance of the child's becoming 'regimented'. She was catapulted from mother to father, from one extreme to the other. Minnelli remained in Hollywood, living out the Hollywood success syndrome, remarrying a socialite, running a formalized home, and attending and giving glittering parties. His wife, Denise, lived in a world of couturier clothes, 'in' restaurants, 'acceptable' people, and current fashions.

For the time being, however, Liza was to remain with her father. All arrangements had been made and the booking confirmed. Judy would open at the London Palladium on a Monday night, the ninth of April, 1951. Abe Lastfogel handled all the details. Once in London, the Foster Agency, representing William Morris (Lastfogel), was to take over. A very nervous and overweight Judy embarked for England on the *Ile de France* with her secretary, Myrtle Tully, and Buddy Pepper, her accompanist. Pepper and Judy knew each other from childhood when they had both attended Mrs. Lawlor's school. A product of vaudeville and a former friend of David Rose (who had been the one to encourage him to become a songwriter), he and Judy had much in common, though they had not seen each other for years; this eased the tension of the sailing.

Reporters boarded the ship at Plymouth and seemed shocked at the weight she had gained. (The next day, after reading their comments, Judy told Pepper, 'From what I've read, I feel like the Fat Lady from Barnum and Bailey's' and roared with laughter.) When Judy disembarked, crew and passengers remaining on board hung out of portholes to wave her goodbye; ships in the harbor flashed signals spelling out her name; and the *Ile de France* gave a long, thunderous blast of its horn. Friends greeted her in London, and that was reassuring. Kay Thompson was appearing at the Café de Paris, and Danny Kaye had just ended an engagement at the Palladium, where he had been received with wild enthusiasm.

To look at her, it was hard to believe that less than six years had passed since the filming of *The Clock,* for in that short time her soft beauty had become harsh neon. She was twenty-eight and looked fifteen years older. She wasn't plump. She was fat, weighing over one hundred fifty pounds – the fat devouring her tiny frame, distorting her features into a gargoyle caricature of herself. Her hair was sparse and dyed an ugly rubber-tire black. Dressed badly, but smiling winningly, she nonetheless captured the press. They loved her with a slavish devotion, and so, it seemed, did all of Great Britain. In spite of her feeling that she had been greeted with open arms, the night before the opening she was sleepless and terror-stricken. By daybreak she was pacing up and down her hotel room, still racked with fear. 'I kept rushing to the bathroom to vomit,' Judy has said of that night. 'I couldn't eat; I couldn't sleep; I couldn't even sit down.'

When the Blitz was at its grittiest, when even the nightingales found it hard to sing in Berkeley Square, there had been Judy singing and dancing up the yellow brick road, giving English romantics, a glimpse of happiness even in the darkest days of the war. A grateful nation would not forget this. Though it was springtime, 1951, there was still evidence of the war wherever you looked. Bombing sites waited reconstruction, their brick and mortar entrails still exposed. Charred and crumbling walls loomed darkly through the cold gray rain. Meat and sugar were still rationed. There was a shortage of cloth, paper, and string. Men tediously home-dry-cleaned their one worn suit; women made do with whatever they had.

Industry had virtually shut down for the war years and was slow now in beginning again. This meant that the entire country still had a look of the late thirties to it. Appliances were outdated by American standards – lighting and heating obsolete; cars and clothes were old-fashioned. The British film industry hadn't yet regained its prewar status, and so

American products and Hollywood stars came in for a great deal of idolatry.

The day of the concert, April 14, 1951, the press gave her encouragement and wished her well. It was the first time any press had been kind to her in years, and she drew some confidence from it. Some of the nervousness began to pass, but she still felt she might not be able to sustain herself without Sid.

After several overseas calls entreating him to join her, he hopped a plane, arriving only a few hours before her first appearance. He stayed close to her side, helping her fight her way into the theater through a cold, gray drizzle – hundreds of screaming, kerchiefed girls snatching at her, kissing her, shoving placards that read GOOD LUCK, JUDY in her face, and scrambling for autographs. When Sid finally got her to her dressing room, she was only half conscious. She kept repeating her fears and reminding everyone that she hadn't worked at all in almost three years and had given a show in public only a few times since she had been a child.

Talking to Joe Hyams (then of *Photoplay* magazine), she said of those last moments before she went onstage, 'There were only minutes left. I had to get hold of myself. I said to myself, "What's the matter, you dope? If you don't cut this out, you won't be able to sing" ... Standing in the wings, waiting to go on, I became paralyzed. My knees locked together and I walked on [stage] like a stiff-legged toy soldier.'

She should have had no professional doubts, for the only things off-key in her entire act were the two dresses she wore. The first, a flared lemon-yellow organza shot with glitter, made her look like a barrel of melting butter. It was still better than the black dress that followed. But that hardly seemed to matter – for when she finally stepped out of the shadows of the wings onto that huge stage, she was welcomed with a real Palladium roar that caused her to stumble. In a moment she had regained her footing. 'Good old Judy!' yelled the audience. She blew them kisses; and when they had quieted, told them, 'This is the greatest moment of my life.' Her voice trembled as she spoke, and her audience rose to their feet and cheered her.

One of the most striking features of her show was its thoroughgoing music hall quality. None of it was accidental. The early years were now paying off. All of Ethel's training, Roger Edens' coaching, Mickey Rooney's goading were put to use. She approached the act in a typical variety manner, treating it as pure entertainment, never allowing herself to be overproduced, placing herself on an equal footing with her audience, consciously working to give everyone a good time, and firmly secure in the knowledge that audiences reacted to good lyrics. She gave each song a clear and lively interpretation.

After the first applause had subsided, she sang an introductory song telling how Danny Kaye had impressed upon her that she must play the Palladium. Then she went into a full-throated rendition of

It's a long, long way to Piccadilly,
But at long last here I am!

Clutching the mike, she joked about her size.

'More to love!' her audience yelled back.

In her first number she was so overly anxious that the fury of her voice made the microphone tremble with her. She opened with 'The Boy Next Door', 'Embraceable You', and 'Limehouse Blues'. Then she kicked off her shoes. 'My feet hurt', she confided. The audience laughed heartily. She thumped around the stage in her stocking feet and kept time to her singing with her big toe. She mopped her brow and wiped the tip of her nose with the back of her hand. 'It's not ladylike but extremely necessary,' she confessed. The audience was in the hollow of her hand.

It was to be a retrospective performance of all her past hits, and she began by being casual, discreetly hoydenish, her voice rich and vibrant – filling every nook and cranny of the gargantuan theater, expressing a new joyousness, a new aspect of herself. Towards the end, all lights but one went out. There was Judy in her stocking feet, sitting on the edge of the stage, the microphone so close to her lips that each tremor was echoed. The eyes were wide with wonder, scanning the darkness overhead, looking for bluebirds. There was an incredible transference. Judy sat trembling in adolescent wonder and hope and trust. She was the universal child of dreams.

In the moment of striking blackness that followed the last soaring note (*Would she make it – would she? Yes! She did! Bravo! Cheers!*) of the song, she replaced her shoes and, doing a small turn as the lights came on, as she began to exit, tripped over a microphone wire and fell flat and hard on her rear. Sid immediately shouted from his box seat out front, 'You're great, baby. You're great!' And Kay Thompson, who was standing at the side of the stage, screamed, 'Get back up! They love you!' The audience rose en masse as Buddy Pepper rushed to her and helped her to her feet. She was laughing nervously.

'That's probably one of the most ungraceful exits ever made,' she said in that voice that often sounded as though it had tripped over microphone cords itself. Then she introduced Buddy Pepper.

The audience shouted back at her, 'Good old Judy!' as they had before. She went offstage, but returned for an encore.

'Good night,' she finally yelled out over their whistles and screams. 'Good night. I love you very much!' But she was brought out again – this time the stage looking like a conservatory, so filled with floral tributes was it.

The next morning the London *Times* reported: 'Miss Judy Garland not only tops the bill at the Palladium this week, she also runs away with the show.'

All the Palladium reviews were raves. Not one faulted Judy's performance, though they humorously criticized her costumes.

With the nightly excitement of her Palladium appearances, she was in very high spirits. After each performance her dressing room was mobbed and at least one

152

celebrity would come backstage to congratulate her. She was up all night and slept most of the day. London was the Ritz Hotel or the theater or the Café de Paris.

When her engagement ended, four weeks later, a severe depression set in. It was a rainy May. London was gray and damp and shabby. For the first time she looked around her. There was a sense of the unreal, and she felt both longing and guilt at being separated from Liza for so long. Tension began between Sid and herself. She was, therefore, in the beginning, anxious and looking forward to the tour before them. Foster had set a tour of the provinces; but she decided to first go to Paris with Sid to buy some new dresses, and came back with two Balmain originals that, at least, were tasteful.

She opened at the Empire in Glasgow on May 21, at the Edinburgh Empire on May 29; spending June 10, her birthday, in Paris; returning the following night to open at the Palace in Manchester. A man in the audience called out for her to sing 'Embrace Me'. 'I'd love to,' she called back. She forgot lyrics to a song – and admitted it, and the audience encouraged her onward. When someone asked for 'The Trolley Song', she said, 'I'm glad you asked for that one – we rehearsed it.'

On she went, the smell of train stations in her nostrils, the sound of thundering applause in her ears. The Empire in Liverpool, June 18; the Royal in Dublin, July 2; the Birmingham Hippodrome, July 9. In Birmingham she even made an 11:30 A.M. personal appearance at Lewis' department store.

So closed her tour of Great Britain.

It took thirteen hours then to fly back across the Atlantic, but all that long distance Judy could recall to mind those last moments in Birmingham.

'Good-night, good-bye, I love you very much,' she called out.

And to the last member of the audience, they stood and sang to her – 'Auld Lang Syne.'

CHAPTER TWENTY-FIVE

IN no fewer than twelve films she had played the wide-eyed, stagestruck girl who did or did not make the Palace. When she returned to New York after her triumph at the Palladium, that celluloid fantasy became her one real, main, and driving force. Walking through the streets of New York alone, as she was now able to do, she would end up always in front of the Palace, sensing more than irony in the fact that the Palace had become a cinema cathedral, and overcome with the injustice of that fact. Somehow, she told friends, the management must be persuaded to reinstate the two-a-day at the Palace – to bring back vaudeville.

No matter how triumphant her Palladium appearance had been, in her eyes she had not yet played the top until she played the Palace. She discussed it with Luft, and he went to Abe Lastfogel.

It was not difficult to understand the lure the Palace had for Judy. From 1913 to 1933, it had been the quintessence of *the tops*, the most refined in vaudeville, with the nation's greatest entertainers performing twice a day, including Sunday. All the great stars of the past had played the Palace – Nora Bayes, Sophie Tucker, Fanny Brice, Eddie Cantor, Eva Tanguay, George Jessel, the Cohans and the Foys, Gallagher and Shean, the Dolly Sisters, 'The Divine Sarah' Bernhardt, Ethel Barrymore, Lillian Russell, Will Rogers – all the top entertainers of the early twentieth century.

Then came the harsh times of the Depression. It was a losing scrimmage, but the Palace fought to keep vaudeville alive and the theater solvent by combining motion pictures and vaudeville acts. After three years vaudeville 'died' more or less officially, and the Palace adopted a straight picture policy, which it maintained until 1949. In that year the theater again combined feature films with live entertainment;

but it had lost the breathlessly young quality, the tingling excitement, the splendor and glory of vaudeville in its vigorous prime.

Judy's success at the Palladium, the phenomenon of the mushrooming Garland Cult, her amazing versatility which enabled her to communicate quivering emotion and follow it with comic pratfalls, the driving vibrato that leaped, soared, swept across the footlights straight up to the second balcony of the great English music hall, encouraged the management of the Palace to go along with Luft and Lastfogel. The Palace could return to a live two-a-day routine, and Judy Garland was the only, the natural choice to launch the historic event. And so it was made public that on October 16, 1951, Judy Garland would open at the Palace, playing two shows a day, Sundays included.

Before her concert years Judy had always portrayed a wholesome, vulnerable, determined, and cheerful young woman, graciously childlike, always seeking to please, smiling bravely in the face of adversity. She was, of course, still that same woman, but now a new side of her personality had emerged. She no longer had to pose. She could do what she wanted: she was able to glut herself with food; say all the outrageous things she had always thought but not said; demand the love she had previously believed she might not deserve; sleep late, dress flashily; and live in an unmarried state with a man she loved. In effect, she was rejecting her past as all those in her past had once rejected her.

A wave of understanding swept across the nation's rejects – the men and women who had never been accepted as they were. Judy's incredible rebirth; the unleashing of her true spirit; her defiance of convention; and most of all, the true beauty of her soul that soared from her in song, the honest pain and anguish she exposed when singing, caused them to rise up and at any cost to reach her, to let her know she was not alone, that they would protect her, that they understood, that they accepted her for *herself* and perceived her need for both a dialogue and an outstretched hand.

This was Judy's new audience. They were to be not only

in the palm of her hand, but also staunchly in her corner. As soon as the announcement hit the papers that she was to reopen the two-a-day at the Palace, they hitched, walked, bused until they reached New York; and once there, they let Judy know of their presence. This army of protectors was a new experience to her. There was no question that she immediately encouraged·their devotion.

It was October in New York – a brisk, beautiful autumn. Vivien Leigh was the talk of the film world with her screen performance of Blanche Dubois in *A Streetcar Named Desire*; Gertrude Lawrence was thrilling audiences on Broadway opposite newcomer Yul Brynner in *The King and I*. Katherine Hepburn had returned to the theater to do Shakespeare in a brilliant production of *As You Like It*; and at Madison Square Garden, Marlene Dietrich startled a circus audience by appearing as ringmaster, dressed in a brief costume of her own design – black tights, top hat, and a scarlet cutaway jacket. She stood in the dark immensity of the ring, took the microphone, and said to the entranced audience in her inimitable deep, warm, cavernous voice, 'He-looo, are you having any fun?'

Harry Truman was in the White House, with Alben Barkley as Vice President. North Korea had invaded South Korea, and the United States had sent in troops. Joseph McCarthy and the Senate Investigating Committee filled the press and the television screens as the 'Hollywood Ten' went 'on trial' before an unconstitutional committee of which a young man named Richard Nixon was a prosecuting attorney. Jacqueline Bouvier had not yet met John Kennedy, but she had just written the winning essay for *Vogue*'s *Prix de Paris* stating that the three men she would've liked to have known were Charles Baudelaire, Oscar Wilde, and Sergei Diaghilev.

Ladies' skirts were at an all-time ugly length – mid-calf; but this time Judy's gowns were designed for her by Irene Sharaff, the well-known MGM designer, and good taste and good sense established a style for the performance that had not existed in her appearance at the Palladium. In fact, there

156

was the ambience of a Metro extravaganza about the entire production.

Under Luft's supervision the Palace had been completely renovated, the decor having an essence of Hollywood grandeur and a heavy-handed Hollywood touch. Judy's act was staged and directed by that old bullwhipper himself, Charles Walters; Roger Edens did all the special lyrics and musical arrangements; and Hugh Martin, who had written the score of *Meet Me In St. Louis* and given her the great hit 'The Trolley Song', accompanied her. All of these artists were mentioned in the program as 'appearing through the courtesy of MGM Studios'. One might, with a sense of irony, say Judy was as well!

Priceless paintings were borrowed from the extensive collection of E. F. Albee and exhibited in the lobby; flashing crystal chandeliers replaced the outdated lighting; walls were painted a creamy ivory and trimmed in glistening gold; and a red velvet carpet was spread from the curb in front of the theater right up to the stage.

Opening night, a solid police cordon was called out to keep in check the mass of fans that teemed Duffy Square. Tickets were a $6 top, and the house was sold out, with signs reading NO STANDING ROOM. Backstage, Judy, pacing nervously amid the huge bouquets in her dressing room and flanked by Luft and accompanist Hugh Martin, was filled with the same last-minute opening-night terror she had experienced at the Palladium.

She was dressed in stylish black; but she was aware that while slimmer than she had been in England, she was still grossly overweight, and that an audience blazing with jewels worn by society figures and film stars – an audience of famous people like the Duke and Duchess of Windsor, Marlene Dietrich, Gloria Swanson, Durante (who had once played the Palace himself), and Jack Benny – now being shown to their seats, had never seen her fat.

She was scheduled to appear in the second half of the program, directly following the intermission – the usual spot

157

for the top act in a vaudeville revue. After an overture led by orchestra conductor Don Albert, which included a medley of Garland hits, a teeterboard group opened the show. They were followed by the youthful Doodles and Spider, who were making their first Broadway appearance – though they had previously scored heavily at The Blue Angel. Then came Smith and Dale, the grand old vaudeville team who had, in 1909, headlined the first All-American vaudeville bill in Europe. Continental dancing stars Giselle and François Szony, a brother-and-sister act, appeared next. Comedian Max Bygraves, who had appeared with Judy at the Palladium, closed the first half.

As the plush and elegant red velvet curtains opened after the intermission, Don Albert raised his baton, and a group of eight young men billed as Judy's Eight Boy Friends danced out on-stage and introduced her. Judy stood, keyed up in the wings, snapping her fingers, tapping her foot to the beat of the music. Stepping from the wings on cue, she remained initially concealed by her chorus line of youthful male hoofers. There was a flash of her black velvet gown as they parted to let her through. On her appearance the audience stood and shouted, applauding wildly. Judy stepped to the footlights. The applause grew. She cupped her hands and yelled, 'Hello!' at the top of her voice. The audience laughed, and Judy with them. Judy was more at ease and in command than she had been at the Palladium. She felt a rapport with the audience; and as Don Albert led the orchestra into her opening number – 'Until You Play the Palace' – they quieted and sat down while Judy remained at the footlights for the opening bars. It was a warm and welcoming gesture.

The 'Palace' number was reminiscent of the Palladium opener – 'It's a Long Way to Piccadilly' – in that Judy was having a musical dialogue with her audience. She related a few facts about her career, kidded the newspapermen about probably reporting that she needed to lose another ninety pounds, and then paid homage to the Palace and the great stars who had preceded her, singing their greatest hits –

Fanny Brice's 'My Man', Sophie Tucker's 'Some of These Days', and Eva Tanguay's 'I Don't Care'.

By now the audience was cheering her on to do her own songs. She was beginning to feel the power, the chemistry the connection between the audience and herself. Tossing the microphone wire over her shoulder in a gesture that was pure camp (she had used a similar gesture at the Palladium but with not so much bravado), she set the mood for the performance to follow. Striding back and forth across the stage, she welcomed Hugh Martin and then launched into 'You Made Me Love You', after which she belted out 'Rock-a-Bye Your Baby', 'The Trolley Song', 'For Me and My Gal', and 'Come Rain or Come Shine'. She picked up her skirt to reveal an orange crinoline petticoat and wiped her brow with a matching orange handkerchief. 'Gotta have some water,' she exclaimed. 'You don't know how hot it is up here.' Then, taking a pitcher and a glass off the top of Hugh Martin's piano, she walked to the footlights with it. 'Anybody want a glass of water?' she asked in a clear, ringing voice. She used a lot of the same dialogue she had introduced into her English performances, but made it sound completely spontaneous. Returning to the piano, she did some dance steps, this time *without* falling, and on an almost blacked-out stage managed a few smooth and humorous pratfalls with Charles Walters.

Leaving the Eight Boy Friends to do a number on their own, she startled the audience on her return to the footlights by having stripped down to black tights, a dashing tuxedo top, and a top hat to sing 'Hallelujah, Come On, Get Happy!' from *Summer Stock*. It was perhaps the most theatrical moment in the show, for despite her weight the Garland legs were still exquisite and difficult to tear one's eyes from. The house rose to a tumultuous ovation at the end of this number, and the continuing applause covered the opening bars of 'This Is My Lucky Day'.

While Judy's Eight Boy Friends once again held the stage, she changed costumes, reappearing this time in chalky tramp makeup and baggy hobo costume and assisted by an

159

agile male partner, Jack McClendon, did the 'We're a Couple of Swells' number from *Easter Parade*. The true gamin in her shone forth. She grinned mischievously through blacked-out teeth, fluttered her battered hat, and batted her painted eyes. The audience screamed out their approval; and she stood there – the lonely tramp: the Chaplain pose Ethel had taught her so many years before – and waited. It was a long time before silence came. When it did, she went down to the footlights, battered hat in hand, sitting down in the footlight trough. Only one light on her face remained; the rest of the stage was in blackness. Cupping her chin in her hands and with tears in her eyes, she sang 'Somewhere Over The Rainbow'.

The theater had never seemed more alive than it did with Judy posed on the edge of the stage in that cavernous darkness voicing a lost child's pitiful lament; and there wasn't a dry eye in the house when she was done. She stood, and for a full three minutes the audience cheered and applauded her. 'I'm not good at making speeches,' she finally faltered. 'What can I say except bless you, good night, and I love you very much.'

At that point the usherettes came down the aisles and filled the stage with floral tributes, and it was many minutes more before the audience would let her leave.

Once again, as in London (though now polished and used to best advantage), her performance carried little admixtures of 'salesmanship' – perhaps Walters and Lastfogel and Luft might have called it 'showmanship'. In many ways this tainted the essential purity of her performance, but it did infuse her with a new image. There was a certain frenzy in her attitude – the quick staccato steps alternating with impatient striding across the stage, the whiplike tossing of the microphone cord over her shoulder, grabbing the instrument itself in an almost desperate manner, the impassioned energy in the delivery of her songs.

There was no question that in an effort to fit up-to-date American entertainment values she had permitted herself to be 'presented' – that is, slightly industrialized. The act was

160

flashy, and some thought it succeeded in spite of this, not because of it.

Quoting Harold Clurman:

> [Judy] is at bottom a sort of early twentieth-century country kid, but the marks of the big city wounds of our day are upon her. Her poetry is not only in the things she has survived, but in a violent need to pour them forth in vivid popular form, which makes her the very epitome of the theatrical personality. The tension between the unctuously bright slickness which is expected of her medium and environment and the fierceness of what her being wants to cry out produces something positively orgastic in the final effect.

This was a historic night for her. She now knew that she had opened a new and exciting door in her career; there was the admiration of her peers, the adulation of her fans, a basket of roses sent by Minnelli in Liza's name to make her feel her child was with her; and there was Sid Luft, glowing, cheering, loving. There had been a call from Ethel, and its effect remained the only tinge of uneasiness she had. Instinctively she knew Sid and Ethel would someday cross swords, and she was honest enough with herself to know who must win and to feel the first pangs of a guilt toward Ethel that would never again desert her.

Backstage was pandemonium. Mobs of reporters, photographers, and well-wishers crowded around her, all telling her how wonderful she was. 'Thank you, thank you,' she repeated again and again, grasping, holding on to each extended hand. 'Are you coming to my party?' she would inquire. 'You *must* come to my party. I'll probably go straight home and collapse, but *you* must go to my party!' Everyone laughed.

Luft had planned a reception for her at the '21' Club. She changed into an ultrafeminine blue tulle off-the-shoulder. The confusion had already set in. She was the toast of Broadway, but she was dressed like a Hollywood starlet at a studio preview.

At least five thousand fans blocked her exit. 'I've been on this beat twenty years,' a policeman said. 'I'm telling you I've never seen anything like it.' Sid and four policemen guided her through the crowd. All around her rose shouts of 'Judy! Bravo! Bravo!' To Judy they must have drowned out even the harsh sounds of nighttime Manhattan.

The sophisticated and crowded interior of the '21' Club looked a bit like a Metro spectacular. It seemed *everyone* was there and toasting Judy in the most expensive champagne. Luft was ostensibly the host, but in fact, Judy was picking up the tab. It did not diminish her excitement as she waited with all her supporters for the morning newspapers to carry the reviews.

But what a grand irony that Robert Garland, the man whose name she had borrowed and then kept as her own twenty years before, was the man chosen by the *Journal-American* to review the show! 'There were shining show people in the good old days,' he wrote. 'There can be shining show people now. Witness Miss Garland. It is as if vaudeville had been waiting somewhere for her to come along, and she, in turn, for vaudeville.'

But perhaps the most moving review was written by Clifton Fadiman and appeared in *Holiday* magazine several months later. 'As with all true clowns,' wrote Mr. Fadiman,

... she seemed to be neither male nor female, young nor old, pretty nor plain. She had no 'glamour' only magic. She was gaiety itself, yearning itself, fun itself ... She wasn't being judged or enjoyed, not even watched or heard. She was only being felt, as one feels the quiet run of one's own blood, the shiver of the spine, Housman's prickle of the skin; and when looking about eighteen inches high sitting hunched over the stage with only a tiny spotlight pinpointing her elf face, she breathed the last phrases of 'Over the Rainbow' and cried out its universal, unanswerable query, 'Why can't I?', it was as though the bewildered hearts of all the people in the world had

162

moved quietly together and become one, shaking in Judy's throat, and there breaking.

For nineteen weeks she played to packed houses. The grind was brutal. On a Sunday less than four weeks after she had opened she collapsed and was rushed to the Le Roy Hospital on Sixty-first Street, and there treated by a Dr. Udall Salamon for nervous exhaustion. By midweek she was back onstage. It was a marathon engagement. Eight hundred thousand people came to see her – breaking every existing record at the Palace.

She closed on a Sunday, February 24, 1952. Jimmy Stewart and Lauritz Melchior, the Metropolitan Opera star, were in the audience. Both joined her onstage at the finale, and Mr. Melchior, who was to follow her into the Palace, led the audience in a music tribute, singing – as her last English audience had sung – 'Auld Lang Syne'.

The past would appear over and done with – swept away, lost, forgotten in the vitality of her new self, her newfound life-style. Luft was by her side. They were living a brassy, late-night life, thriving on nightclub smoke, surrounded by new faces – Broadway folk, nightclub habitués, musicians, and gamblers. She had earned $20,000 a week at the Palace and had never seen a penny of it, trusting Luft and Lastfogel to handle the finances. The Garland bandwagon had greased its motor and refueled, and the world was once again climbing aboard. But Judy loved the feeling of being 'surrounded'. She was very happy. Liza was on her mind, but she dreamed of a new future for the child, and she was looking forward to their being reunited.

She was, in fact, heading toward California. For on April 26, she was to open at the Philharmonic Auditorium in Los Angeles.

Hollywood columnists Sheilah Graham, Hedda Hopper, and Mayer's old friend Louella Parsons all announced from their Hollywood perches that Judy was on 'the *comeback road*.'

CHAPTER TWENTY-SIX

IN an interview before her Los Angeles opening Judy told the world, 'Sid has done it for me; that's my fella.' And Luft had added: 'I love Judy. I want to protect her from the trauma she once knew. I don't want her to be bewildered or hurt again. I want her to have happiness.'

Judy was desperately in love and experiencing new sensations. There was a certain abandon in her feelings toward Luft that she had never felt before. Sid was tough, strong, and opinionated. From the onset of their relationship he was Number One and Judy the follower. She lovéd the role. It made her feel extremely feminine. She told herself she would be protected now, cared for, understood. But at heart she remained dreadfully insecure. Accordingly, she found herself constantly testing him. Therefore, there was never truly a time when they didn't have 'spats'.

While still with Luft, she wrote an article for *Coronet* magazine titled 'How Not to Love A Woman', in which she stated, 'We [women] must know, beyond doubt, that we're safe with you [men]. That you can take it, that you are not bluffing about your strength and most of all, that you *care* enough to win.' And in another part of the article she writes, 'We will seem to be fighting you to the last ditch for final authority ... But in the obscure recesses of our hearts, we want you to win. You *have* to win. For we aren't really made for leadership. It's a pose.'

Luft was not about to yield his leadership or hand Judy the reins, as she might have feared. Yes, there were moments of confusion, twinges of alarm, an instinct that perhaps she should pull back. Always moved by the passage in the Bible in the Book of Ruth, 'Whither thou goest, I will go, and where thou lodgest, I will lodge', she comments at the end of her *Coronet* article on this philosophy: 'We weep because we think of it as a beautiful description of woman the follower. To many of us it means that you [men] alone must be the leader. If you are, nothing else really matters.'

There was, however, that key word 'Leader' – its interpretation and the confusion it brought to Judy. Luft had a strength that was born of toughness, not courage, and an ability not so much to lead as to *drive* others who could help him satisfy his own needs. In Judy's case and at this point in her life, the latter worked as a positive force. Luft craved the limelight, a showy, ostentatious life – wanted to be 'in the big time'. He had already come to terms with his own inability to gain these ends by himself. All of which gave his one true talent – *the art of promoting* a thrust forward.

Luft was, however, no Mike Todd or P. T. Barnum. Lacking their genius, he had to first have a presold product. Where he could not succeed in making Lynn Bari a star of the first magnitude, he could take a star – Judy – and keep her in orbit. There were perhaps other agents, managers, promoters (who would have come into no more than 10 percent of the take) who could have done the same thing. But no one was willing to take the time, give the dedication, and risk the chance of personal jeopardy that working with Judy imposed. This was Luft's additive – the extra ingredient that enabled him to get Judy on her feet, bigger, better, and more of a money-maker than ever before. In effect, he took over her life on a twenty-four-hour-a-day basis. He bullied her, pushed her, praised her, beat her down, picked her up – at each turn carefully weighing which would in the end get her up on that stage playing to packed houses.

Until the very end of her affiliation with Luft, Judy claimed she never saw any of the money she made and in the early years never inquired about its disposition. Her feeling that Luft had to be Number One was a good assessment of his personality. By the time they were headed for California, he exerted full control over her. His ability to do this was one of his greatest attractions for Judy and certainly a complete reversal of the passivity of David Rose and the aestheticism of Vincente Minnelli. Only Mayer – and before him,

Ethel – had ever made her sense that another power was greater than her own. Mayer was ostensibly out of her life, but Ethel was waiting for her in Los Angeles. Judy had not seen her in a year, and Luft and Ethel had not yet met. That meeting was scheduled shortly after their arrival in California. Depending on whose viewpoint one subscribed to, it was both fatal and highly successful. Each took an instant dislike to the other, and Ethel was made to understand that she was now the complete and total outsider.

Ethel was bereft. She was also aware that she stood no chance of cracking through the wall Luft placed between Judy and herself, because he would be on constant guard. She was extremely disturbed. She developed a painful ulcer, and her own resources were now shrunken so that her standard of living had to be altered. She had become fearful of her financial future – having always relied on Judy's support, she feared Luft might influence Judy to withdraw it; but she was also concerned that he might exert other influences on Judy and that she might be losing her place in her daughter's life.

Sought out by the press, Ethel made some unflattering remarks about Luft, ambiguously saying she thought he was bad for Judy but not specifying how or why. As soon as the newspaper report appeared, she had second thoughts on what she had done and tried to contact Judy, but to no avail – being told her daughter could not be reached. Asking the stranger to whom she was speaking (who was someone obviously in Judy's employ) if Judy was disturbed by the newspaper report, Ethel received the reply that she was not. But, of course, this did not represent the truth. Judy was bitterly hurt and very protective of Luft. She refused to see Ethel while she was in Los Angeles. Fate stepped in and decreed that they were not to see each other again, though their tremendous mutual ability to create deep-rooted disturbances in the other's life was far from over. Luft could pressure Judy not to see Ethel, but later it was beyond his capacity to exorcise Ethel's ghost from her daughter's psyche.

Judy could not have perceived it at the time, but her record run at the Palace had already made her a legend. The resurgent star now found herself with a frenzied following. Scalpers were getting $100 a pair of tickets to the opening at the Los Angeles Philharmonic Auditorium, and all seats were sold out to the premiere performance weeks before April 26, the scheduled date. Opening night was a replay of the Palace opening – wild applause and shouts of *Bravo!* rang through the huge old hall – and the engagement was sold out for the entirety of its four-week run.

There was nothing Hollywood despised more than failure, and nothing it venerated more than popular success. Having grown up in this selfsame society, Judy was geared to its values. Each day she rose with the terrible anxiety that *that* night the show would fail and Hollywood shake its success-oriented head. 'Well, we were right,' she was afraid people would say. She also began to question the meaning of her concert success, for Hollywood people were fairly contemptuous of any medium through which only scant thousands could be reached. Their power remained in packaging for millions; and among themselves they cast doubts that Judy, looking fat and matronly, would have succeeded without the power of film magnetism that *they* had invested in her. The whispers were not kept in private corridors, and so their innuendos came back to whistle like a stubborn wind beneath her dressing-room door.

Even Luft's encouragement and Liza's proximity could not ease the rumblings of anxiety that she was beginning to experience. No sooner had she arrived in Hollywood than she began to push to leave it. Luft was working on a San Francisco appearance to follow, and that gave her something concrete to look to.

Her record *Judy at the Palace* (Copyright 1951, Decca Records, Inc.) had just been released and was selling extremely well, and she had signed a five-year contract with RCA Victor Records. There was no reason for her to feel insecure – but nonetheless, she did. Her final decree of divorce came through before she completed her Los Angeles appearance. She was a free woman. To Judy that meant only that she was now free to marry the man she loved.

On June 11, 1952, Judy took one day away from her San Francisco concert appearance at the Curran Theatre and she and Luft were married in a simple, five-minute ceremony at the Hollister, California, ranch of a wealthy friend. That night Judy was back performing at the Curran. It was a preview of what their married life was to be like.

Only hours after the ceremony Luft was sued by Lynn Bari, claiming that Judy had earned $750,000 in 1951 and that Luft as her manager, had received a large portion of it. Miss Bari asked the court to raise Luft's $200 monthly support payments to their son to $500. Judge Burke in Superior Court in Hollywood ordered that the amount of $400 monthly be paid over.

Their court problems did not end there. Ethel – angry, pressed by her own fears and financial needs – now went to court to claim nonsupport from her 'high-salaried' daughter. Judy was profoundly disturbed and confused. In the end, incensed that Ethel would trot their differences out into public and into court, she stood her ground, declaring that her mother was a capable piano and singing teacher, having instructed her, and was qualified to run a movie theater as well. She then had records produced to show what moneys had been paid to Ethel in the past. Ethel's case fell through. A greater estrangement was created between mother and daughter.

It did not help that on July 19, Ethel 'bared her soul' to columnist Sheilah Graham in a coast-to-coast interview. 'Judy has been selfish all her life,' she declared. 'That's my fault. I made it too easy for her. She worked, but that's all she ever wanted, to be an actress. She never said, "I want to be kind or loved," only "I want to be famous." ' She added that she wanted nothing further from Judy and that she wished the press would forget her as Judy most obviously had done.

Ethel then took a $60-a-week job at Douglas Aircraft, working on the assembly line, and immediately confided this news to a few of her friends who happened to be members of the press.

Judy was pregnant and had been since her San Francisco concert. In the advanced stages of the pregnancy she took very sick. She was swollen with edema and dangerously overweight. Luft was seldom at home, his twenty-four-hour-a-day supervision ending with her inability to appear on-stage. The honeymoon was over. Judy has said, 'From the beginning Sid and I weren't happy. I don't know why. I really don't. For me it was work, work, work; and then I didn't see much of Sid. He was always dashing off to places lining up my appearances. I wasn't made any happier look-ing into mirrors seeing myself balloon out of shape from liquids trapped in my body.'

The doctors claimed her condition was caused by a metabolic imbalance and that the weight was, indeed, liquid trapped in her body. New fears set in: she would lose Sid; she would lose the baby; her concert career was over – having been only a flash in her life; she would die in de-livery. (There was still the painful and frightening remem-brance of Liza's birth.)

On December 8, 1952, she gave birth to a little girl. They named her Lorna. The child was healthy and beautiful, and Judy seemed to feel renewed and happy. It was to be the one bright and happy spot in her life for quite a while; for on January 5, 1953, less than four weeks later, Ethel fell dead in the parking lot of Douglas Aircraft of a heart seizure that had occurred at seven-thirty in the morning. She was discovered between two parked cars on her hands and knees, as though desperately trying to crawl for help.

Judy collapsed. It was not one of those convenient 'collapses' famous stars have in order to avoid the press. She was not hiding under a bed so that she did not have to answer questions – though to be sure, the whole sordid, un-savory story of Judy's 'abandonment' of Ethel in these last days of dire circumstances was rehashed in the press. For-gotten was the Judge's just decree after studying all the evidence: that Judy *not* pay Ethel support. It made a far more dramatic story for the press to ignore that.

The irony, of course, was that Judy had been supporting her mother since she had been a very small child. All their lives their roles had been reversed in that respect. And had Ethel been cautious with the money Judy gave her, neither of them need ever have had financial insecurities. The further irony was that only in the last six months of Ethel's life had Judy withdrawn monthly support, having maintained Ethel at times when she herself was deeply in debt. Actually, Ethel had more security than Judy, having received cash for a theater she and Gilmore had owned in Dallas and having a small income from investments made with Judy's early earnings.

It is hard to understand why, if Ethel felt she must work, she chose a factory assembly-line job when there were many more lucrative jobs open to her. She could certainly have secured a position in publicity, costuming (she was still an expert seamstress), theater management, booking, or, as previously mentioned, as a piano teacher or coach. She also had a large family whom she, through Judy's bounty, had been very good to all the years of Judy's career and whom she certainly could have called on had she truly been in need.

The court suit for support, then, appears to have been a vituperative action initiated in anger and meant to censure or embarrass Judy on one hand and on the other, threaten Judy – as the old hotel-room-desertion act had once done – into complying with Ethel's will. In short, it was a form of emotional blackmail.

But Judy's feelings regarding Ethel were too deep-rooted and too complex to permit her to see anything clearly. Once more she had 'misbehaved', causing grievous results, and there was no longer any way to get Ethel to forgive her. It should not have mattered. But it did. For the rest of Judy's life it mattered.

Somehow she managed to fly to the funeral, though doing so was entirely against the doctor's orders. Midway through the service she broke down. Luft held her up until the end.

Then, leaning heavily on him and another friend, Judy managed to make it to the car. Immediately afterward, she went to pieces and took to her bed. It was the beginning of a two-year-long relapse – the worst breakdown she had suffered or would suffer in her life. Any chance she and Luft might have had of a successful marriage appears to have been snuffed out during this period.

It was a lonely time and a monotonous time. She seemed to have been beaten back and deserted by the world. Luft was constantly away from home on business trips. Once more she was immersed in debt, and in her present condition she could not imagine how she could ever rise above it. Her morale was never lower; and to add to this, whenever Luft was home, it seemed he had come there to appear in court to receive scoldings from a judge for not paying child support or alimony to Lynn Bari.

Luft began to press her to pull herself together so that she could work. Whatever his true motives might have been, the result did at least get Judy to her feet. She could not without returning once more to the pills, the crash diets. Luft now believed Judy should return to films in a package that they owned and in a film of which he would be the producer. If successful, it would establish him as a film producer and mean he could take over the family's support. It was something to grab hold of for Judy. The immediate search for a film property began.

Back in the early 1940's, Judy had done a great many radio shows. In January, 1941, she had appeared on the CBS *Silver Theatre* program in *Love's New Sweet Song*, for which she wrote the original script that True Boardman adapted for presentation. In December, 1942, she had starred on radio with Walter Pidgeon and Adolphe Menjou in the CBS *Lux Radio Theatre* adaptation of *A Star Is Born*. At the time she had felt it was the finest performance she had given, and it had led to her first yearnings to play a full-fledged dramatic role. She had, in fact, discussed the idea of her doing a remake of *A Star Is Born* for the studio at that time but was told a radio appearance was one thing, a film

171

role quite another. She was too young and the image all wrong. In a way, though, thanks to the seed that performance had planted in her head, it had led to her starring in *The Clock*. Now it all came back to her.

If she was to do an independent film – why not a remake of *A Star Is Born*? Something must have clicked in Luft's promotional mind. Instinct probably told him the property was right for Judy, but that it had to be a musical version. With that decision, he set about the first phases of getting such a tremendous production into operation.

CHAPTER TWENTY-SEVEN

Up to the time of the publication of this book, Sid Luft has had only two films under his production aegis. Both were produced in the same year (1954) and at the same studio (Warner's).

One film was the brilliant musical version of *A Star Is Born* directed by George Cukor, starring Judy Garland and James Mason. The other was a substandard Western entitled *The Bounty Hunters*, which starred Randolph Scott and was directed by André de Toth.

Directed by William Wellman, and starring Fredric March and Janet Gaynor, the original *A Star Is Born* had been a Hollywood classic and one of the film industry's top grossers.

If it was Luft's decision to petition George Cukor to direct this version with Judy, then, indeed, his contribution to the final product is insured. Cukor's cinema is a subjective cinema, consistently exhibiting his exquisite taste and style. He is never fearful of a commitment and he is masterly in his direction of women. By 1954 he had already directed Katherine Hepburn in *A Bill of Divorcement*, *Little*

Women, Sylvia Scarlet, Holiday, The Philadelphia Story, Adam's Rib, and *Pat and Mike* (a very comforting knowledge to Judy); Garbo in *Camille*; Norma Shearer in *Romeo and Juliet*; Crawford in *Susan and God* and *A Woman's Face*; Bergman in *Gaslight*; Jean Simmons in *The Actress*; and Judy Holliday in *Born Yesterday*.

Never having directed a musical (since, he has contributed *Les Girls, Let's Make Love*, and *My Fair Lady* to that form), Cukor was hesitant about accepting the assignment. The Moss Hart script, however, was a literate and moving adaptation of the original (by Dorothy Parker, Alan Campbell, Robert Carson, and Wellman); and it dealt with actors, a subject that holds a large attraction to Cukor, who had used it in many films to very good advantage (i.e., *The Royal Family on Broadway, Sylvia Scarlet, The Actress, Dinner at Eight, Les Girls, A Star Is Born, Let's Make Love*, and *Heller in Pink Tights*).

In *A Star Is Born*, Judy was once again to play a girl named Esther. Esther had also been the name of the character she portrayed in *Meet Me in St. Louis* – certainly her best performance in her Metro years. The coincidence appeared to be a good omen. The story dealt with the love affair and marriage of an aging, alcoholic movie star (Norman Maine) and the young woman (Esther Blodgett) who, in their first encounter, saves him from making a drunken spectacle of himself before an audience of his own peers. Later Maine discovers Esther has a voice with a quality of true greatness and helps her in her own climb to the top of film stardom, renaming her Vicki Lester. But as she ascends, he slips badly – drinking so heavily he has to be institutionalized. Vicki decides that to save Maine she has to give up her own career. Overhearing this decree, Maine martyrs himself and frees her by walking out of their elegant Malibu Beach house and drowning himself, leaving Vicki to continue her ascent to stardom.

The film was an important one for Judy in more meaningful ways than as a career vehicle. The story, which twelve years before had intrigued her as a dramatic opportunity,

173

now bore a deep relationship to her own life. The more she studied the script, the more painful, the more *impossible* it became for her to chance losing it. The peregrinations of her mind might seem difficult to map but not in the final analysis to understand, for the script enabled Judy to play out two of her own fears and fantasies. She was at one time both Norman Maine – the star who in a desperate need for love devoured all those around him – and the great star's 'lover', giving completely, unselfishly, and with complete understanding. She had great compassion for the character of Maine – the great star who was alternately being called a has-been and then having to fight the terror of one new comeback after another; the great star who could not fight his greater weakness (alcohol) and so allowed it to become his excuse, his crutch, and in the end, his true executioner. By playing Vicki Lester (Esther Blodgett) she was able to show the world how self-sacrificing love *must be* if one does love such a star. In the melodramatic but moving last part of the film Norman Maine commits suicide to save those he loved. It was a romantic notion, but from that point forward in her life Judy would consider that possibility many times.

She had been off the stage two years, away from films four years; and though her last film, *Summer Stock*, had been a success and her last concert a smash hit, the press now treated her as a has-been and she had suffered the poorest public relations. It had started with Ethel's interviews; and had been compounded by Ethel's court case and untimely death. But Judy's public image seemed smashed beyond repair more by the airing of all her financial woes than by anything else. She did, indeed, appear a spoiled, unthinking, irresponsible woman. She had made more money in one year than any newspaper reporter could have dreamed of making in a lifetime, and she had spent it foolishly – and not paid her taxes – which reporters most assuredly *had* to do each year. Edema had given her a bloated, drunken look. It was insinuated that Judy Garland was an alcoholic and that the reason she had not appeared

174

in two years was that no management would risk a drunken performance.

The fears, the fantasies – they were a Garland pattern; and they were the basis of Norman Maine's character and of Judy's strong identification with that role. They were the impetus that gave her own role such force, poignancy, and urgency. She *had* to convey to the world how much Norman Maine must be loved and accepted. She had to make the public understand how lonely and cold it was at the top. In essence, her stunning performance was a closing plea before a worldwide audience for her own defense.

Cary Grant was initially set to play Norman Maine. It was fortunate for the end product of the film that his own good sense caused him to withdraw. It would have been unreal for an audience to believe that Grant – the suave, million-dollar movie idol who was known to be a health nut – could be an alcoholic has-been. Ray Milland had done it in *The Lost Weekend*, but Milland's screen image had not been so well established as had Grant's. James Mason was cast. It was a brilliant and successful choice. Mason's portrayal stands out as one of his best in a career filled with great performances.

In all her Metro years Judy had never been given the opportunity to submerge herself completely in a role, for no part had demanded that of her. She had been able to rely on a simple understanding of the character she might be playing (for they were never deep or complex). By interpreting the character with a basic honesty and being able to graft her own personality onto that character, she had been totally believable even in the most inane of roles. Vicki Lester was her first true challenge as an actress. (*The Clock* had been a departure, and *Meet Me in St. Louis*, sensitive; but neither performance had demanded so much of her.) Not only was the role complex, but her own need to *be* Vicki Lester and to convince her audience of the honesty of Vicki Lester's great love and of the sincerity of her intention was of a very complex nature.

Norman Mailer, in *Marilyn*, attempting to throw light on

175

that star's ability to *become* a character she was playing, states:

> In the depths of the most merry and roistering moments an actor can have on stage there is still the far-off wail of the ghoul. For a good actor is a species of necrophile – he makes *contact* with the character he is playing, inhabits a role the way a ghoul invests a body. Indeed, if the role is great enough, the actor must proceed through a series of preparatory acts not unrelated to magical acts of concentration, ritual, and invocation.

So, as the first days of shooting passed, as Judy became more and more mesmerized by Vicki Lester, as Vicki Lester began to take over from Judy Garland – the torment, the concentration, the invocation that was to plague her for the long, long duration of the film's production began. Every night before a scheduled morning scene she would have to more or less invest Vicki Lester's psyche in her own. And all the time this terrible confusion, the first identification with the role of Norman Maine was there to haunt her. Vicki simply could never sway in her love and devotion for Maine. If she did, somehow it was a betrayal of Judy's own self; for after all, she was also Norman Maine. And the deeper she got into the film, the more inevitable Norman Maine's – and, therefore, her own – destruction and suicide seemed to be. It was a harrowing and debilitating experience, and there were nights when the exhaustion overwhelmed her and mornings when she simply could not face the pain of the scene she was to play.

Within a few weeks of the commencement of photography, the trouble began. She had had to submit to a crash diet before she stepped in front of the cameras. Diet pills and sleeping pills once more became a pattern and were interspersed with the severe emotional highs and lows of her performance; the extreme hard work the part required; the tough, unrelenting direction of Cukor; and the total professionalism of James Mason. Then came the incredible decision to reshoot the entire first month's footage in

176

Baby Frances at three years old (*Kobal Collection*)

Judy in *The Wizard of Oz*, 1939 (*MGM*)

With Mickey Rooney in *Strike up The Band*, 1940 (*Rex Features*)

The famous Garland legs. *For Me and My Gal*, 1942
(*Kobal Collection*)

Top Judy with her husband, Sid Luft, after the première of
A Star is Born, 1954, (*Rex Features*) and *above* with Mark Herron
after their marriage in Hong Kong, 1964, (*Rex Features*)

Judy Garland arriving in London with her children,
Liza Minnelli and Joe and Lorna Luft (*Rex Features*)

Top Judy and Liza (*Rex Features*) and *above* rehearsing for
a show together at the London Palladium theatre, 1964
(*Camera Press*)

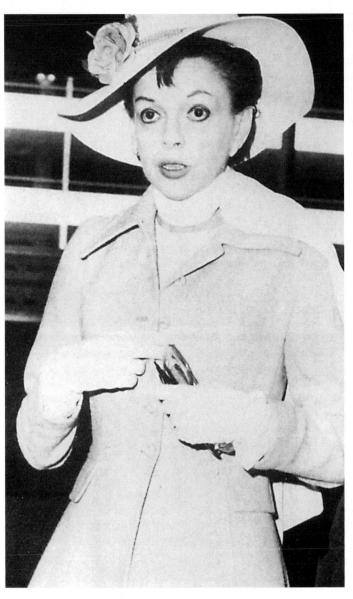

Returning the last time from New York, only six days before
her death, June 1969 (*Kobal Collection*)

Cinemascope. From that point, Judy, though she was the only one to adamantly object to this scrapping of a full month's work and starting over, had Luft always at her heels, pushing her on, giving her no chance to stand still. In a unique agreement, Luft's deal with Warner Brothers stipulated that the entire negative cost of the film be recouped before he and Judy received their share. Originally budgeted at $2.5 million, by the end of principal photography the film's cost had soared to over $6 million. Luft and Judy were broke during most of the production and deeper in debt than ever at the end; and as the cost rose, so did Luft's desperation.

The pressure was felt by everyone connected with the film. Some broke beneath it. Hugh Martin, who was the arranger and composer for the film, walked out. (Harold Arlen and Ira Gershwin did the final score with special outside material by Leonard Gershe and Roger Edens. This was the famous 'Born in a Trunk' number which Luft had bought outright for Judy.) In all, five cameramen and four costume designers also walked off the film; and new key people had to be found who could still maintain a sense of continuity to the production.

The press had a holiday. Judy was once again, as in the past, blamed for all the problems a production was having. Finally Judy confronted the reporters. 'I'm a little tired of being the patsy for the production delays on this film,' she told them testily. 'It's easy to blame every production delay on the star. This was the story of my life at Metro when I was a child actress. When some problem came up and they couldn't lick the delay, no matter who caused it, it was always blamed on the star. Whoever was responsible figured that the star could get by without a bawling out. They couldn't.'

Cukor at least had a sense of humor. 'First they said it would never start,' he commented, 'then that it would never stop.'

Ten months from the first day of shooting it finally did stop. By that time Judy was irrevocably rehooked on pills,

177

and her love for Luft had turned to a churning and extremely painful hostility, a grave sense of betrayal and rejection. To Luft this must have seemed incongruous. He was, after all, only attempting to make her once again top of the heap and the two of them rich. In the end he was to blame Judy for his inability to get another picture off the ground.

The film premiered simultaneously at the Paramount and Victoria theaters in New York. The opening was televised with Judy as guest of honour. The ads for the film said, 'Just about every celebrity in town will be there!' – and they were.

'*Star* is a massive effort,' *Time* magazine said.

The star, Judy Garland, was a thirty-two year old has-been as infamous for temperament as she is famous for talent. What's more, all the producers' worst dreams came true. Day after day, while the high-priced help – including Judy's husband Sid Luft – stood around waiting for the shooting to start, Judy sulked in her dressing room. In the end *Star* took ten months to make, cost six million dollars. But after Judy had done her worst in the dressing room, she did her best in front of the camera, with the result that she gives what is just about the greatest one-woman show in modern movie history.

And *Time* closed with the line '. . . Judy Garland makes a stunning comeback.'

There was that word 'comeback' again! Well, at that precise moment, in spite of the difficulties in her marriage, the financial harassments, the physical exhaustion, and the super-dependence once again on the pills, her audience loved her; the press forgave her.

Now the future did look beautiful. She was once more standing at the top looking down. True, the film would never make her rich; the money the production had cost made that impossible. It would not even help her get out of debt with the Government; the interest and penalties mounted terrifyingly on her back taxes, making the amount owing astronomical and seemingly impossible to repay.

But there was a new interest in her records; she was up for an Academy Award; and she was once again pregnant.

The night of the Awards she had just given birth to her third and last child, Joseph Wiley (called Joey from his birth), in the new maternity wing of the Cedars of Lebanon Hospital in Hollywood. She was touted to win, and the excitement in Hollywood was high. Feeling it was right for Judy and good for the film, Luft had gotten both Judy and the hospital to agree to permit a television crew to come in and at the proper moment, when the Price-Waterhouse man at the Awards show opened the sealed envelope for the name of the winner of Best Actress of the Year, to relay Judy's reaction from her hospital bed across the nation.

Makeup men, hairdressers, and technicians swarmed in her room, and filled her doorway. She was propped up in the bed and nervously waiting as she watched the television monitor that had been set up in her room. The moment came. The envelope was opened and the contents read.

Grace Kelly had been selected by the members of the Academy as Best Actress of the Year for her performance in *The Country Girl*.

There was an insane, surreal moment. No one said anything. Then the crew immediately began dismantling the hookup. In less than ten minutes it was all over and they had left with all their equipment. She was a loser and alone. It was after ten o'clock, and all the hospital-room lights were turned off.

Judy was still propped up, still made up for the television cameras when the night nurse came in with the sleeping pills.

CHAPTER TWENTY-EIGHT

THAT night ushered a new terror into her life – a series of phobias: fear of appearing onstage, of entering stores and cars, of flying – that was to be difficult for her to overcome. And there was serious trouble at home. Realizing that *A Star is Born* was not going to ease their financial problems and unable to get another film off the ground, Luft convinced her she must go back to doing concerts. The doctors could not trace the problem, but she had not felt well since Joey's birth. What she needed was rest, home, a sense of roots, and someone to take care of her. Luft's answer was to leave her home with the children while he traveled from one end of the country to the other to find her work.

And he succeeded, for in July – nine weeks later – he booked her for a seven-city West Coast tour. In each city she thought she might not make it through her performance, but she did. In San Diego, during one of her best shows, she asked her audience, 'Do you think this kind of figure will ever come back?' She was once again as heavy as she had been four years before at the Palladium; and though she was both starving herself and relying heavily on diet pills, she could not lose weight.

Before the end of the summer and without a respite, Luft booked her into the New Frontier at Las Vegas for her nightclub debut. She sang for forty minutes straight out of the sixty-eight minute show and broke all the New Frontier's existing records. Then on September 24, 1955, she entered television with a *Ford Star Jubilee* one-and-one-half hour spectacular. Ostensibly the show was a replay of her Palace performance. She was under pressure, not well, and exhausted. Still she was what *The New York Times* called 'tremendously appealing', and in the view of the *Journal-American* she was also 'the greatest natural talent in show business'. The show was a success, but Judy was once again near collapse. To add to her tension the Government had swooped in, claiming most of her large earnings for the year yet, because of interest and taxes, still leaving her with a debt close to $300,000. What remained of the salary she was permitted to keep got hacked away by staff expenses, travel expenses, and Luft's percentage.

At home there were the three children – Liza, nine; Lorna, not yet three; and Joey, five months. Judy desperately wanted to remain at home and be a mother. But the acrimony between her and Luft grew more intense each month. 'We were losing our ability to communicate with each other,' Judy has said of that period. 'I had learned how to handle audiences again, how to be an entertainer. But I didn't seem to be learning much from my marriage.'

For the next few years Judy and Luft were to part, file suit for divorce, and then dismiss the suit again and again. The first time was on February 4, 1956, just three and a half years after they were married. Three days later they were reunited.

This was a period in which Judy claimed Luft was violent. Peter Lawford tells the story of being called over to her house late at night by a hysterical Judy and arriving there to find her with small jagged cuts all over her face which she insinuated Luft had inflicted and which in privacy the maid confided that Judy had inflicted on herself.

Whether Judy or the maid spoke the truth, on March 4, 1958, Judy again filed suit for divorce – this time charging that Luft 'has beaten and attempted to strangle the plaintiff on many occasions, the last occasion being on February 21, 1958.'

Directly after this – on March 25 of that year – a tax warrant was filed against her by the New York State Tax Commission. And on April 3, a warrant was issued for her arrest for failure to pay $8,000 New York State tax on income earned in 1952 at the Palace which Luft had never paid. She had to hand over to the court, for bond, personal jewelry and her costumes. The press made much of the matter.

The 'Marie Torre incident' followed. Miss Torre was television columnist for the New York *Herald Tribune* at the time of the 'incident' and in an article quoted an unidentified Columbia Broadcasting System executive as saying that Judy 'is known for a highly developed inferiority complex.' Judy sued for over a million dollars, and Marie Torre was ordered by the judge to reveal her source. It was a test case. Miss Torre refused to do so and was sent to prison for ten days for contempt of court. It did not make Judy any more popular with the American press.

It was understandable that she suffered a great fear of insecurity along with all her other phobias. There were literally dozens of reasons for this, but the most basic at the time was her terrible indebtedness when she had earned so much money and her suspicion that Luft was riding the Garland bandwagon like everyone else in her life had and that he did not truly love her. As always, she blamed herself. She was fat and ugly, and she was not able to perform. The Ethel-Mayer self-recrimination pattern was reset into motion. It was a year after her first television appearance – a year of marital strife, self-loathing, and growing dependence once again on pills – before she was to make a major public appearance again.

In September, 1956, for the second time, she played an engagement at the Palace. As she entered her old dressing room, she was overcome by the shiny gold plaque that hung over the door: THIS WAS THE DRESSING ROOM OF JUDY GARLAND WHO SET THE ALL-TIME LONG-RUN RECORD, OCTOBER 16, 1951–FEBRUARY 24, 1952. R.K.O. PALACE THEATRE. Her appearance, as received by critics, was not so triumphant as her previous engagement. She seemed to lack the naturalness she had had before. Her weight certainly slowed her movements, but there was something mechanical in her performance that all the critics called attention to.

This point in her life also saw the phenomenal rise of The Garland Cult. It had begun years before. There had been followers like Wayne Martin – lonely people who worshiped her in the privacy of their homes; fans; collectors – but the

slavish devotion of what was to become the full phenomenon of The Garland Cult did not swing into frenetic
motion until the mid-fifties.

For a complete understanding of Judy and the Garland
Cult, this period in her life supplies the most valuable clues.
For years she had suffered pill addiction, insomnia, multiple
neuroses, pressures, tensions, armies of creditors, ill health,
traumatic relationships, and lost illusions. Her personal
fears were at a peak, and she had fallen prey to such acute
stage fright that Luft had to push her out onto the stage to
perform. She did not perspire, according to her own words,
but *sweated* so profusely during a concert that the costume
changes were a necessity; and even so, when she came
offstage, her body odor was so gamy that stagehands often
visibly backed off. She would drench herself in Joy perfume,
its pungent sweetness often causing fits of nausea right in the
middle of a performance. Compounding all these horrors
was the new fear plaguing her that her voice would go.
There were times when it would crack or slip away during a
performance. She was never sure when she could depend
solidly on it. No longer the wide-eyed, dreamy Dorothy of
The Wizard of Oz, she was now a woman who had been
through it all and knew what it was about. Yet no matter
how great the indignities she suffered offstage, onstage she
exuded a sense, a feeling of dignity even in her lowest, her
worst moments of performance.

It was this last that might be called her magic quotient –
the ingredient that whipped her audiences into a frenzy and
had such a hypnotic effect upon them. Judy appeared to be
super-strong, able to endure superhuman trials. That was
why when she was good, audiences went wild; why Luft and
her musical arrangers made her test herself in each performance, allowing her no respite once she was onstage, setting her keys so that end notes were tough to reach; why
with each concert her production was staged more and more
with an eye to playing up this magic quotient; why, in the
end she made her entrance very often from the back of the
audience, looking small, ill fitted, and proceeded down

the aisle to stand alone on a huge, barren stage, one small light picking her out, clinging to a microphone as though it were her only connection to life. This was the image that the Garland Cult was dedicated to. Audiences reacted, were mesmerized and frenzied alternately. When those high notes at the end of a song seemed out of reach, they would pray softly, 'Please, please make it!' If she did, they would cheer wildly; and if she did not, they would still cheer wildly to let her know they knew she could and would next time.

Jerry Lewis once said it very well:

People now know the troubles Judy has been through. Who among us isn't plagued with troubles too? So people of all kinds, with worries and problems and heartaches, go to see her; and they identify with her. And when she sings, she is communicating for them all the emotions they can't communicate themselves because they don't have a stage and a microphone and talent. The stout women in the audience identify with her; and the people who remember their own unhappy childhoods identify with her. All the people whose insides have been torn out by misery ident-ify with her, and she is singing for all of them. In a way, she's singing with a hundred voices.

There were a lot of concerts in the years between 1956 and 1959 and too many ups and downs to even recount, but the press diligently did so, dogging her heels and rehashing the old sordid stories whenever they related any new crisis in her life. Seldom was a review of a performance printed in which her personal tragedies and problems weren't dragged in, and always it referred to her as being 'on the comeback trail'. During all this time her marriage to Luft had become a series of psychotic actions and reactions. She could not live with him and she could not live without him. Luft certainly did everything possible to achieve the latter, for he had set himself up in control of her finances, her career, her health.

On October 29, 1958, Louis B. Mayer died at the age of

seventy-two of acute anemia. That previous July he had embarked upon a fight to regain a voice in the operation of MGM – or Loew's, Incorporated. Mayer had joined with millionaire Canadian road builder Joseph Tomlinson, a Loew's director, and the two men had initiated what was termed the Mayer-Tomlinson Scheme to obtain control of the company. Court fights had followed, but Mayer was terminally ill and could not conduct the final battle. Richard Nixon, then Vice President, made a public announcement of sympathy at Mayer's passing: 'I was among those fortunate enough to be a close, personal friend to him,' he began; then told of Mayer's genius. Mayer's death deeply affected Judy. She slipped into a period of depression. The past must have come flooding back to her then; and much of it was hard to face, painful to recall, difficult to bury.

For New Year's 1958, she returned to Las Vegas, appearing at the Flamingo Hotel. It was a drunk and celebrating audience, and she wasn't at her best. After she had struggled through five numbers performed in a jam-packed, smoke-filled room, having to compete with a noise level that forced her to overreach for her notes, a woman screamed out from the audience: 'Get outta here. You're too overweight and we don't want to hear you anyway!' Then two women climbed over the footlights and began to dance. Judy walked offstage – and into another lawsuit for breach of contract. Luft declared he would never allow her to appear in a nightclub again.

Finally in 1959 he chose the massive Metropolitan Opera House for a concert, and after that the Chicago and San Francisco opera houses. It would seem he did so simply because they were the largest houses available. By fall her voice suddenly deserted her, and her body swelled up monstrously. Suffering severe pain, she was rushed to New York's Doctors Hospital. The doctors there believed she had hepatitis. She remained in crisis and under treatment several weeks. She came very close to death. Luft took a room at the hospital to be close to her. The doctors confided in him that Judy might not be able to perform again.

It is difficult to know what went through Luft's head. Judy gave out a number of interviews in which she asserted that the doctors' proclamation rather pleased her and that she was looking forward to retirement. However, in their circumstances at the time, retirement would not have been what Judy fantasized. They were several hundred thousand dollars in debt with no assets or capital, and at no time in their marriage had Luft proved he could support the family – certainly not in the style they both enjoyed! He must have been fairly frantic with concern, especially when her condition worsened before it got better. Getting her to agree, he came up with the money-making idea of Judy's writing her autobiography (with a ghostwriter).

Always a good promoter, he left Judy in a very weakened condition at the hospital and went to see Bennett Cerf at Random House, whereupon he talked Cerf into agreeing to advance him $35,000 against a signature by Judy on a contract to cooperate fully in the writing of her autobiography. Luft then convinced Judy she should sign, but as her health improved, she had a change of heart.

Upon her release from the hospital, they returned to Los Angeles and the heavily mortgaged home in Holmby Hills. Judy, semi-invalided, was forced to remain inactive for over four months. Once again she gained heavily, tipping the scales at one hundred fifty pounds. She had a few sessions with a ghostwriter, but now felt her signature had been obtained under undue duress and refused to complete the interviews. Random House did not take a complete loss on the $35,000, as the interviews were turned into a two-part article, sold by Cerf to *McCall's*.

Judy was in a severe state of depression and hating Los Angeles. There were constant unpleasant articles about her, and she was always being deluged by bill collectors and creditors and pressed for money that she did not have. Recalling her happiness in England and the kindness of the British press, she decided she would like to return there. Luft and the three children accompanied her. Her fans – who had now reached cult proportions – rose up en masse on both sides of the Atlantic. For the first time they became truly active, physical, *seen*. Her ability to return to the stage after her serious illness and ill fortune, their own desperate need to see and hear her, was paramount – the only thing in their minds. Her life became theirs, her suffering their own; and in this transference her failure to *overcome* would mean their own failure. They now moved in to become part of her life, and Judy permitted – perhaps welcomed – it. Wherever she went from this time there were members of the Garland Cult, each one living only in the hope of somehow touching her life and so gaining some small measure of importance to their own lives by so doing.

After six months in England during which she was trying to be 'just a housewife and mother', the true situation came clattering down on her head with the harshness of hailstones. No money had been coming in for the entire time they had been in England. They were in desperate straits. There was only one thing for her to do if the rent was to be paid: sick or not, she had no alternative but to allow Luft to arrange another concert.

In the fall of 1960 she returned to the Palladium and did two concerts. They were a departure for her in one way: she occupied the entire evening and was the only artist on the bill. Rather than being a vaudeville appearance, the two concerts were truly 'An Evening with Judy Garland'. The concerts were successful, but her marriage was near its end. Knowing the only way she could break with Luft was to find another manager, she signed with Freddie Fields of Creative Management Associates. Fields flew over to London to close the deal, and Judy liked him. He was personable, charming; had a sense of humor; and – most important – assured her he could get her out of debt.

She left London without Luft, returning to New York in the midst of one of its worst blizzards and on a New Year's Eve; and according to her own words, she had 'fallen out of love'. She went on to say: '. . . During that awful blizzard of January, 1961, I went for a walk in the snow one night. I thought *I* was the blizzard. Suddenly I realized I didn't give

a damn about him ... for a few hours there it was difficult –
like being shot out of a cannon. It was really terrifying.'

That was understandable. For ten years Luft had been in
absolute control of her life – his influence perhaps even
more powerful than Ethel's or Mayer's had ever been. For a
decade he had been as necessary to her survival as her pills
had been, and she was not at all sure she could make it
without him.

CHAPTER TWENTY-NINE

IN order to help her become financially solvent, Freddie
Fields and his partner, David Begelman, involved her in two
years of such intensive activity that only a superwoman or a
robot could have survived. First they settled a three-year
legal batle that had raged between Luft and CBS, setting up
two television spectaculars for her. Then they negotiated a
$50,000 contract for a cameo role in Stanley Kramer's film
Judgment at Nuremberg (it had been seven years since *A
Star is Born*) and a voice-over in an animated film called
Gay Purr-ee in which her voice was that of a little cat named
Mewsette; signed her to star in two films – *A Child Is Waiting* and *I Could Go On Singing*; booked her first on a four-
teen-city, six-week concert tour (to end in New York at
Carnegie Hall); followed that with a second concert tour
which brought her one-night concert appearances to a total
of forty-eight in the time span of one year; and arranged for
the recording of what was to be a best-selling album. It was
almost humanly impossible, but Judy did it all, managing at
the same time to receive a nomination for an Academy
Award for *Judgment at Nuremberg* and giving a concert
(Carnegie Hall) that would go down as an all-time great in
entertainment history. She had become a living legend; but

the price she was to pay was to be excruciatingly high. Daniel Webster never made a worse deal with the Devil.

The harder she drove herself, or Fields and Begelman drove her, the more towering her fears became. She relied upon the same arrangements, always sang in the same key, and seldom introduced new material. For her audiences, who loved the ritual of the familiar, there most probably would have been a riot if she had not sung her standards, but the truth was that she felt safer with old material.

'It was practically impossible for Judy to learn anything new,' Bobby Cole (who was her musical director in many concerts in the sixties) states. 'She was afraid. And I tell you something, you take forty Dexedrine a day, fifteen miligrams, and you're going to be afraid too. She was a medical phenomenon. Forty Dexedrine in one day – that's enough to keep a horse up for ten years! Honey, how are you going to sleep unless you take downers too? You've got to take Seconals and then you take something else – ten, twelve downers; and even then you're going to wake up. To get her to go to bed you had to use a narcotic sledgehammer. She'd take them and sit there for fifteen minutes, and we would have to carry her to bed. It ruined her. It killed her.

'You can't explain anyone who lives on speed. Heavy speed. It is complete, total paranoia. I don't mean she wasn't conscious of her performance or her audience. She knew everything she was doing. I'll tell you something: a performer is like a fighter, you know; the bell rings and you're on. I've seen her. She had a little [dressing-room] tent at the side of the stage. We used to walk through the little tent before she went out. I threw up my hands – *that's it*, I thought. I was going out and killing myself. I would walk through and there she was! She was on. That operates. When you're a performer, that operates.

'I'll never be able to say that Judy Garland was not aware of her audience – *never*,' Cole continues. 'She was always aware of her audience – *always*. As a matter of fact, she was thoroughly other-people-oriented. So that's not what speed does. What speed does is to make you very nervous, very paranoid. If there was one guy in an audience of thirty thousand who didn't clap quite as hard as somebody else, she'd know that. That's what she felt.'

There is no way of soft soaping the brutal truth. Judy was a confirmed and habitual addict; and during all the years she had been one, no one close had done anything about withholding pills from her or helping her get assistance to withdraw. Many of those financially dependent upon her aided and abetted her habit, with or without evil intent. It was no longer easy for her to obtain pills, as it had been during her MGM days when pills were made available to her. Fearing she might not be able to make a performance without 'ups' (thereby jeopardizing their own security), some of those closest to her made sure she had an adequate supply at hand during these times often withholding them from her until she was in her dressing room or wings, to ensure that she would appear.

A former U.S. Commissioner of Narcotics, Harry J. Anslinger, once recommended to MGM executives that she be given a year's rest because of her drug problem. It was rejected by the studio and Anslinger was told, 'We have fourteen million dollars tied up in her.' That was after a Los Angeles policeman, knowing Judy's problem, reported it to Anslinger. Anslinger met with Judy, and Judy confessed a doctor was supplying her with vast amounts of morphine and amphetamine; but his agency was unable to move in because of the studio's intervention. Then Anslinger had gone to Charles Seragusa, former Executive Director of the Illinois Crime Investigating Committee, and then his superior. They managed to get the doctor's license revoked, but another immediately took his place.

And that was how it was. One supplier would replace another. Judy never dealt with these people directly. It was always through someone exceptionally close to her, and that person was generally the recipient of much of her love and dependence.

She gave her first concert without Luft and under the aegis of Fields and Begelman in February, 1961, in Dallas,

Texas. It was essentially the same show she had given six months before at the Palladium, but the performance was harder-edged, better. What gave the show a new quality was the overpowering chemistry between Judy and her audience and the exultation her appearance brought out in them. They shouted encouragement, screamed their love. 'No entertainer has ever given such a show in Dallas,' a Dallas newspaper declared.

Two nights later she was in Houston, and so were many members of that same Dallas audience. The Garland Cult had swung into action. They gave her four standing ovations in Houston; and a stagehand, carried away along with the audience, unwittingly entangled himself in the curtain, struggling for ten minutes before his muffled cries for help were heard.

After the Dallas debut, Judy complained that she had made a lot of money in her life but had never really touched it. Fields and Begelman came to her hotel after the concert with a large brown paper shopping bag filled with the night's receipts – ones, fives, tens, twenties – and throwing it into the air, let the money cascade down and around her. Judy roared deliriously with laughter. They stayed close to her on tour and often thought of similar antics to make her laugh. It helped her through, for Judy had a great sense of humor and never, never lost her ability to laugh.

Twelve cities and fewer weeks later, Judy returned to New York thirty pounds lighter, nervous, but tremendously excited about the last concert of this tour – Carnegie Hall. Backstage before the performance, Judy was more keyed up than usual. It was not only because this was New York and Carnegie Hall, not only because she would be singing before a star-studded audience comparable to the one that had greeted her first Palace appearance – but because she had one new number, 'San Francisco', to sing, and because the song included a tough comedy opening. New material always frightened her. Those close to her managed to reduce the potency of her pills without her knowledge, but she was still heavily on speed. The concert was to be recorded live as well. It remains as testimony to the incredible heights to which Judy rose that evening.

Inside, Carnegie Hall was filled to capacity. Outside, those Garland fans who could not get in waited on this cool, brisk evening (April 23, 1961) for comments from those who had been fortunate enough to secure seats. All were ready to rush around to the stage entrance at the end of Judy's performance – to comfort her if she failed, to cheer her if she succeeded.

Speaking on a Barry Gray radio show, Rex Reed, who was shortly thereafter to become a noted film critic and columnist, recalled his own impressions. 'I'd just come to New York, and that was the thing I wanted to do all my life – to see Judy Garland. I think it was probably the greatest experience I've ever had in the theater. I had never seen that much love given to a performer. I had a marvelous seat – right next to Eli Wallach and Anne Jackson. I only knew them by reputation. I wasn't writing then; I was working as an office boy in some publicity office.

'Eli Wallach and Anne Jackson grabbed me. We were holding on to each other, and Tony Perkins was right in front of me; and [Leonard] Bernstein ... even Hedda Hopper was there – and Betty [Comden] and Adolph [Green] and Lauren Bacall – just everybody I'd ever heard of; and they were all really with this lady. And it wasn't just the cult who supported her. This was show business and this was the hardest audience to please – really an audience of hard-nosed professional critics. And it was the greatest triumph in anyone's life. I mean, it was something unequaled to me.'

And Judith Crist recalls on the same program, 'I remember Bernstein, the tears running down his face, screaming. But not just Bernstein, but Hank [Henry] Fonda, who is normally an impassive man – "Bravoing".

'No one had any intention of leaving the theater,' she continues. 'It was absolute pandemonium. It ended and the *entire* audience, instead of rising to leave, ran to the footlights like moths attracted to a screen door. They ran to the footlights with their hands in the air, screaming, "Judy! Judy!" and she touched all the hands she could. Then Rock Hudson lifted Lorna and little Joey on the stage, and she hugged them and leaned down to kiss Liza, who was in the front row, and the audience screamed for more; and the children were touching people's hands and it was like a sea. You couldn't tell where the seats were and where the aisles began because the entire Carnegie Hall was a sea of People. She came back out to kind of throttle the emotion and the pandemonium. People couldn't get back to their seats so they sat in the aisles, disobeying all the fire laws of New York City – and they all just sat there together bathed in perspiration.'

And John Springer, who handled her public relations and spent part of the night backstage and part out front, added, 'It was like the lemmings. They just moved in one mass forward.'

She came onstage, svelte-looking, vibrant; her hair was in an upsweep; she was back to a measure of her once-slim self and wore modish black toreador pants and a blazing-blue-sequined Mandarin jacket. Behind her was Mort Lindsey conducting one of the largest orchestras she had ever appeared with.

She began the first half with 'When You're Smiling' – and for forty-five minutes, without pause, went on singing one favorite after another. No tricks, no gimmicks; set aside were the chorus boys and the tramp routines. There was just Judy on that cavernous stage, a microphone clutched in her hand and that symphony-sized orchestra backing her up. She looked like some small tropical, glittering bird perched in the center of a massive black forest.

The first half of the concert ended with 'That's Entertainment'. Her audience was exhausted, and yet on some sort of emotional binge. Strangers were grabbing each other's hands. Yet when the house lights went out after intermission and the stage lights came on, and as they waited for Judy to reappear, there was once again that unexplainable terror that she might not make it – that she had nothing left to give.

And Judy, if consulted, might have agreed with them. Staggering to her dressing room, she gasped and held her arms tightly about herself as if in excruciating pain. Near sobs, she told anyone close she was too exhausted – that she didn't see how she could go back on. In her dressing room she tore off her drenched and unpleasant-smelling outfit, then sipped a glass of white wine as her hairdresser blew icy air over her heaving back and shoulders with a portable dryer. Yet within ten minutes her makeup had been repaired, her soggy hair dried and repuffed, and she had been zippered into another costume.

Someone commented that she had made a miraculous physical recovery. 'Well, you know, I'm like Rocky Graziano,' she replied. Then, managing a nervous laugh, she headed back for the stage, where the curtain was about to rise.

'You stand there in the wings,' Judy reflected a few weeks later, 'and sometimes you want to yell because the band sounds so good. Then you walk out and if it's really a great audience, a very strange set of emotions come over you . . . A great reception can really throw you. You can lose control of your voice and it takes two or three numbers to get back into your stride. I lift my hand in a big gesture in the middle of the first number; and if I *see* it's not trembling, then I know I haven't lost my control.'

When she stepped back out onstage, she ran nervous fingers through her stylish hairdo, causing it to collapse. Standing center stage, she smiled as she waited for the encouraging applause to fade and then, with a toss of the microphone wire and her head, sang 'I'm Gonna Love You Come Rain or Come Shine' with all her heart. In the middle, she raised her hand in that famous palm-out, exaggerated gesture. It wasn't trembling. For forty-five incredible minutes she sang as she had never sung before – bringing down the house with her new number, 'San Francisco'. Near the end she asked, 'Aren't you tired of hearing me sing?' Her audience screamed back their denials. And she went on singing, closing finally with 'Chicago'. The applause, the screams were thunderous. She called out to them, 'Good night! I love you very much!' They screamed louder. 'Good night! God bless!' she called from the wings. That was when the audience moved down to the edge of the stage and she returned to touch their hands. 'I don't ever want to go home, do you?' she had said to them earlier in the evening. No one seemed to want to.

There was an evangelical frenzy in the auditorium. The crowds were screaming hoarsely, 'We love you!' and Judy, leaning over the footlights to touch them, seemed incapable of holding anything of herself in reserve.

'There was an extra bonus at Carnegie Hall last night,' Judith Crist wrote the next day (April 24, 1961) in the New York *Herald Tribune*.

> Judy Garland sang ... And she sang, let it be reported, as she hasn't in years – not at the Palace and not at the Met: she sang with all the heart that has been her hallmark, but added to it is a happy self-confidence that gives new quality and depth to her performance. It's a performance that deserves all the pre-commitment her very name evokes.

And Shana Alexander, writing for *Life*, reported:

> Judy Garland is not only the most electrifying entertainer to watch on stage since Al Jolson, she has moved beyond talent and beyond fame to become the rarest phenomenon in all show-business. Part bluebird, part Phoenix, she is a legend in her own time.

CHAPTER THIRTY

ONCE again Judy was near the top of the roller coaster. She went back to California to shoot a television spectacular with Frank Sinatra and Dean Martin. And the small, key role in Stanley Kramer's *Judgment at Nuremberg* followed. She appeared in the climax of the story in three brief scenes in which she touchingly created the wretched German hausfrau Irene Hoffman. The film was about the second of the Nuremberg Trials and zeroed in on the final cases against four members of the Nazi judiciary. Irene Hoffman, a plump, middle-aged woman, testifies that on account of his innocent friendship with her during her girlhood an elderly Jew was executed and she herself imprisoned. Her heartbreaking court appearance helps to convict one of the judges on trial. It was an electric performance, and once again she was placed in nomination for an Academy Award (this time for Best Supporting Actress) and once again she was the loser. But Hollywood was ecstatic about her film 'come-back'.

'She's a great technician,' Kramer told the press. 'There's no one in the entertainment world today, actor or singer, who can run the complete range of emotions, from utter pathos to power and dimension, the way she can ... She's like a piano. You touch any key and the pure note of that emotion comes out. She knows how to laugh and to cry on cue. When we made *Judgment at Nuremberg*, I'd just have to say, "Judy, register hate and fear like a German hausfrau who had been persecuted by the Nazis," and the hate and fear would be there.'

In the hands of a studio again (this time United Artists), she was requested and expected to appear at both the world premiere of the film in Berlin and the English premiere (before the Duke of Edinburgh) in London a week before Christmas, 1961. Only a few weeks before, she had ended a series of one-nighters that had brought her concert apperances up to forty-eight in that one year, the last concert being performed to a capacity house (13,909 seats) at the Boston Garden. She was coming close to the end of her physical endurance, but somehow she managed to get to Berlin. Directly after the premiere she was flown to Rome, where she was taken to the Excelsior Hotel. Thereupon she collapsed. She was suffering severe pain, and the Italian doctors diagnosed her illness as a serious case of pleurisy. Confined there, she did not reach London and, when able, returned to the States.

Her 'comeback' appearance in *Judgment at Nuremberg* had proved so successful that Kramer had come up immediately with a second offer, for her to play the lead opposite Burt Lancaster in a film about a state institution for mentally retarded children. Judy was in no condition to appear before the cameras in a taxing, emotional, full-length role. Once again her pill addiction was brutalizing her body and overwork taking its toll. But once she had read the script it was impossible for her to turn down the roll of Jean Hansen – music teacher on the staff of the institution. It brought back all the memories of her stay at Peter Bent Brigham Hospital and of the little retarded girl who had broken through a wall of silence to speak her name. She told Fields and Begelman to accept.

The film, *A Child Is Waiting,* went into immediate production and was shot at the Pacific State Hospital in Pomona, California; and except for the lead boy, all the children in the film were patients. Judy gave her all before the cameras and then would entertain and talk with the children in any spare minute she found. She was reliving a time in her life, and it had not been a happy one. By the end of principal photography, she was in a severe state of depression, far from well, and totally and irrevocably dependent on pills to survive a day. The roller coaster was beginning another precarious descent. Fear and desperation grasped hold of her. Work seemed to be the only answer. It was one of the few times in her life that there was not a man by her side; and so she retreated into the old routine of calling friends in the middle of the night – including John Kennedy, whom she had once campaigned for and who had been kind to her during one of her previous sieges of depression and illness.

Stuart Millar and Lawrence Turman (who later did *The Graduate*) submitted a script (by Mayo Simon) for her to read. At that point it needed a great deal of work – but the character of Jenny Bowman hit a tender and aching void. There was much of herself in the role, and it struck Judy that perhaps through this film she might be able to explain away a lot of her own foibles.

The script was then called *The Lonely Stage* (later it became *I Could Go On Singing*) and dealt with a short, traumatic period in the life of a world-famous singer. It was to be shot in England and released, like her last two films, through United Artists; Dirk Bogarde was signed for the male lead. Judy wasted no time in signing along with him and packing up the children to leave immediately for England.

She stopped en route in New York, checking in at the Stanhope Hotel into an eleventh-floor suite. There she was confronted by Luft (who was at the same hotel in a sixth-floor suite), who demanded that she leave his children Lorna and Joey with him. They had a violent argument and Luft claimed that then two 'hired goons' burst through the door of his suite and held him in a tight grip while Judy went off with the children. Terrified, she later claimed she feared that Luft would somehow snatch the children from her, for he had threatened to do so and to bring court charges against her to declare her an unfit mother, Luft, in a statement to the press, said that he would fly to London soon to see his children. 'They won't be there long,' he added, but he did not elaborate.

That September she had filed suit for divorce once again – this the fourth time in Las Vegas, Nevada – charging Luft with extreme mental cruelty. He then had filed a divorce complaint at Santa Monica, California, shortly thereafter obtaining a restraining order prohibiting her from proceeding with her divorce action. Directly after this New York confrontation with Judy, he filed charges in Las Vegas against Judy alleging that she had concealed $2 million in 'community property' earned since their business severance.

He also charged that she 'is presently suffering from mental illness as a result, in part, of her use of barbiturates to the degree that, in the absence of prolonged rest and hospitalization, she is unable to care for her minor children.'

The 'community property' assets that he charged were concealed were identified as royalties or percentages from the films *Gay Purr-ee* and *A Child Is Waiting*, her Columbia record albums, and contractual future payments and percentages on *The Lonely Stage* (not yet called *I Could Go on Singing*). And he asked for custody of the children.

What he was suing for was 50 percent of Judy's income since she had left his management, claiming it as marital community property.

Judy was not due in London for several days, but she was frightened Luft might take the children away from her. Pale and distraught and suffering from an attack of laryngitis, she huddled them together and with three burly hired private detectives as guards, bundled them off to Idlewild Airport (now Kennedy). The decision to leave sooner than planned was so precipitate that Liza was wearing slacks and sandals and had slips, dresses, and sweaters draped over her arm and told reporters that she hadn't had time to get her clothes for the trip. Liza now had a career on her own mind. She had been studying dancing at the New York High School of Performing Arts and had given a moving portrayal of Anne Frank in a school production. On a high school guidance card Liza wrote that she wanted to be a dancer and film actress.

Once in London, Judy feared Luft might follow and spirit the two youngest away. She declared to the London press that she and Luft had been estranged for two years and that the marriage was over. Almost immediately she moved to have Lorna and Joey made wards of the British court – so that Luft would have a legal battle on his hands and face a possible jail sentence if he did try to take the children from her illegally.

Her worst fears were realized. Just before filming began on *I Could Go On Singing*, Luft arrived in London. They had been estranged for two years, and in that time she had zoomed right back up to the top of the ladder and reconquered both stage and screen. She had earned over $1 million (though not the $2 million Luft had claimed) and for the first time in decades was finally out of debt, even being able to put aside a small amount of money for the future. She believed very deeply in her upcoming film and she loved London and the English. But she was physically once again at breaking point. Fields and Begelman had given up playing constant and private nursemaid to her, and she truly did not know how to fend for herself. Not being able to publicly face her addiction, she was never able to secure her own pills. And she had a mammoth, taxing, important role to perform.

Luft, in Las Vegas, had filed a countersuit for divorce against her; and the marriage was never to be repaired.

CHAPTER THIRTY-ONE

AT the start of shooting on *I Could Go On Singing*, the crew, according to co-star Dirk Bogarde, called Judy 'Miss Garland'. By the end, they referred to her as 'It'. He claims the crew hated her. 'They had had a wallop of her. She would keep them waiting hours and hours. But when she delivered, no one else delivered like her. She lived with an intensive *I, I, I*. There seemed to be no other life but hers. And she simply could not take stress.'

Judy, badly off center because of the pills and her health and the emotional roller coaster her daily confrontations with Luft kept her on, was indeed almost impossible to work with. Yet in the film Judy gives a performance equal in stature and intensity to her performance in *A Star Is Born*; and had the story allowed, it could have been a truly great film. All of the scenes between Judy and Bogarde were written with her cooperation, and often by Bogarde and herself

– and came as close to expressing the truth about Judy, in terms of the character she portrayed, as any she had done before. The part was that of Jenny Bowman, an aging but great performer who has sacrificed her personal life for her career. Then, during an engagement at the Palladium in London, she makes a last grasp for both her son and her lover, whom she had long ago let go. Bogarde, her lover and father of their illegitimate son, tries to stop the boy from disrupting his life to follow Jenny.

'I know how much fun she can be to be with,' he tells him, 'how good and wise – and life would be more exciting. You'd go to places you've never seen before. You'd fly; you'd catch boats; and you'd laugh a lot. I loved her – I still do love her. But mark this: Jenny gives more love than anyone but takes more love than anyone can possibly give.'

The lines in the script were very close to the truth, and Judy was aware of it. All the neuroses the pills had induced had made her a monster. The more someone gave, the more she demanded. By giving, the person had proved she could trust him; there weren't too many people she could trust, and her needs were overwhelming.

'You see,' Bobby Cole has stated, 'anybody that becomes a friend of Judy is working all the time – working keeping this one away from her; don't let So-and-So do this. "Delores, [Cole's wife]," she'd say, "you've got to get Sid away from here." And [the producers] would say, "Delores, you've got to make sure she's at the Saint Regis at four o'clock." "Delores, we're counting on you," and before you know it Delores is working her ass off. Delores is counting Dexedrines. No matter how it drove you crazy, there was something – Judy was like the eternal victim . . .'

The most powerful scene in the film occurs after she is told by her son that he will not join her. Due to appear at the Palladium, she gets outrageously drunk, trips, hurts her ankle, and is taken to the hospital. Her lover (Bogarde), who is a doctor, is called.

'No more coffee,' she screams at him. 'I couldn't take any

more coffee. You'd have to feed me through the veins. I'm full to the brim with it. I'm full to the brim with the whole damned world.'

Bogarde calms her and moves in very close, and the camera seems to be on top of them.

'Have you come to take me home?' she asks pitifully (for Jenny really has no home).

'No, I've come to take you to the theater.'

'Oh, no, you haven't. I'm not going back there again – not going back there ever, ever, ever again.'

'*They* are waiting.'

'I don't care if *they're* fasting. Give them their money back and tell them to come back next fall.'

'Jenny, it's a sellout.'

'I'm always a sellout.'

'You promised.'

'The hell with them. I can't be spread so thin. I'm just one person. I don't want to be rolled out like pastry so that everyone has a nice big bite of me. I'm just me. I belong to me. I can do whatever I damn well please and no one can ask any questions.'

'You know the last is not true.'

'. . . and that's final! It's just not worth all the deaths that I have to die.'

'You have a show to do,' he reminds her. 'You're going to do it and I'm going to see that you do.'

'You think you can make me sing? You can get me there, but can you make me sing? I sing for myself. I sing what I want to, whenever I want to – just for me. I sing for my own pleasure. I'll do whatever I damn well want. You understand that?'

'I understand that. Just hang on to that.'

She sobers almost instantly, and her voice becomes desperate. 'I've hung on to every bit of rubbish in life there is and thrown away the good bits. Can you tell me why I do that?' she asks.

And before the scene ends she tells him, 'There's an old saying: When you go onstage, you don't feel any pain; and when the lights hit you, you don't feel anything ... It's a stinking lie.'

I Could Go On Singing was the only film for which Judy had worked on the screenplay. From that point of view it satisfied some of her desire to write. But it was an emotionally draining experience. She was at one time analyzing herself and then having to demonstrate her findings before a full film crew, exposing every weakness, every source of inadequacy she had. She was aware throughout of the delays she caused. At one point in the shooting she purportedly fell and hit her head in her hotel bathroom and was hospitalized in London Clinic while filming was held up a week.

She was also aware of the growing hostility of the crew, of the lack of patience on the part of Bogarde and the executives; she could not seem to help herself. She was particularly fond of Bogarde and feared losing his friendship. Before she completed the film, she warned him, 'One day you'll have your back to me. You won't walk away facing me. No one does.' Bogarde said afterward, 'Judy is a schizo; Judy is a mess; Judy is a genius.'

The film was not a successful one. It is difficult to understand why, for with all its failures, it was (and remains) an exciting film portrayal and a beautifully mounted picture. Judy looked ravaged – time and trauma had eroded her. It was a real, moving, and revealing look at one of America's living legends. It was being filmed at the same time the Marilyn Monroe–Arthur Miller film, *The Misfits*, was in general release. Judy was beginning to see some parallel in Marilyn's and her lives. She was aware that Marilyn was almost as desperately addicted to pills as she was. 'Why don't they stop her,' she was heard to comment angrily. And *The Misfits* disturbed her. 'It's like seeing someone naked and exposed,' she said. She felt that Miller's screenplay was drawn from his wife's (Marilyn's) own character. Her objection was not that Marilyn should expose herself, but that someone else was doing the exposing. Perhaps it had some bearing on her working so closely with the script of *I Could Go On Singing*.

'You'll see her in close-up,' Judith Crist said in the New York *Herald Tribune*.

... in a beautiful, glowing technicolor and striking staging in a vibrant, vital performance that gets to the essence of her mystique as a superb entertainer. Miss Garland is – as always – real, the voice throbbing, the eyes aglow, the delicate features yielding to the demands of the years, the legs still long and lovely. Certainly the role of a top-rank singer beset by the loneliness and emotional hungers of her personal life is not an alien one to her.

It was her thirty-sixth – and last – film and stands alone as the only one that reveals the true essence of the mature Judy Garland. Shown as an aging woman in it, nonetheless she exposed her own high-strung vitality, her tensely gay personality. She had that elusive, indefinable attribute known as star quality; and at no other time, except in *A Star is Born*, did she so dazzle one with it.

London critic Philip Oakes, in his review of *I Could Go On Singing*, summed it up:

She is a star; the genuine outsize article ... She is an actress of power and subtlety; a singer whose way with a song is nothing short of marvelous ... She is a great artist. She is Judy. She is the best there is.

Yet the failure of the film at the box office led one to ask many questions. Where was the support of the Garland Cult? Was her career coming to an end? Had she lost her audience and their love? Judy fretted about all these things and about most of the other unhappy circumstances in her life. English director Carol Reed lent her his country house in Epsom; but she was terrified to leave the children alone there. First she hired round-the-clock guards. Then she moved them into her London hotel. Luft now alleged they had been kidnapped. She initiated out-of-court negotiations with Luft, agreeing to give him a percentage of her earnings. Whatever the final agreement was, Luft seemed satisfied.

She had the British wardship lifted and, having received permission for the children to leave the country, departed England for Lake Tahoe, Nevada, where she intended to rest and wait out her divorce in familiar surroundings. It was the first of August.

On the night of the fifth of August in Hollywood, Marilyn Monroe took to her bedroom without eating dinner. She was alone in the house except for her housekeeper. The telephone was by her bed and she made a number of calls. A light shone under the door (she did not like to be in the dark). She had been deeply depressed. Her marriage to Arthur Miller had failed. Her last film, *The Misfits*, had been unsuccessful. She had recently been fired from another film. Friends were deserting her, but perhaps worst of all, she was wholly dependent upon pills – and upon those people either in her employ or close to her who could supply her with the pills. Before morning came, her housekeeper had become apprehensive and called for help. They had to break through the glass door of the bedroom from the garden. Marilyn was lying nude on top of the bed. She was dead, and on the bedside table was an empty pill bottle and a silent telephone.

Judy had known Marilyn through her early years in Hollywood – before she had become the blond sex symbol of the world. She had commented to Marilyn and others that there was a similarity between them as women and as performers. In an interview with *Ladies' Home Journal* she tells the following story:

> I knew Marilyn Monroe and loved her dearly. She asked me for help. Me! I didn't know what to tell her. One night at a party at Clifton Webb's house, Marilyn followed me from room to room. 'I don't want to get too far away from you,' she said. 'I'm scared.' I told her, 'We're all scared. I'm scared too.'

The incident had occurred just before Judy's return to England.

The news of Marilyn's death sent Judy into a deep depression. For several weeks she kept very much to herself and to her room. Liza, at sixteen, had decided to go to New York and try to break into the theater. There were just Joey and Lorna with her now. It preyed on her mind that *somehow – somewhere* – she had to make a proper home for them. Having paid all her current and past-due taxes out of what she had earned these past marathon-earning years, and then splitting what was left with Luft, she had a clean slate but certainly not enough money to retire on; and the strenuous nature of her work in those years had left her feeling physically depleted. She did not see how in her present condition she could cope with another concert tour, and no one was submitting film scripts for her approval. Fields and Begelman were discussing television, but it was all tentative. Still, she was heavily on pills and dieting to lose weight if and when it did come through.

Once again, in *Ladies' Home Journal*, Judy comments:

> I don't think Marilyn really meant to harm herself. It was partly because she had too many pills available, then was deserted by her friends. You shouldn't be told you're completely irresponsible and be left alone with too much medication. It's too easy to forget. You take a couple of sleeping pills and you wake up in twenty minutes and forget you've taken them. So you take a couple more, and the next thing you know you've taken too many.

And later in the article she adds:

> There have been times when I have deliberately tried to take my life . . . . I think I must have been crying for some attention.

'Care must be taken; attention must be paid,' Arthur Miller said of the aging salesman Willie Loman in *Death of a Salesman*, and Judy had commented on the play, 'That's the way I feel about myself, too: "Care must be taken; attention must be paid." '

On the morning of the fifteenth of September, 1962, not quite six weeks after Marilyn's death, Judy was discovered unconscious on the floor of her room and rushed to Carson-Tahoe Hospital. The chief of staff of the hospital, Dr. Richard Grundy, saved her life; and noting certain medical warnings of serious trouble, ordered a complete examination to determine her true physical condition. He found that she was suffering from acute pyelonephritis in her right kidney, which produces a severe pain similar to that of kidney stones and which she must have been suffering over a long period. To the press he reported that his patient had taken an accidental overdose to stifle the pain she had been suffering and that there had been absolutely no suicide attempt whatsoever. Dr. Grundy prescribed rest and treatment; but Judy was now growing fearful of the future.

Liza tells stories of their life at this time – of how, whenever reporters or photographers wanted an 'at home' story on Judy, she would borrow a friend's house and, bringing pictures and personal memorabilia with her, place them all over before the interview and then whisk them away directly afterward. Life was truly a series of borrowed houses and hotel rooms during this period, and Judy fretted constantly over this way of life.

The following February found her with Lorna and Joey at the Sherry-Netherland Hotel in New York and Luft there at the same time. Liza was appearing out of town in *Carnival* at the Mineola Playhouse. One night when the younger children had gone to see Liza, Judy was found unconscious on the bed by the hotel maid. She was suffering cuts on her forehead and mouth, and was rushed to Mount Sinai Hospital. The first editions claimed she had once again attempted suicide, but the doctors counterclaimed that she had suffered a fall (Judy had said she had tripped and fallen in the bathroom and could not recall how she had gotten back to the bed). They had feared cerebral bleeding but in the end, released her after treating her for minor wounds.

A few days later Judy and Luft were reconciled, the divorce action seemingly set aside. They flew together to

London for the premiere of *I Could Go On Singing*; then, rushing back to New York, gave a large party for Liza, who had just made her New York professional theatre debut in *Flora, the Red Menace*.

The Lufts were now registered at the St. Regis Hotel together, but Judy appeared to be alone most of the time. Once more she was found unconscious. Again the press shouted 'Suicide!' and another time a doctor issued a statement of denial adding, 'Miss Garland is just suffering from exhaustion.'

Luft was taking back the reins of her career. Fields and Begelman were ostensibly her agents, but Luft was her manager. All of them convinced her she had to remain before her audiences. They booked her into Harrah's in Tahoe as a compromise. She managed to get through the first week of the engagement, but then collapsed. Mickey Rooney stepped in and finished the engagement for her. Just barely recovering, she flew back to London to do a live television spectacular at the Palladium (a very popular English variety show called *Sunday Night at the Palladium*). Twice she missed song cues, and once she went to leave the stage by the wrong exit. She was confused and appeared out of it. Directly after the show, which was kindly but poorly received, she flew back to the States to do a television special there.

It was infinitely better than the English show, but the press still found it disappointing; and because of it, negotiations that Fields and Begelman were having with James Aubrey for her to do a weekly sixty-minute television show on CBS were temporarily set back.

The roller coaster had gone over the top and now seemed to have no place to go but down.

CHAPTER THIRTY-TWO

JIM AUBREY, then president of CBS, was responsible for the final decision to sign Judy for a weekly one-hour series at $30,000 a show. After paying the huge entourage that wound up in her personal employ, Sid's managerial fees, agents' fees, and taxes, Judy cleared perhaps $5,000 a show. But as she did not shoot one each week (the first thirteen took twenty weeks), that amount was actually reduced to approximately $3,250 take-home – not much of a percentage, and a far less awesome figure than $30,000, but a fairly solid chunk of money all the same. Judy returned to the Coast and moved into her house on Rockingham Drive in the Holmby Hills area of Los Angeles.

Mel Tormé functioned as musical arranger on the show. He was brought in by the producer, George Schlatter, and from the first rehearsal, Judy felt insecure with him. Their music followed two separate philosophies: as musical arranger Tormé felt the need to introduce new material all the time, and Judy preferred to rely on her standards. There was professional hostility that carried itself over to their personal relationship.

However, there is no question that Judy was as emotionally off center and difficult to work with during the filming of this series as she had been during the filming of *I Could Go On Singing*. Both crews must have experienced the same unbearable conditions. She was, for one thing, trying to maintain a crash diet in order to remain slim for the cameras; was heavily on 'speed'; suffered insecurity because of her lack of knowhow in this new and devastating industry; and though she refused to face the *whys* of it, experienced excruciating physical pain.

There is also no question that in the last six years of her life Judy Garland fought for her survival with superhuman endurance – and that there were periods when it appeared she had won the battle. It was during these periods that she gave her best performances, and it was because she could bounce back so rapidly that those around her were often unaware of or insensitive to her grave physical condition.

Judy now drank only small quantities of hard liquor due to her recent past history of hepatitis, when she had been told alcohol would kill her. She drank Liebfraumilch, sipped wine or vodka mixed with tonic or juices, but actually consumed very little. However, even a small quantity of alcohol combined with the amount of narcotics she took a day (and she was now taking morphine along with her heavy dosages of 'uppers' and 'downers') would give anyone who might not know her true condition the idea that she was drunk.

According to Bobby Cole, she would ask, "Will you fix me a drink?,' then would take two sips, put it down, and ask, 'Will you make me another?' As Cole tells it, 'By the end of the evening there would be eighty bucks' worth of vodka and six bucks' worth of tonic sitting around in stale glasses, but she never drank it. The only reason she drank was because she was being dehydrated. Dexedrine dehydrates you. Some people who didn't understand might not have seen the truth . . . she was never drunk. I wish she had been drunk as a skunk. At least with booze you go to bed; you wake up the next morning. But all the time she was on pills.'

In his book (*The Other Side of the Rainbow*) Tormé recalls an incident when Judy takes what his wife fears is an overdose of sleeping pills and is out cold. Tormé frantically calls the doctor he knows has been treating Judy and the doctor is calm and refuses to come to see her, claiming she is used to the dosage she took. In the morning Tormé goes off to CBS figuring he will have to make excuses for her not showing up at rehearsal, but not too much later, he reports, Judy came literally *bouncing* in looking sharp and singing great. He deems it a 'miracle'. Perhaps – if the use of twenty to thirty Dexedrines taken at one time to wake up from a sledgehammer of Nembutal could be called a 'miracle'.

The producers in the beginning decided Judy should talk and do skits as well as sing. With seven cameras glaring at her from all angles and one looking down her throat as she sang, Judy felt anxious and threatened. She always had a slight stutter under trying conditions; now it became more pronounced. And every week she had the weight over her head that the show's rating might not be so high as that of the top-rated program *Bonanza*, which was on NBC, the competitive network. Judy commented with humor at the time, 'You know, I used to watch *Bonanza* all the time; and if my show doesn't get better, I'll go back to watching *Bonanza*!'

The series' first executive producer, Norman Jewison, commented after the show's first shift in personnel, 'This show is the *Cleopatra* of television.' Certainly nothing was spared once Schlatter entered the picture. A forty-by-one-hundred-ten-foot house trailer, air-conditioned and emblazoned with red and white candy stripes, was hoisted to a second-floor ramp and converted into her dressing room. Behind the trailer's kissing-Cupids door knocker, an interior decorator had created a miniature replica of the star's home, complete with wall-to-wall carpeting, antique marble tables, and indirect pink lighting. The furnishings included a piano, and stereophonic sound system, a tape recorder, a serving bar, and a refrigerator containing Judy's favorite wine, Blue Nun Liebfraumilch.

Adding to that extravagance, nearly $100,000 had been spent to raise the stage and to embed a separate revolving stage with new electronic Marconi cameras that the technicians claimed removed wrinkles from faces. Workmen had also painted the long corridor from her dressing room to the stage door to resemble the winding yellow brick road in *The Wizard of Oz*.

An amusing incident occurred shortly before the series began shooting. Facing a gathering of several hundred representatives of stations affiliated with CBS, Judy sang a parody of the Carolyn Leigh song 'Call Me Irresponsible,' to wit: 'Call me irresponsible/ Call me unreliable/ But it's undeniably true/ I'm irrevocably signed with you.' All present cheered loudly.

The show premiered on September 29, 1963. 'What should never happen to Judy Garland did last evening in the premiere of her weekly program over the Columbia Broadcasting System,' said Jack Gould, the *New York Times* television critic.

The busybodies got so in the way that the singer never had a chance to sing out as only she can. To call the hour a grievous disappointment would be to miss the point. It was an absolute mystery ... The thinking of C.B.S. executives was to develop a 'new' Judy, one who would indulge in light banter and make way for suitable guests to share the weekly tasks ... Those telephones on the twentieth floor of C.B.S.'s home should buzz this morning with but one directive to Hollywood – *Free Judy*.

And CBS talent chief Michael Dann replied with this statement: 'We have decided that she [Judy] should never appear in sketches and never play any character but herself. And she'll be singing more medleys, more standards. Songs are her babies. We told her what we think and she's listening. She's far too insecure about television to exercise her own judgment. She knows what's good for her.'

And Judy replied, 'I'm the original take-orders girl.'

But now that was no longer true. She had a temperament clash with Jim Aubrey which she could do nothing about, but she could try to get rid of other unsympathetic personnel. She wanted familiar faces around her – people she felt she could rely on. Thus there was a mass 'firing' after the fifth show, and for whatever reasons – personal or professional – she had turned against Tormé and was demanding a new musical arranger.

Finally asserting her own wishes, she brought Mort Lindsey and the orchestra onto the stage and, with an onstage tent in which to change costumes, did a one-hour concert which highlighted many of the great numbers she had performed at Carnegie Hall. She was alone except for one number in which she sat on the edge of the stage singing 'Happiness Is Just a Thing Called Joe' to Joey, and a very beautiful new lyric, 'Lorna', put to the show's theme music by Johnny Mercer, to Lorna. She also sang 'Liza', but Liza was not present on that show. That hour was one of the greatest ever recorded for television. (It was recently re-aired, to overwhelming enthusiasm, and received an exceptionally high rating.) But unfortunately, as many shows were already shot that had not been shown, and as CBS had high-salaried commitments to the stars it had lined up as future guests, Judy was not allowed again to get out there in front of the band to sing.

The decision was to appeal not to her cult, who they felt wanted to treat her like a goddess and not share her, but to the 'camera and sneaker clan'. An attempt was made to dispel the legend surrounding her. Instead of guests' flattering her, they would 'bring her down'. 'Judy, you used to be so fat', guest star Steve Lawrence needled. 'This isn't the original, this is the twelfth Judy Garland; the original went over the rainbow years ago', resident comedian Jerry Van Dyke quipped, adding, 'There's a little farm in Pasadena that grows Judy Garlands.' Often Van Dyke would repeat the same 'joke': 'What's a nice little old lady like you doing on television?'

'The absurd notion of debasing Judy's reputation as a legendary figure,' television critic Richard Warren Lewis said in *Life*, 'and molding her show into an imitation of other prosaic variety shows has been a disaster where it hurts most, in the audience-rating polls.'

But her producers never gave up. She was forced to make chitchat with her guests and to take a back seat while they performed. Only one guest show truly stands out. In that one she had Barbra Streisand and Ethel Merman as guests, and there are two classic numbers – one in which all three ladies try to 'outbelt' one another, and one in which Judy sings 'Get Happy' as Barbra sings 'Happy Days'; and according to Tormé's book, that idea was Judy's.

'I went down to see her,' he writes. 'She was playing Streisand's record of "Happy Days Are Here Again" on a portable phonograph. She took the arm off the record, invited me to sit, and said, "Listen." Then she began to play the record from the beginning again. As Streisand's voice came through the speaker, Judy started to sing "Get Happy" in counterpoint to "Happy Days". The result was electrifying, one of those chance discoveries in which two great songs jell into one extraspecial opus.'

When Barbra came into his office. Tormé writes that he told her, 'Since you sing in any key, try "Happy Days" in this one.' Then, beginning the introduction in a key suitable to his own range, he motioned to her to start, whereupon he joined in, as Judy had, with 'Get Happy'. 'Barbra kept singing as she half-turned to me, a wide smile on her face. When we finished she exclaimed, "That's terrific! I mean it! Your idea?"

'No. Judy's,' Tormé replied honestly.

During the time of the filming of the television series, Judy was seeing and appeared to be very much in love with Glenn Ford. He was very attentive, and Judy dropped small hints that they might marry.

By the end of the series, the affair was over and Judy in romantic limbo. Luft was in Calfornia and they once again had drawn swords. And Judy, in fear – by her own admission – of being bodily attacked, hired a bodyguard. Perhaps it was good that the personal side of her life was as traumatic as it was then; for after Judy had gone through twenty-six torturous shows and nearly a year of exhausting work; of having to fight through the cyclone winds of her addiction and her physical disabilities; of suffering monstrous tensions, crash dieting, in-fighting, and the insecurities caused by the ups and downs of television ratings, *The Judy Garland Show* was dropped. But it seemed destined to happen. A weekly hour format for Judy Garland was never a feasible idea. With her physical and psychological problems, there was no way to ensure that she could be consistent each week. And had she been able to hold up, and had she been presented each week alone and 'in concert' – her best format – no audience could have sustained such a weekly assault on their emotions.

Norman Jewison had said when he began the program: 'Judy is a legend in her own time. She is a combination of Sammy Davis, Jr., Aimee Semple McPherson, and Greta Garbo.' Recognizing that, it is difficult to understand why both Jewison and CBS would then try to turn her into a combination of Crosby, Como, and Shore.

What was wrong with the genuine, the legendary Judy Garland?

CHAPTER THIRTY-THREE

DIRECTLY after the cancellation of the television series, Judy was booked on a Far East tour to begin at Melbourne, Australia. For the first time on any such extended tour, she was to go without a manager or agent close at hand. But she had met a tall, dark, slender, aesthetically attractive young man, recently returned from Europe where he had performed a walk-on part in the Federico Fellini film 8½. Mark Herron, who was then in his late twenties, had graduated from theater groups in Los Angeles and Arizona and was now a Hollywood film hopeful. A friend, former child star Roddy McDowall – who was also close to Judy – introduced the two. Nervous about making the long trip 'un-chaperoned', Judy asked Herron to join her as her secretary or tour manager. Early press reports referred to him, however, as her 'traveling companion'.

In looking back, it seems inconceivable that sensible men like Fields and Begelman would have arranged such a strenuous tour for Judy at a time when her health was failing badly and her addiction ruling her mind and body. But one must also be aware of Judy's incredible ability to pull herself together time and time again and to appear so vibrant and full of energy (as she had during the shooting of the television series) that her true condition was masked and visible only to those sensitive enough to perceive the truth: that her 'highs' were induced by grit, guts – but mostly pills. It was difficult for those on the outside to grasp the truth of her physical condition. Many of her hospital visits were attributed to nerves, exhaustion, or pills; and observers were prone to chalk up her 'indispositions' as emotional disorders rather than physical warnings. For those close to her, it was another matter. Their own needs took precedence, coloring their final judgment. Any other man or woman in Judy's state of health would have been hospitalized for a complete medical rundown, institutionalized for drug addiction, and finally retired – or at the very minimum, restricted to some less demanding work.

Liza said, after her mother's death, 'Mama was just like a beautiful flower that withered and died.' That was now exactly what was occurring. She was withering. Her liver and kidney were both diseased. She had the beginning of a colon obstruction which made digestion painful – later she was to have a rectal obstruction, causing excruciating pain; she was plagued by anemia; and her nervous system was badly shattered. The pills had created a serious imbalance – a lack of coordination, at times, which caused her to fall as often as she did, requiring medical attention over twenty times. There is no way of knowing how often she hit her head during those falls, perhaps suffering minor concussions.

As though she were not beset by enough trials, her stutter had grown increasingly noticeable. She became terribly self-conscious about it – but finally was able to employ the disability to her advantage, playing it up for humor or effect, covering it by adding a little circular, swinging gesture of her hand whenever a word was difficult to enunciate. The stutter, accompanied by that gesture, was to become a private 'trademark' that all those close to her eventually aped even in her presence. In fact, one could pick out any person close

216

to Judy by the use of Judy's mannerism. The hand would seem to stutter with her, moving forward in tiny jerks. Finally the letter or word would roll out, and the hand would roll forward with it in a flourishing circular movement. The palm would open, the fingers spread – and the word would be freed.

From the time of the Far East trip, she had no weight problem. It was quite the reverse – as with each passing year, she grew frailer, more birdlike. It is difficult, in fact, to know or understand what kept her going and even more difficult to comprehend how she was able to perform at all. For a Garland appearance was as physically debilitating and exhausting as a fighter going ten stiff rounds.

The flight to Melbourne, because of her fear of flying and the imbalance produced by the nineteen-hour time difference, nearly did her in. In order to remain awake at the proper hours so that she could appear when scheduled, she had to take an extra large dosage of amphetamine. This made her unsteady on her feet and caused her to be an hour late at her concert. When the impatient and massive crowd of seventy thousand in that giant outdoor amphitheater saw her stumble from the wings, they assumed she was drunk and began to yell insults at her.

'I love you too,' Judy called nervously back at them, but her audience was not in the mood for humor. They continued to heckle her. 'Sing, sing! Get on with it!' they shouted.

Judy stood unsure of herself for a few moments. Her hand was shaking and she had trouble with the mike. She was keenly aware of a hostility from her audience and she was badly thrown by it.

Not being in her best voice, she nonetheless gave them a vital and conscientious performance lasting forty-five minutes. Considering her physical condition at the time, the performance was a miracle; but the Australians, set back by the delay and still suspecting she was drunk, as her footing was unsteady, could not be warmed up. They reacted indifferently, occasionally calling out a rude remark. Finally, during the song 'I'll Go My Way by Myself', Judy put the microphone down on the edge of the stage and, in her own words, 'got the hell out of it'. It was an upsetting experience. It was the first time she had *run away* from an audience and the first time she had ever felt she had to.

The Sydney concert that followed went on without incident, but Judy was finding the trip exhausting and perilous. Her next scheduled stop was Hong Kong. There had been typhoon warnings, but in order to arrive in time, she had flown through extremely bad weather – reaching the Mandarin Hotel just before ninety-mile-an-hour gale winds began battering the city. Feeling very strange on arrival, she chalked it up to the strain of the last two concerts, the terror of her recent flight, and the unnerving sound of the storm winds beating at the hotel shutters outside her room, and asked to be left alone to rest. Some hours later Mark Herron checked to see if she was all right. Finding her unconscious on her bed, he rang for help, whereupon she was rushed to a nearby hospital. Local doctors, finding she had already been in a coma many hours, administered oxygen and worked over her body in a desperate effort to save her life. Finally, after fifteen long, critical hours, she gained consciousness. At that time a sobbing Herron spoke to the press. 'She is very bad, very bad. The doctors won't tell me anything,' he cried, and he asked the reporters – who had access to Telex machines – to immediately notify Freddie Fields in California.

By the following day Judy was able to speak; she smiled; but she was pathetically weak. The press now hinted at an overdose of sleeping pills. Herron and the hospital denied this, as they did reports that it had been a heart attack. Exhaustion was given as the cause of her serious collapse. Fields had flown Dr. Lee Seigel in from Hollywood. Dr. Seigel diagnosed her ailment as 'pleurisy, a chest inflammation usually accompanied by high temperatures and difficulty in breathing.' Rest was prescribed; and Dr. Seigel, after assuring himself and Judy, too, that she would be all right, returned to Hollywood. Judy weighed a frail and

218

dangerous seventy-eight pounds. She was very weak, but she told the press with a smile, 'I'm going to be all right.'

Then on June 11, just fifteen days after her traumatic fight for life, Judy and Herron appeared in a local nightclub, wearing matching jade rings, and announced they had been married. Her 'recovery' seemed incredible enough; but her marriage was unexplainable, as she was not yet legally divorced from Luft. Still, she insisted, 'We've been married five days now,' and added, 'I'm very happy.' Then, though still frail, Judy appeared able enough to join in the entertainment and sing a rather breathy version of 'Over the Rainbow', to overwhelming applause. She beamed and leaned heavily on Herron's arm as they left the club.

Reporters piled in on them at the hotel, and Herron was quoted the next day as saying, 'We were married about six days ago – I don't know what day it was. It was on board a ship. We had rented it for the day. We were just anchored in the harbor here in Hong Kong. It was sundown. I don't know the name of the ship. A very nice Chinese fellow stood up for me. I don't know his name. Judy wore a tan suit and she looked lovely. We're both very happy and excited.'

Herron and Judy returned to Los Angeles, where Luft wasted no time in filing an affidavit for the custody of the children, claiming that Judy should be denied the custody because 'she is emotionally disturbed and imbalanced'. He claimed in the same affidavit that Judy had attempted suicide more than twenty times. Judy was present in the courtroom when the charges were read, but left the courthouse extremely distraught.

She had been met on her homecoming with the distressing news that her sister Sue had died while she had herself been ill in Hong Kong – word having been withheld from her at the time. A week later, she was back in the hospital (Cedars of Lebanon, where Joey had been born), and the doctor in attendance declared to the press that she had been suffering severe abdominal pains and that he was conducting further tests. There was some speculation about the possibility of appendicitis, but nothing further came of that.

Following her hospital release, apparently well enough at least to travel, Judy and Herron flew to Copenhagen and then to London. It was supposed to be a holiday, a vacation away from all her woes – but on her arrival in London, she appeared in a very distressed state. Shortly thereafter she was admitted to the casualty department of St. Stephen's Hospital, suffering from injuries to her wrists – which she claimed had occurred while she was using scissors to open a trunk bound with metal. Ninety minutes later, she was released, but she entered a nursing home.

Receiving an invitation to appear at the biggest charity show of the London season, *Night of a Thousand Stars*, Judy disobeyed doctors' orders and left the nursing home on her own recognizance, appearing only a few hours later backstage at the Palladium, where the show was being held. She told the show's director that she could not sing, but that she would simply take a bow and say a few words. Following the Beatles, she stepped out of the wings into a single spotlight. As soon as the audience saw her, they went absolutely wild. A spokesman for the Palladium said, 'I think if Judy hadn't sung, there would have been a riot.' They cheered and stamped and shouted, 'Sing, Judy, sing!' with far different meaning in their voices than when her Melbourne audience had shouted similar words, and Judy reacted emotionally to them. There were tears in her eyes, and she kept mumbling, 'Bless you – bless you.' There were cries for 'Over the Rainbow'. Judy beamed, but shook her head and waved as she began to back away from the microphone.

But the cheers continued, and she returned to stand alone on the gargantuan stage, the huge Palladium orchestra in the pit below her. Pitifully small, very pale, and weighing only ninety pounds, she looked as if she might need support. Taking the mike in her hand, she sat down on the edge of the stage – her huge eyes seeming vast in the frailness of her tiny face as the spotlight hit them. The audience hushed immediately. You could have heard a match strike. The band played the familiar introduction, and Judy began to sing in a

220

soft, breathy voice that became more vibrant as the song progressed. Never had she sung the song 'Over the Rainbow' more poignantly; never had an audience been more moved. They jumped to their feet when she had finished and cried and cheered, refusing to let her off the stage, then hushed again as she laughed nervously – to encore with a rousing performance of 'Swanee'.

Shirley Bassey was to follow, but Judy's encore had ended in such wild acclaim that it was impossible to do anything but end the show with Judy onstage, thereby cancelling Miss Bassey's number. There was the same audience madness that had occurred at Carnegie Hall. The Beatles and all the other stars, including Miss Bassey, came out onstage and massed around her, congratulating her as the audience surged forward in an effort to come as close as the pit orchestra would permit.

And once again the press stated, 'Judy Garland sang her way back to the dramatic comeback of the year . . .'

Happy in London, she remained there throughout the summer; but things were not right between Herron and herself, and he was often away (later Judy was to say that Herron had 'conducted our relationship from a moving telephone booth'); and by September she had taken ill again – September 24 finding her back in a nursing home with an 'acute abdominal condition but there is no danger'.

Within a month, Luft's charge that she was an unfit mother came to Superior Court in Santa Monica, California. Judy was in London. The portrait sketched of her in the courtroom was a frightening one. Luft had as witness a young man in his employ, Vernon Alves, who was to function later as his 'production assistant'. Alves claimed Judy used barbiturates, had once tried to jump from a hotel window, and many times had spoken to the children in a loud and intoxicated voice. He also claimed he had seen Judy in a hotel suite in Philadelphia 'running around without any clothes on . . . from room to room, screaming and accusing everyone of everything. I spent most of my time trying to catch her as she was bouncing off the wall. The last thing I did was catch her before she got out the window and throw her down on the couch.'

The second witness was a maid – Rhoda Chiolak, who was in the Luft's employ from 1954 to 1960 and from 1962 to 1963, and who substantiated Luft's charges. It was a wild picture of Judy and was made more bizarre by Luft's introducing Glenn Ford's name and also asking that Judy's money be held in receivership for the two children on the ground that she was squandering 'the family fortune' on her current companion, Mark Herron. With all of this, Luft still failed to win any portion of the case, and Judy retained custody of the children. But Judy in turn, dropped a 'petition for contempt' order against Luft.

Liza joined her mother in London and on November 8, 1964, shared the bill with her at the Palladium. It was Liza's first major concert appearance, and Judy gave her full rein. Liza, long-haired and teen-aged, youth and talent brimming over, showed more than future potential. She was the stuff of star material, and sometimes it was difficult to tell the two voices apart.

The concert with Liza seemed to be a turning point. Judy returned to the States on a concert tour, but it was obvious that her health was on the decline and that her performances were being badly affected. Many concerts were either cancelled or postponed. During one in Cincinnati she had to walk off in the middle of a performance; this time, though, it was because she had become too ill to stand on her feet.

In April, 1965, she appeared at the Academy Awards Show in Hollywood, not as a contender, but singing one of the nominated songs. The awards were being held in a large auditorium in Santa Monica. Until the time she appeared, the audience had seemed very complacent. But as she strode out onstage with a mike on a long, trailing cord, flipping it over her shoulder – something in the way she looked making them fear she might lose the words, that any moment she might just trip over that wire and collapse – her audience became one. For once in their egocentric lives, the Hollywood 'elite' wanted someone else to succeed. Her voice was off, but she must have felt the great concentration of passion on the part of her audience for her to 'do it', and somehow she managed to come through brilliantly for them.

On May 19, she received word that she had been granted a divorce from Luft. Refusing any comment to the press, she continued her concert appearances, singing to critical reviews. If the press was against her, it was quite the opposite with her audiences. The cult was in full swing. Good or bad, they cheered her on; and Judy tried to give them the best that was in her. If she was badly indisposed, the performance would be off; but her American audiences, from this point, were sympathetic. Judy has said, 'I try to bring the audience's own drama – tears and laughter they know about – to them. I try to match my lifelong experiences with theirs, and they match their own sadness and happiness to mine.'

One month later she was back in the hospital – this time the Neuropsychiatric Institute of the U.C.L.A. Medical Center. The press release issued was that 'Miss Garland has had a nervous collapse'. But she was scheduled to appear at the massive Greek Theatre in Los Angeles. She insisted she could make it, although her doctors felt she should not. Make it she did, but not until after tripping over one of her pet dogs and breaking her arm the day of her appearance. In the grand 'the show must go on' tradition, she made the curtain – appearing with a cast on her arm – but the pain became too severe, and Mickey Rooney, as though in true-life replay of their old Metro musicals, rushed in to take over the remainder of the show for her.

Part Four

During the bad days I'm sure I would have perished without those wonderful audiences. Without *that* and a sense of humor, I would have died ... I think there's something peculiar about me that I haven't died. It doesn't make sense but I refuse to die.

—Judy Garland

CHAPTER THIRTY-FOUR

'WHEN I was eleven,' Liza says, 'I was hiring Mama's household staff. God, it must have been hilarious. Out comes this eleven-year-old kid and says, "May I see your references, please?" ' Liza was now twenty, and she had been so old, so responsible so long that it seemed she had never been a teen-ager. At this stage she was, in a sense, the mother of the family. Extremely loyal to Judy, she was, as well, fiercely devoted to keeping the family intact. There was a high degree of camaraderie between mother and daughter, and the similarities between the two extended deeper than the arched body and outflung arms both employed to end a song, or the quavering high notes and deep-throated sadness in their voices. They shared a marvelous sense of humor, binding love, career dedication, and the enigma of continually reaching out to grasp life and just as constantly withdrawing from it.

Both had quick-to-rise, emotional temperatures, and neither could veil the truth. There were volatile blowups between them even when Liza had lived at home, times when Judy would lock Liza out of wherever they were living and Liza would stand outside the door until, finally, Judy would open it and they would fall into each other's arms crying. It was during one of these lockouts that Liza left for New York (she was sixteen at the time), having saved enough money for her fare and $100 extra. She never returned 'home', nor did she ever again ask for support, for the next two years living first in the Barbizon Hotel for Women ('I went bananas!' Liza comments about that experience); spending two nights on a park bench in Central Park; and bedding down on a friend's couch for the rest of the time.

227

The Palladium appearance had briefly reunited them, but it had been a worrying experience for Liza and a shock to both mother and daughter – for Judy suddenly realized she had a grown-up daughter and, as Liza comments, 'She became very competitive with me.'

But Judy was eventually able to push back the competitiveness she felt. Liza held a very special place in her life. And at the same time, Liza was responsible for some of the guilt she suffered. If she could have done it all over again, she would have – just so it would *perhaps* have been different for Liza. So she did try to contribute what she could to Liza's happiness. Liza was a professional in her own right, and Judy did not hesitate in helping her.

In a *New York Times* interview with Tom Burke (December 7, 1969), Liza reveals the following episode:

I was up for a television show, *Ben Casey* or something, and the part was a pregnant girl who had had an abortion that had gone wrong, and she's in the hospital. I knew how I wanted to see it, but not how to *be* it. So I sort of gingerly took the script to Mom, and said, you know, 'Mama, help me'. We sat down on her floor, and she said, 'Now, read me your lines, and the doctor's lines, both.' His line was, 'Did you want to have the baby?' I read it and Mama said, 'All right, he's a doctor, he isn't getting personal – but how *dare* he intrude on you, how *dare* he ask you that, how *dare* he be there, how *dare* you be in the hospital, if only you could have married the father, if only he'd loved you, which he *didn't*. Now, *did you want to have the baby?* ! ! ! !' All I had to say was, 'No,' but it came out right. Because she had given me the thoughts – the pause, not the line. Then she said. 'Read me his line again,' and I did, and she said, 'Now this time you are going to concentrate on *not crying*. That's all you have to worry about, not letting him see you cry. Your baby is dead, your life is ruined, but you're not gonna cry, you're a strong girl, your parents have told you, your teachers have told you, *you know it, you know it, you're not going to cry!*' And my 'No' came out even better. She taught me how to – fill in the pauses. And if there's a way I act, that's the way. From that one day there on the floor. And now, if maybe another actor will say, 'What are you using in that scene,' I'll say, 'Well, I'm playing that I'm not gonna cry.' They say, 'Whaaat?' But *I* know!

But Judy's concern for Liza's career was not as strong a force as her fear that Liza might not escape her own pitfalls. 'Watch my mistakes,' she would warn Liza. Liza seldom drank and did not take drugs, being adamantly opposed to even common pills such as aspirin. Dean Martin's daughter Gayle has said, 'Rather than a fear of what drugs can do to you, Liza has a knowledge.' Liza was fighting at a very early age to ward off any dark maternal patterns.

While on her ill-fated Australian tour, Judy had met a young, attractive Australian singer-comedian, Peter Allen, and had encouraged him to come to the States, promising him a spot in her nightclub act. The following year, Allen was in London at the same time as both Judy and Liza. Judy now saw this young man as the white prince come to rescue Liza. Perhaps she was attempting to live vicariously through Liza, but she considered it a good, maternal, loving gesture to introduce the two young people and was pleased when she observed a mutual attraction. Judy turned her attention to Lorna and Joey, heaping perhaps more on Joey than on Lorna because Joey always seemed to need more. He was less self-sufficient, less coordinated, a poor student. But it was Lorna who Judy truly believed would someday be the second-generation star, not Liza.

But to say the children occupied her mind entirely in the years between 1960 and 1967 would be a complete untruth. Judy was occupied mainly with the very essentials of survival. Her drug addiction was destroying her body, and the parasites were undermining her future. Once again she could not call her soul her own. Once again she turned in desperation to the nearest man who offered help. And once again that man was Sid Luft.

229

And it seems incredible, but by 1967 Judy was again hopelessly in debt – and that in spite of the impressive salary she had been paid by CBS and the fact that she had appeared in concert at a high salary very frequently. With the exclusion of the periods of time when Fields and Begelman were in charge and when Mark Heron was part of her life (1961–65), Luft was never far from her side. However, let it be said that Judy, through her sporadic dependence on Luft, encouraged the situation.

Repeatedly, close observers have stated that there were times when no one else but Luft could get Judy onstage or keep her there. Though she was out of love with him in the physical sense and highly resentful of his associate, Vernon Alves, she nonetheless felt *rooted* to Luft. He was, after all, the father of two of her children, and she could not believe that his intentions were other than to protect his family, even when she was devastated by his actions. There was also a pattern that had established itself very early in her life, back in the days when she was on the road with Ethel. She was expected to be the family supporter and all others were accepted in the role of dependents who did everything within their power to help keep her working. They did so in pursuit of their own survival as well. A pattern of threat and rejection if she erred – and reward if she *behaved* had also been vested. Therefore, though it might seem inconceivable that after all the anger and disillusionment and hostility she had suffered with Luft she could reunite with him in her career, it was not an illogical action in terms of her well-entrenched behavior pattern. How many times had she felt the same things about Ethel? About L. B. Mayer? About Minnelli? And in varying degrees, about all the people in her life who had been aboard the Garland bandwagon? But the most poignant, crucial, and fundamental fact to remember was Judy's total dependence upon those close to her. They were her lifeline to the outside world and they were the only comforters in her distress.

By 1967, Judy was fully aware not only that she was hooked, but also that her body was moldering, necrosis setting in to each vital part. Where once she had thought in desperate moments of ending her life, she now hung on to any outstretched hand that might promise to keep her afloat. She became almost savage in her desperation. A quiet, ferocity overtook her actions and responses. Her nails would tear like tiger's claws into the palm of anyone who meant to leave her; her demands became insistent threats; she was a very frightened, terrified lady.

Not only was all the money she had made gone by '67, not only was she in debt – she was several hundred thousand dollars in debt, most of it again to the government. The pattern had repeated itself. Her earnings would go to her managers, but her taxes and many of her road expenses would not be paid; nor was she ever trusted with any of her own earnings. Now she was back in a position in which the government could seize her earnings as she made them, leaving no money for her. Something drastic had to be done, and Luft was right at her elbow to insist it be done his way.

Two years later, Judy gave a deposition to a London court about the circumstances existing in her life during the spring of '67 and about the Group V contract that Luft proposed, had drawn up, and had her sign. The following, a direct excerpt from Clause 4 of this deposition, given by Judy in the High Court of Justice, Queen's Bench Division, on December 29, 1968, and signed by Judy and by a Commissioner for Oaths, is presented verbatim so that some clarity can be given to the murky transactions that were to come:

... The alleged contract with Group V Limited came into being in June 1967 when I was approached by Mr. Sid Luft to whom I had formerly been married but from whom I had then been divorced for some four years. He suggested to me that an organization should be set up to be called Group V, the 'five' to consist of me, my daughter Lisa [Liza] Min[n]elli, the two children of Sid Luft and myself and Sid Luft. He explained to me that Group V would act as agents and representatives, pay us reasonable living money and enable us to build up trust funds for the children and otherwise obtain financial security. He also explained that there would be certain tax advantages. I accepted his suggestion and he then asked me to sign. He gave me one page to sign and as I trusted him I signed it. I was in a hurry to travel to a performance. I was subsequently shown the complete contract in which the first fifteen pages had been put in front of the page which I had signed. I was then told that Group V Limited did not include my children and myself but rather Sid Luft, Raymond Filiberti, and three other persons whose names I cannot remember. Despite the circumstances I continued to work for Group V because they had by that time made many advance bookings for me to appear and I felt that I was under an obligation to the audiences who were expecting me to appear. I continued to fulfill bookings made for me by Group V for a year after the contract was signed and a further two months after that. I mention the further two months because I had expected to receive from Group V some form of letter or notice renewing the contract but to my knowledge no such letter or notice ever reached me. I was waiting for such a letter because it would have given me an occasion to deal with Group V because throughout the year after the contract was signed I had fulfilled engagements made by Group V but had received no remuneration from them. I would find in each case that Group V had made the booking and received payment and that I would be left to appear and not be paid. At no time during the period of fourteen months mentioned above did I receive any payment at all from Group V in respect of the moneys I was to receive under the contract. I only continued to fulfill engagements which they had made in the knowledge that they at least were being paid and that I was entitled to an accounting from them. I was thus at least working and meeting obligations to the audiences.

Not only was I not paid but Group V failed to pay my expenses. A large quantity of my baggage was impounded in New York because Group V failed to pay my hotel bill. In December 1967 I met an engagement in Las Vegas and was then booked to appear in New York. I had no money of any kind and was obliged to borrow. I asked Filiberti for a loan as he knew I had not been paid and he gave me a cheque for $2500 drawn on his bank in New York. I flew immediately to New York but on presenting the cheque found that payment had been stopped.

Raymond Filiberti and two men named Leon Greenspan and Howard Harper were to play a Machiavellian role in the last year of Judy's life. Filiberti had a police record. Greenspan and Harper were acquaintances to whom Luft owed a large sum of money. Harper, whose real name was Howard Harker, also had a long police record and had been found guilty by the State of New Jersey on various dates of disorderly conduct and of strong-armed threats.

But in June of '67, Judy had never heard of any of them. What she knew was that she could not be alone, nor could she deal with any business problems or financial pressures; and Luft was there by her side assuring her that if she signed the paper he was handing her, she need not worry about anything except her performances. Her desire to trust him overriding her sensibility, she signed.

One is inclined to believe that Judy's respect for authority and the law compelled her to be as truthful as memory permits in her deposition. Presuming that to be so, the contents of the fifteen pages that were placed before the page containing Judy's signature (on which appear only Judy's and Luft's signatures and one sentence – 'In witness whereof, the parties hereto have executed this agreement as of the day and year first above written') constitute a diabolical travesty of personal rights. They contain twenty-six clauses, each of them designed to rob Judy of any rights in her own career, no matter what path that career might take. She was, from the date of the contract, owned by Group V in a prohibitive and exploitative fashion – was chatteled to a group of suspect men whom she did not even know.

The Group V contract had Judy sign away all rights in and to not only her services as a performer but 'any and all incidents, dialogue, characters, action, material, ideas and other literary, dramatic and musical material written, composed, submitted, added, improvised, interpolated and invented by Garland pursuant to this agreement' and granted the Corporation without limitation rights to 'transmit, publish, sell, distribute, perform and use for any purpose, in any manner, and by any means, whether or not now known, invented, used or contemplated (specifically including, but not limited to), by means of motion pictures, radio, television, televised motion pictures, printing or any other similar or dissimilar means all or any part of the matters and things referred to in this article.'

In Clause 13 of the contract Judy is denied the right of free speech:

Garland will not at any time without the Corporation's prior written consent issue or authorize the publication of any news stories or publicity relating to her employment hereunder or to the Corporation . . .

But perhaps one of the most bizarre clauses in the agreement is Clause 17:

As used in this agreement, the term 'incapacity' shall be deemed to refer to any of the following events occurring at any times during the term of this agreement: the material incapacity of Garland arising out of her illness or mental or physical disability or arising out of any accident involving personal injury to Garland; the disfigurement, impairment of voice or any material change in the physical appearance or voice of Garland, the death of Garland; and the prevention of Garland from rendering services by reason of any statute, law, ordinance, regulation, order, judgment or decree.

Garland will give the Corporation written notice of her incapacity within twenty-four (24) hours after the commencement thereof, and if she fails to give such notice, any failure of Garland to report to the Corporation as and when instructed by the Corporation for the rendition of her required services hereunder may, at the option of the Corporation . . . be treated as Garland's default.

This meant that Judy would be held responsible for any loss of income to the Corporation if she could not fill a commitment because of, for instance, a stroke, or any serious and sudden illness, and that her estate would be held responsible in the case of her death unless a twenty-four-hour notice could be given!

When Judy signed the Group V contract she was hopeful that some of her problems would be solved by its existence. Instead, from that date to the end of her life, it was to cause her privation, humiliation, and a shattering of her self-dignity.

CHAPTER THIRTY-FIVE

HER world was now a sky crowded with dark and threatening clouds. When one came close enough, the clouds were seen to be clusters of maggots. They swarmed about her in the nighttime because she had come to be a nocturnal creature. Not that she liked the night. She feared it with such an intensity that she could not sleep until it had passed; nor could she be alone – or in the dark. All night, wherever she was, the lights would blaze and the radio would blast and there would be people making her drinks she seldom touched, drinking her liquor, milling about, feeding their own convoluted dreams on her desperation.

Liza was living with Peter Allen in an apartment in central Manhattan. Her career was zooming ahead and she was very much occupied. But Luft, on the road again as Judy's manager, did not complain if she kept Lorna and Joey. Liza has said of her early years that it was difficult to know who was mother and who was daughter. The pattern was repeating itself with Lorna, whose maternalism overlapped her mother's and encompassed her younger brother. In 1966–67 they really had no home and were constantly on the move from one hotel to another. Judy still controlled the mortgage on the Rockingham Drive house, but its ownership was in serious jeopardy.

Mickey Deans came into her life as early as 1966, though they did not get together until more than a year later. Deans was managing Arthur, the fashionable discotheque owned by Sybil (the ex-Mrs. Richard) Burton. He had been a pianist at Jilly's, a well-known local bar that had always attracted famous theatrical personalities. He was a good musician, very personable, an ardent conversationalist with a winning small-boy smile – the kind that said, *Yeah ma, I'm guilty, but I love you and I didn't mean to do it!* He was very ambitious. Perhaps his job at Arthur was tough for him to accept in view of his showbiz ambitions; but he fed upon the knowledge that he was where the action was – and he was able to meet the top celebrities and entrepreneurs in New York City.

His world was also a nighttime world, a world of wild music and frenetic sound, of booze and pills, of theater people, gay people, prostitutes, celebrities, musicians, the hangers-on and the con men. And his world did not shut down until four in the morning, at which time he was too wound up to go to bed.

In an article he wrote for *Look* magazine, Deans describes his first meeting with Judy at a time when Judy could not pull herself together to fly to a performance.

I first met Judy Garland in 1966. A mutual friend called me from the West Coast and asked if I would take an envelope to be delivered to me by a doctor over to Judy, who was in trouble at the St. Regis Hotel in New York.

236

I agreed, and a little later, a doctor dropped by Arthur, the discotheque I was then managing. He left a small package with me, and I took it to Judy. When I knocked on the door of the hotel suite, it was opened by little Lorna Luft. Behind her stood her brother Joey, eyes wide with fear and apprehension.

Judy stood across the room. Her hair was undone and obviously graying at the roots. She was wearing a cocktail dress but no shoes. In an attempt at graciousness, she started woozily across the room only to trip and fall across an ottoman. We both laughed, and this relieved the tension. As we smiled at each other, I heard Lorna telling Joey not to worry as this was the doctor.

I gave Judy the envelope, which contained 'ups', pep pills. She popped them into her mouth along with some of her own pills, pulled herself together and made the plane she had been in danger of missing.

Deans was not to see Judy again for quite a time, and by then she had blocked out the circumstances of their first meeting as she had been able to block out most of the unsavory day-by-day happenings in her life at this period. During the long, torturous months that were to intervene, she was, however, seldom alone. Luft and Alves, after the signing of the Group V contract, were at hand when a concert was imminent and during a performance. Bobby Cole had come back into her life as musical director, and he and his wife, Delores, were always on call. There were to be two semiserious romantic liaisons: with Tom Green, who also functioned as publicity assistant to Luft and Group V, and with John Meyer, who was likewise involved in publicity; there were those members of the Garland Cult who called themselves 'The Garland Group' and who lived vicariously and by any means, simply to be close to Judy; there were the various doctors who ministered to her; and there were members of her public relations firm.

In the spring of 1967, Judy came to New York and stayed at the St. Regis. It was a very joyous occasion: Liza and

Peter Allen were to be married. But also, she had been cast in the film version of the best-selling Jacqueline Susann novel *Valley of the Dolls*. The role she had signed to play was that of Helen Lawson, 'an aging queen of Broadway musicals who had the talent to get to the top – and had the claws to stay there.'

A press conference was arranged at the hotel by Twentieth Century-Fox, which was producing the film. 'So I'm cast in the part of an older woman,' Judy told the press. 'Well, I am an older woman. I can't go on being Dorothy for the rest of my life.'

John Gruen, interviewing her for the New York *Herald Tribune* in the chaotic shambles of her suite at dinnertime, asked her how she felt about being called a legend. 'If I'm a legend, then why am I so lonely?' she shot back.

He observes:

> ... She stood rail thin, her sleeveless black dress emphasizing the thinness. Her face is gaunt; the eyes enormous. There is electricity in her presence, but she seems disconnected just now. She reels around a bit, her speech comes in splutters, but she is cheerful, friendly, apologetic for the mess ...
>
> ... Suitcases are open on the beds. Clothes hang from hangers or lie on chairs and couches. Phonograph records, mainly of Judy and Liza, are strewn around the room, there are flowers, letters, bills, messages, photographs and empty glasses on the various tables of the three room suite.

She had just heard the news that the banks had foreclosed the mortgage on her Rockingham Drive house and her furniture and private possessions were in danger of being lost. The news had come while Gruen was interviewing her. 'Well,' she joked nervously, 'if worse comes to worse, I can always pitch a tent in front of the Beverly Hilton and Lorna can sing gospel hymns! That should see us through. ... Lorna is already showing signs of becoming a fabulous singer.' She added, 'I think Lorna will make it very, very big one day.'

According to Gruen, Lorna, then fourteen, pale blonde and blue-eyed like her father, stood close at hand during the interview, as did eleven-year-old Joey, his dark, slender face shadowed with private concern. Liza, the Coles, Tom Green and assorted others were present. Judy was not shy about discussing the truth openly.

'Why should I always be rejected?' she inquired. 'All right, so I'm Judy Garland. But I've been Judy Garland forever. Luft always knew this, Minnelli knew it, and Mark Herron knew it.'

Judy left New York to continue work on *Valley of the Dolls*, accompanied by publicist Tom Green, who was being referred to as her 'fiancé'. From the very beginning, Judy felt accepting this role had been a mistake. The further she continued into the film, the more convinced she was. With an instinct that the film could do nothing for her career and that in the end it would be a commercial but dirty film, she decided to do what she could to get out of the contract. A curious dichotomy of values and morals guiding her actions, she refused to appear on the set when she felt that a scene was either dirty or that she did not believe the dialogue. There followed accusations that these 'delays' were caused by her drug addiction and her drunkenness. It certainly was true that she was as reliant as always upon the pills (she was not drinking, however) and that the daytime work schedule of a film caused a difficult imbalance to her nervous system, but Judy, unless physically incapable (and a translation of this phrase would mean *totally unable to stand on her feet*), could always fulfil a commitment if the drive – the true desire – was there.

Having relied on others in the decision that she appear in *Valley of the Dolls*, she had been guilty of not reading the script until the cameras were ready to roll. When she did, she was appalled. 'That very strange Jacqueline Susann doesn't seem to know any words with more than four letters,' she commented, adding, 'I just can't stomach it.' And the night before she was to shoot her first scene, she tersely said of Helen Lawson (her role), 'That broad has a dirty mind.' After the scene, which involved a confrontation with Patty Duke as Neely, she cracked, about Miss Duke, 'That broad has a dirty mouth.'

She wanted a release from her contract, and since the studio refused to give it to her, she in turn refused to appear before the cameras. Finally, the studio was forced to fire her, paying her $40,000 in settlement and replacing her with Susan Hayward. (The film subsequently did very little for Miss Hayward's career.) She was also given the $5,000 sequined paisley pants suit that Trevilla had designed for her to wear in the film. The suit – which was as spectacular as it was heavy and almost painful to wear – was to become a major costume for all her future appearances.

Shortly thereafter, Judy signed the Group V Ltd. contract and Luft booked her on a backbreaking musical tent tour during the hot months of June and July, ending with a stand at the Westbury, Long Island Music Fair, where the box office took in a record-breaking $70,000 in six days.

On July 31, 1967, Judy, under Luft's auspices, appeared for the third time at the Palace in a Group V Ltd. production called *Judy Garland, At Home at the Palace*. It was a family affair. The program proclaimed that 'During the course of Miss Garland's performance she will introduce her protegés, Lorna and Joey Luft.' Luft's staff included Vernon Alves, Assistant to the Producer, and Tom Green, Director of Public Relations for Group V Ltd. Appearing with Judy were the immortal black vaudevillian John Bubbles (the original Sportin' Life in George Gershwin's *Porgy and Bess*), who had shared the bill with Judy when she had appeared at the Met; comedian Jackie Vernon; and a former Ringling Brothers–Barnum & Bailey Circus star, Francis Brunn.

She entered from the back of the theater in the now-famous sequined pants suit, looking fragile (she weighed ninety-six pounds), 'jogging down the aisle, hugging admirers, shaking hands and just plain shaking' (*Time*, August 18, 1967).

'This is going to be an interesting performance,' she told her audience from the stage in a hoarse voice, 'because I have absolutely no voice. But I'll fake. Oh well, maybe I'll hit the notes because you're so nice and because it's so good to be home.'

'I love you, Judy,' screamed a man from the balcony. 'I love you too,' she called back. Then, moving to stage center, looking like some lost but beautiful blue jay on that vast stage, and singing in a warm and certain lower register, she opened the show with 'I Feel a Song Coming On'. It ended in a powerful crescendo, and after the wild applause quieted she laughingly commented, 'My! I'm a loud lady!' She struck a saucy hands-on-hips pose. 'No crooner I,' she added.

Later in the program she asked the audience, 'What should I do now?'

Again shouts from the balcony and a man's voice, 'Just stand there, Judy.'

'I get too scared to stand here,' she replied. 'Guess I'd better sing.'

And sing she did, belting out the old favorites, bringing a terrible intensity to songs like 'The Man That Got Away' and a moving poignancy to 'Over The Rainbow'. She was in rare form – much of the old Judy was on display – and there were shrieks and bravos when she made her first exit. 'Don't ever go away,' her audience shouted. She cried as she lifted the mike from the stand and held it trembling and close to her mouth, brushing tears away from her cheek with the other hand. She looked totally drained, ill, her cheeks flushed as if with fever. The costume she wore appeared to have become intolerably heavy for her and she to have shrunken inside it; the flashing sequins in the spotlight made one think of a lizard about to shed its skin.

'Thank you, God bless, I love you very much,' she said in a croaking, tired, emotionally spent voice. The audience began its surge forward, reaching out for her tenderly, as if to touch the last frail leaf of November.

'Audiences have kept me alive,' she confessed, and then leaning in close, confiding, 'everything I want is right here,' she told them.

In the audience that night and seeing Judy for the first time was nineteen-year-old Edward Baily III. He was a young man on the edge of despair. He had not been a dedicated Garland fan, had never seen her in concert, but he had heard her on records. Somewhere about midway in her performance he says, 'I don't know what happened – but I was hooked.'

After the show he raced around to the stage door, where about two hundred other Garland fans were gathering, standing there until two in the morning, when Judy left the theater. He drew back so that she wouldn't see him, feeling she must not think of him just as a fan.

Judy had been in good form that night, and though one could not say either the performance or the audience had risen to the evangelical frenzy they had at the Carnegie Hall concert, still the divine winds of revelation seemed to sweep from the stage to the last balcony of the Palace that night. Baily uses the word 'hooked' as one might refer to an introduction to a drug or to a religion. He had gone to the theater as one might, in desperation, approach the tent of a faith healer – and for him, the miracle had occurred. Having never seen Judy in a film, Baily's sole identification was with a middle-aged woman more than twice his age. Judy, by seeming to be able to see past all exteriors and into the soul, became the fantasy mother of his dreams. From the moment he became 'hooked' he had been at-the-ready to do her bidding.

At the Palace stage door, Baily met, for the first time, the Garland Group. He and they were an instant brotherhood. Standing together for hours in the hot night waiting for Judy, they shared thoughts and confidences. Baily was immediately taken in, made au courant with all of Judy's trials, and apprised of all the 'members of her court'. According to

242

Baily, it was implicit that one treated all of Judy's round table with as much persuasive charm as could be mustered. What Baily had found was an adhesive, conjunctive, symbiotic relationship that encompassed all the members of the Garland Group and Judy as well. For the first time in his life he felt accepted, a part of a family.

When Judy did leave the theater that night, Baily was moved by her smallness, her apparent exhaustion. He knew he was now pledged to remain close to her and that he must both cheer her and protect her at the same time.

CHAPTER THIRTY-SIX

'I CAN live without money,' Judy said, 'but I cannot live without love.' That was the symbology beneath the public announcements of 'enduring love' for all the young men who shared her last years. It was like shouting, 'I am not afraid!' as loudly as she could in a cavern of echoing darkness. By loudly proclaiming, 'I am loved; I am in love,' Judy could, for short periods, convince herself that this was the truth.

In her public disapproval of Arthur Miller – 'I don't approve of Arthur Miller,' she had stated to the press, 'because I don't think he understood Marilyn Monroe very well' – she revealed the true raison d'être for each disenchantment. She had finally come to believe that Mark Herron did not understand her. Now she was certain that was true about Tom Green.

There was a great deal of newspaper coverage involving some rings that Judy claimed Green had stolen. It is more likely that Judy had given him those rings when she was in a drugged state and that at a later date, feeling misunderstood, could not recall giving him the jewelry. The problem was

243

finally resolved out of court, but the Green-Garland liaison was over. According to Judy it had never been an important relationship, but the twenty-nine-year-old Green had been a steadying influence for over six months, and members of the 'circle' and of the Garland Group claim Green was the only man they knew who had tried to wean her off pills. Judy was in the state she considered 'intolerable' – she was attempting to live without love. A new young man, John Meyer, entered the scene, but this too was never to become an intense or meaningful relationship.

One night, after a Palace performance and with Judy still dressed in the sequined pants suit, Bobby Cole took her to an elegant Manhattan restaurant – where she was refused admittance because, in those days, it was still considered a breach of etiquette for a woman not to wear a dress. She was more amused than angry, but she did not feel like going back to the hotel. Cole called Mickey Deans and asked if women in pants were permitted at Arthur. Deans told him to bring Judy right over and was waiting at the door when they arrived. Judy appeared not to recall that they had previously met and Deans did not remind her, but there was a warm and instant interchange between them; Deans sat with her until after four in the morning, although Arthur had closed hours before. But Deans was, at the time, deeply involved in another relationship, and although there was a mutual attraction, and they found they both liked and laughed at the same things (Judy was most struck by Deans's easy ability to laugh), a tacit understanding that the time was not yet right passed between them.

After the Palace there were a series of concerts across the country that Luft, acting for Group V Ltd., arranged. Early on, Judy became aware of the deal she had received. But there seemed no one to turn to and little she could do to extricate herself from the situation. For though quite often during this period her hotel bills were unpaid, she was being supplied with the necessary pills to feed her habit. Legally, there was no way to obtain twenty to forty pills a day, and Judy was incapable of dealing with the situation on her own.

But on the second night of a stand at the Back Bay Theatre in Boston, she refused to leave the hotel for the theater. Some two thousand fans were both disappointed and disgruntled. 'Too many things have happened in the past. I couldn't come,' Judy said to the press through a lawyer, Barry Leighton, but she did not elaborate, and Luft, with no apparent care about Judy's public relations, contradicted a statement by the theater management that Judy had been ill and made a point of declaring that he did not know why she did not appear and that '... my ex-wife was in good health the last time I talked with her, which was a few minutes before she was scheduled to appear at the theater.' What had really occurred was that Judy had become aware of the gross exploitation of her, due to the Group V contract and was questioning Luft on it. She was now demanding that Luft arrange to pay her before each appearance.

Throughout what was to be her last American concert tour the Garland Group was constant – traveling by any means possible to get to her concerts, cheering her on, waiting for her after the shows, remaining in the lobbies of her hotels as though on guard.

Ed Baily never missed one performance. He was, by now, totally dedicated to Judy, and even Judy was becoming aware of his dedication. It was, in fact, going to be impossible for her to be unaware of it, for at each performance Baily managed to have either yellow or pink roses (her favorites) delivered to the theater for him to carry up onstage and present to her at the end of the concert. She assumed Baily was a young man with some personal income that allowed him to 'travel with' her (Baily's phrase – and as explained by him, meaning on the same train or plane, stopping at the same hotel; but never in an authorized capacity or in the same company as Judy) and to overwhelm her with roses.

In one year's time Baily sent Judy $100,000 worth of roses. (Christmas, 1967, he had a large Christmas tree designed and made entirely of pink roses and presented it to her onstage.) He sent roses not only to Judy but to all those members of her entourage whom he felt he must win over in his bid to enter their private circle. Long-stemmed roses were then about $15 to $18 a dozen, and never did he present Judy with less than five dozen.

In late 1967 and early 1968, Judy's performances left a great deal to be desired – leading *Variety* to comment: 'Nagging question is how long can Judy Garland keep it up. How long does she want to? Audience affection and good will are there, but there can be a limit to how long folks will watch a well-loved champ gamble with her talent.'

She appeared to be down once more. She was booked into the Garden State Arts Center in Holmdel, New Jersey, from Tuesday evening, June 25, to Saturday evening, June 29. She had a new conductor, twenty-two-year-old Gene Palumbo, and Lorna and Joey were appearing with her along with a group called the Tijuana Brats.

She stepped out onto the immense outdoor stage with the four thousand people in the audience not knowing what to expect. It was hot and she was perspiring and in her 'sequined uniform'. She weighed ninety pounds and looked pale, but it was one of those evenings to be remembered. (Critics claimed it was her best performance in ten years.) She belted or caressed twenty songs and, according to *The Asbury Park Press*, '. . . carried a non-stop show with grace and charm, despite the moths buzzing around her face, the strings hanging from her sequined pants suit, and a too bright spotlight to which she complained, "No lady likes to be seen in that light!"'

The audience went wild and flocked to the stage at the end of each song; they jumped up and down on their seats; they screamed, 'Bravo!' and 'We love you!'

She pranced out onstage at the ten-fifteen opening with 'Once in a Lifetime'. Her short hair was drawn back behind her ears, only a stray lock falling on her forehead. Tucked into the loose neck of her glimmering suit was a shocking pink chiffon scarf, and her shoes each sported a matching rose. She wore mammoth crystal earrings and a matching knuckle-sized ring.

246

'As long as I have love I can make it,' she sang; and then afterward she told the audience: 'You're a marvelous audience; *I feel you*. I've been around so many years, and I've loved you all that time.'

Someone screamed, 'You still look great!'

'I don't want to look like Mount Rushmore,' she replied, 'just beautiful.'

Halfway through, she hopped up onto the piano for a drink. 'I don't want to break my image,' she croaked, excusing herself and offering a toast to the audience and to Palumbo.

She sang 'How Insensitive' sitting on the center-stage steps; did a soft-shoe dance with several limber Rockette kicks to 'The Trolley Song'. Her rendition of 'What Now, My Love' was tender; then she smashed into 'I'll Go My Way by Myself'. At the end, mountains of roses were carried up onstage to her by Baily. 'I'll take anything I can get!' she said. The audience then sang 'Happy Birthday' (it had been June 10 two weeks before), 'God Bless!' she called out – and finally disappeared.

The next day, she gave a very 'up' interview at her hotel, The Berkeley-Carteret, to *The Ashbury Park Press:*

> *How do you like singing outdoors?*
>
> 'I dont mind it, but I don't like it in the summer. The bugs, you know. They fly into my mouth.'
>
> *What do you do in that case?*
>
> 'You park the bug like this.' She tucks her tongue into one cheek.
>
> *How's your autobiography coming?*
>
> 'It's been quite a packed-in life. It will take years.'
>
> *Would you choose show business if you had your life to live over again?*
>
> 'No! It's a brutish business.'
>
> *Why do you attract a cult-like following?*
>
> 'Maybe I'm some kind of female Billy Graham.'
>
> *Are you going swimming here?*

'I'm afraid of water. I'm also afraid of flying,' she added.

How do you get around?

'Dogsled,' she joked.

Who are your favorite singers?

'Tony Bennett, Peggy Lee and Liza Minnelli!'

Your favorite food?

'Chicken, any way but fried, and ice cream cones. They never let me eat them at M.G.M.'

By night, a terrible storm had moved into the area. But the exterior turbulence was no more violent than the storm that was taking place in Judy's hotel room. She had just discovered that on May 19, Luft had assigned her Group V Ltd. contract to Howard Harper and Leon J. Greenspan as security for a debt. She was appalled, furious; she refused to step out of the hotel until she had it on paper that she would receive money for her performance (her salary was to be $1,500 nightly, plus a percentage of the gate). Knowing she would not budge otherwise, Luft, using a piece of hotel stationery and crookedly printing the words, drew up a letter agreeing to pass over to her the amount of $1,200 (holding $300 for federal taxes) each night *before* her performance.

Judy was, thereupon, given a $1,200 check and got up to go to the theater. Arriving late, during the height of the storm, she nonetheless managed to make it onstage, throwing her hands up to her face as she did, blinded by the lightning, deafened by the thunder.

'Well,' she said, gasping, 'We'll press on together.' But the storm grew louder and the rain fell more heavily. It was a losing battle; until the closing songs her performance lacked spirit, and she was painfully off-key. She told her audience that they had pulled her through. But on Thursday night even they did not appear to help.

She was suffering from an ulcerated sore on the sole of her foot. For Friday night's performance she steeled herself with a massive dose of painkillers. These plus her usual pill intake caused her to be heavily drugged. Yet the performance almost came up to that of her opening night, and her audience, unaware of her problems, went wild. Then, on Saturday, arriving thirty-five minutes late and appearing sluggish (the drugs again having taken their toll), she sat on the stage, attempting to sing most of her repertoire from that position, and because of the severe pain in her foot that the drugs now seemed unable to mask, she had to be helped to her feet by Palumbo. At ten-fifty, after twenty-five minutes of pure endurance, she collapsed violently in a heap on the stage and was rushed to a hospital.

She had received no injuries in her fall, but her foot was found to be seriously infected. Fearing blood poisoning, she returned to New York City, where Dr. Udall Salmon placed her in the Le Roy Hospital.

In her dressing room the night before her collapse, wearing a long, frayed blue terrycloth robe and chain-smoking menthol cigarettes, she had confessed to reporters that what she would like most of all was to star in a Broadway musical. It had been more than idle daydreaming. Hal Prince was casting the musical *Mame*, and Judy felt that she was perfect for the role. She embarked on a concentrated campaign and did, at least, seem to have Prince interested. For the next few months, winning the part was the most important thing to her. With the final realization that Angela Lansbury had the role (Miss Lansbury had supported her in *The Harvey Girls*), Judy then went on a campaign for the London *Mame*. Ginger Rogers won that role.

It is difficult to fathom how Judy thought she would have been able to sustain a strenuous musical like *Mame* night after night and for a long run; but it was easy enough to understand why she was attracted to the role. Mame, like herself, was a larger-than-life personality who raised a child under exceptional conditions. Mame was an aging eccentric with 'pizazz' and at the same time a lovable, loving woman.

Not getting *Mame* was a deep disappointment – a personal rejection. Everything in Judy's life, after that one

Hotel Berkeley-Carteret
ASBURY PARK, NEW JERSEY
PROspect 5-5000

JUNE 26, 1968.

It is hereby agreed that JUDY GARLAND
will be PAID her NIGHTLY SALARY
of $1500.00 minus $300.00 that must be
RETAINED for the INTERNAL REVENUE,
that amount being $1,200.00 BY 4:00 P.M.
EACH day of the entire engagement, that eng.
BEING AT THE GARDEN STATE ARTS CENTER, JUNE 25 – JUNE 29.
If MR LUFT is not AVAILABLE to
PAY MISS GARLAND, MR. JOHN LARSEN will
ADVANCE ABOVE SAID SUM to MISS GARLAND

MISS GARLAND'S ABOVE
MENTIONED SALARY will
BE PAID to MR WES
FULLER AT ABOVE
MENTIONED TIME NIGHTLY.
IF MR. FULLER is UN-
AVAILABLE, the money will
BE PAID thru MR.
CALUMBO or
MR. Gilsworth for MISS GARLAND

Sid Luft

John Larsen

for Garden State Arts Assoc. Inc.

shining night at the Garden State Arts Center, seemed to be falling apart. Her disillusionment with Luft was the most grievous thing she suffered.

She was ill, and following her hospitalization at the Le Roy Hospital she went to Boston (borrowing money from a close friend) to seek help at Peter Bent Brigham Hospital. She and Luft had had a final and irrevocable fight, and he had returned to California. She was between men. Humiliating things had happened to her. She had been locked out of her New York hotel, and all her clothes had been impounded for nonpayment of the bill by Luft. Baily and the Garland Group had found her huddled pitifully alone in the lobby. 'I'm Judy Garland and I don't even have a clean bra to my name,' she had wept.

Joey had returned to California with Luft; Lorna enrolled in the New York Professional Children's School ('I must have gone to about eight hundred schools,' Lorna says. 'Every place we went, Joey and I had to be put in school. I never had any friends as a child.') For the time of the last tour, Lorna and Joey had been with Judy. It had been a difficult, a bad time. What followed was worse.

Judy's health was failing quickly, and she was in desperate straits. Lorna, sixteen at the time, had been exceptionally close to Judy. She was incredibly reminiscent of Judy as a youngster: all show-biz out front, but insecure, frightened and withdrawn in reality. And although it was Liza who appeared to resemble Judy the most, Lorna had the essence, the vulnerability, the injured look so indelibly identified with her mother. There is no question that in the spring of 1968 Lorna was suffering. Judy begged her to join her in Boston, but Lorna finally decided to fly to California to be with Luft and Joey.

'Mama called again,' Lorna says in a *McCall's* interview, 'I told her I just could not come to Boston. She didn't understand. She kept asking "Why?" I said I wanted a life of my own.'

And so at the same age as Liza had been when she left

251

home, the youngster flew to the Coast. Judy was on a sinking ship without a captain, crew, or passengers. And she was very sick.

CHAPTER THIRTY-SEVEN

IF there is one allurement of the past, it is that it is the *past*. Judy was back in Peter Bent Brigham, old friend Kay Thompson supportive and close by; but it was as though her life had not been given notice that the curtain had fallen. With Luft three thousand miles away in California, Judy thought she might be able to cast him from her thoughts. But it was impossible. She was living in the most abject humiliation: penniless and dependent upon the kindness of friends; homeless – her furniture and personal possessions now impounded by an appalling assignment of the Group V Ltd. contract by Luft to Greenspan and Harper. Intense hostility bound her to Luft. Any dependence or sentiment was gone. There was no more lingering tenderness – no more 'romance that would not die'. It was dead and even difficult to recall what had killed it. Yet burial was hopeless. She blamed Luft. How she blamed Luft! But even more, she blamed herself. Vanity made her feel an equal sinner; ego gave her a gnawing conscience.

Pledged to appear at the Pavilion in Columbia, Maryland, on September 16 and 17; the Mosque Temple in Pittsburgh, Pennsylvania, on September 30; and at the Springfield Music Fair in Springfield, Massachusetts, on October 2 and 7, she was now aware that if she did appear she would receive no remuneration. And that if she did not she could be turned over like a piece of loan collateral (which she was) to Leon Greenspan and Howard Harper. For back in May, just previous to the Garden State Arts Center appearance, Luft and Raymond Filiberti had so desperately needed $18,750 that they had made an assignment of her contract to Harper and Greenspan.

It was to be one of the most controversial documents in her life. In it, Judy was 'assigned', 'sold', 'transferred', and 'set over' to Harper and Greenspan for the fee of one dollar, along with an old film script called *Born in Wedlock* and 'certain coal deposits located in the counties of Grundy, Scequatchie, Bledsoe, and Cumberland in the state of Tennessee.'

The specified ninety days had expired and Luft and Filiberti had not been able to repay the loan. On the twenty-eighth day of October in the Supreme Court of Westchester County, New York, Harper & Greenspan filed a Summons and Complaint against Group V Ltd. and Raymond Filiberti. Harper and Greenspan now wanted either their money or Judy Garland (also certain coal deposits in Grundy, Scequatchie, Bledsoe, and Cumberland, Tennessee, and the film script *Born in Wedlock!*). It is interesting that Leon Greenspan acted as his own notary public on the assignment and were it not so thoroughly chilling to think of a human being parceled and sold along with some coal deposits and a script with an inane title, the situation might have an essence of hard-core black comedy.

It was a bleak and cold New York autumn when she returned from Boston after the Springfield engagement – broke, terrified, and alone. Yet it was curiously like other times she had come to New York by herself. There had been the time she had left Minnelli and MGM – that was when she had met Luft. And there had been the January when she had left Luft and signed with Fields and Begelman. Each of those times she had found solace in walking the city streets alone, trying to find some true corner of her own identity. However, it was not as easy to walk now. She was weak. There were physical things happening to her that alarmed her. She was not steady on her feet. Her vision had grown dimmer. The nightmares and sleeplessness had returned. And though she was finally so painfully thin that she should

253

ASSIGNMENT

KNOW ALL MEN BY THESE PRESENTS, RAYMOND FILIBERTI and GROUP V LTD. with offices at New York, New York.

in consideration of the sum of ONE (($1.00) DOLLAR and other valuable consideration, to them in hand paid, the receipt whereof is hereby acknowledged, does hereby sell, assign, transfer and set over unto HOWARD HARPER and LEON J. GREENSPAN, all his right, title and interest in and to the property known as "Born in Wedlock" and certain coal deposits located in the counties of Grundy, Scequatchie, Bledsoe, and Cumberland in the State of Tennesse and; all right, title and interest in and to a certain contract made the 8th day of June, 1967 by and between GROUP V LTD. and JUDY GARLAND for the exclusive use of her services; and further that said properties have not been previously conveyed, assigned or pledged and that the contract with Judy Garland is in full force and effect and will not expire until June 8, 1969, the same having been extended until that date.

to be held in escrow until ninety (90) days from the date hereof which properties shall vest absolutely in said LEON J. GREENSPAN and HOWARD HARPER unless a certain note, a copy of which is annexed hereto and made a part hereof is paid in full with interest on or before said date.

IN WITNESS WHEREOF, said RAYMOND FILIBERTI and GROUP V LTD. have set their hand and seals this 17th day of May, 1968.

GROUP V LTD.

(Raymond Filiberti)   By: (Raymond Filiberti)
Raymond Filiberti   Raymond Filiberti - President

STATE OF NEW YORK : COUNTY OF WESTCHESTER : ss.:

On this 17th day of May, 1968, before me personally came RAYMOND FILIBERTI, to me known to be the individual described in and who executed the foregoing Assignment, and he acknowledged to me that he executed the same.

(Leon J. Greenspan)
Notary Public

have been able to eat what she wanted (she stopped at the carts of street venders and bought hot dogs she could not eat), solid food sometimes gagged her, and when she was able to eat it she would suffer excruciating stomach pains, accompanied by such extreme constipation that she found herself waking up on the floor of the hotel bathroom not knowing how long she had been lying there unconscious. Nor was she ever sure she would not come back to the hotel to find her belongings impounded. One possession – a mink coat – she wore constantly, loving the elegant feel of it. She had posed in it for Richard Avedon for an advertisement for Black Glama Mink, and afterward it had been presented to her.

She was fighting a game battle for the survival of her spirit and therefore tried to concentrate on those things that would 'get her through'. She read the Bible, learned long passages of it by heart; memorized some of Shakespeare's sonnets; and tried to 'get straight' all she could remember about her father. Frank Gumm, in fact, was occupying much of her thoughts. She related him to a feeling of gaiety and hope. In retrospect, it seemed to her he was the only man who had truly loved her.

Most family photographs had been lost in the impounding of her personal possessions through the years and by the gypsylike existence she had lived, and so she could not find a picture of him. For the first time in a number of years, she contacted members of the family. No one had a picture of Frank. It came to her as a shocking revelation that her only memory of her father was as a man who had looked younger than she now looked. He had been a laughing, fun-loving Irishman with a full head of dark hair and a lithe, graceful body. His image, however, seemed confused with other images: those of Tyrone Power, for one; Mark Herron; and now Mickey Deans.

Reverie kept bringing Deans to her mind. In the few times she had been with him she had been able to forget her troubles. His enthusiasm and laughter had been infectious. There had been a rapport. They had liked the same things, had had the same offbeat sense of humor, the same ability to be silly without embarrassment. He was thirty-four and that was young, for she was forty-six. But her father had died young, and she could recall how small and protected and female he had made her feel when he took her that first day to MGM; how he had walked right in and faced all those big-time executives; how he had *that* time defied Ethel; how he had looked at her in her dirty slacks and no makeup with dancing eyes that said, 'What do *they* know? I think you're beautiful' – how he had, indeed, made her feel beautiful.

She had spoken to Deans from Boston. She rang him again on her return to New York, and they began to see each other. The last man in her life had now appeared. Being Judy, she was to believe and to publicly state that he was the true love of her life.

Deans was born Michael DeVinko in Garfield, New Jersey, on September 24, 1934, the youngest of three children in a Greek-American family. His father was a textile worker who had a hard time supporting the family. Deans hated the smalltime, lower-class life in Garfield. His only thought from the time he hit his teens was to leave it. Good-looking and with an outgoing personality, he was certain he could make it in show business if he had the opportunity.

When he was fourteen he took the $35 he had earned working in an appliance store near the small DeVinko house and bought an upright piano with fourteen broken keys. His father forbade him to bring it into the house, but his sister spoke up in his defense. All the living-room furniture had to be crowded together to make room for it. The piano was impossible to play in the condition it was in. Deans, therefore, went to a professional tuner and talked him into allowing him to apprentice until he could learn how to fix and tune the old upright himself, continuing to work afternoons and weekends to pay for classical lessons and for a television set. He deemed the set an important addition to his training, studying the performers on the small screen as assiduously as he had observed the piano tuner. Ethel had done much the same thing in that old movie house in Grand Rapids.

256

By sixteen he felt he could make it on his own in the jazz world, left home, and began a long line of small-time club 'gigs' – Club Lee in Fort Lee, New Jersey; the Jungle Club in Union City; The Tender Trap in Fairview. It was a nomadic, nighttime world. He was young and ambitious and tough enough not to care what was happening around him or to him if it meant steamrolling himself to his final goal: a club date in New York. People moved into and out of his life, but he had learned how to chop things off, how to keep his eye leveled on the main goal.

Then came Jilly's. He got his first close-up view of the 'bigtimers'. They came while he played and talked through his sets and never really saw him through the dense clouds of cigarette smoke. He knew club playing was not what he wanted. He had to be out front, where the action was – where the stars were.

From Jilly's he went to the Tenement in New York, then traveled out to Harold's Club in Reno, Nevada, hating what he was doing; feeling servile ('Play "*Melancholy Baby*" '), rootless, losing back his pay to the casinos where he was the 'bar pianist'. The years passed. He wasn't sure how he was going to do it, but he was determined to make a pitch for the 'big time'.

He had heard about Judy Garland, seen a concert of hers in Newark, New Jersey; but her music had not reached him. He was still very much a part of the jazz world. When he thought about her, it was in neons. He admired her star status and understood her use of pills.

No photographs of him in the late sixties do him justice. They are static, and Deans never was. Not handsome in the general sense, he had incredible charm, a disarming boyishness for one so worldly, a strange symphysis of audacity, youth, and humility. Slim and vital, he stood in attitudes and gestured extravagantly. His eyes would dart, a smile break open his face; his laugh would roll out unrestrained, uninhibited. He paced a lot, drummed his fingers on static surfaces, doodled whenever he had pencil and paper, and used his hands whenever he spoke (language coming from him rat-a-tat-tat; ideas, words shot out before being carefully aimed). His voice was deep-timbred, words were mumbled or jumbled, but the flow did not stop. Occasionally he would sing at the piano in an untrained voice, surprising his audience with an innate and creative sense of phrasing. He was natively intelligent, alarmingly sensitive, deeply emotional – the emotion playing hide-and-seek with the laughter revealed in his dark, rather myopic eyes. He had all the appearance of a downhill racer trying with all his lifetime experience to avoid a dangerous and sudden stop. As he reminded Judy so strongly of Frank Gumm, perhaps one can visualize through Deans a clearer picture of Judy's father fantasy.

When Sybil Burton opened Arthur, her idea was to create a club where performers, the famous, and the infamous would have a sense of 'grooving'. The decision was made to use young actors and musicians who wanted to be seen – as waiters.

Deans started as a captain and then became Night Manager. He liked the role, and found being on social terms with the star clientele exciting.

If Judy had blocked out the 'pill meeting', Deans had not. What had remained in his mind from that night at Judy's hotel was Lorna. 'Are you all right here alone with your mother?' he recalls asking her. 'I'm fine,' she replied grimly. There had been something painful in her face, he says; something old, yet still vulnerable in her straight and honest returning glance. It had made him feel sick, and he was glad when he reached the fresh air. He knew without questioning further that there had been many other semidark, middle-of-the-night strangers with pills; that the youngster had protected and cared for a 'stoned-out' mother many, many times, knew the symptoms, helped in finding the cure. And there was her 'wise mother' protection of the little boy. He was aware that Lorna had been playing this role from the age of no more than eight or nine. For all those years since then, Lorna had been a firsthand 'attender' to her mother's deep needs.

After that evening when they had talked until four in the morning at Arthur, Judy had sent Deans tickets to see her at the Palace. He had attended; joked with Bobby Cole, who was a friend of his; but had not gone backstage to see Judy. She had come into the club a few times. Each time he had sat with her. Until her return from Boston they had not spent any time privately together. He was still involved in another relationship, but now she began to frequent the club, and Judy would say, as she did in her concerts, 'I don't ever want to go home, do you?' They'd have breakfast together would go shopping at five in the morning, and Judy, tiny as she was, would sit in the basket and Deans would push her around the all-night market, neither of them caring what anyone else thought.

Judy began to feel very secure. She saw Deans mostly at Arthur while he was at work and in command, greeting customers, handling crises, attending to her needs. She felt he was strong, and she liked the feeling of power he exuded. He did nothing to control her pill intake, but he did get her to eat, to sleep, to push aside terror. She was depending upon him a lot; she found he was a good musician, knew about lighting, had good taste in clothes, was tough, ambitious and audacious, and possessed the natural instincts of an entrepreneur. She told someone there was a bit of Mike Todd about him.

The phenomenon of Arthur was beginning to run its course. Everyone with an interest in the club began to blame the others, but the truth was that the parade had simply passed it by. The party was over, and yet all of Deans's efforts went into an attempt to keep it going. At the same time, he was seeing more and more of Judy; becoming more and more enmeshed in her world, her life; trying to help her at least get back on her feet. He was with her when she appeared on the Merv Griffin show (as was Margaret Hamilton, the witch in *Oz* and her old 'friend'); the Johnny Carson show as well. He felt she could come back, could even make it financially big again. He was enough of a musician to also realize her voice and endurance were shaky, but

259

astute enough to be aware that the ring of stardom to her name could allow her to cash in on side benefits. It was these side benefits – ventures in which her name would sell a product – that he believed would bring her back into the big chips. He had an idea for miniaturized cinemas to be called The Judy Garland Theaters: that was a first step.

She signed a new contract for recording and was offered a month's engagement at the first-class theater restaurant The Talk of the Town in London. She had told him nothing about the Group V Ltd. assignment, and so he convinced her she should take it, but Luft had her musical arrangements and refused to release them without a sizable figure's being paid for them. Deans told her to 'tell Luft to fuck it! I'll get you new arrangements.'

It led to her hopefully suggesting he accompany her to London and help her organize the show. They were in Arthur. It was four in the morning. The place reeked of stale liquor and burnt-out cigarettes. It was time to close up, go home; but neither really had a home to go to – for Judy was staying at a hotel, and Deans, up until that time, still shared an apartment, not having yet been able to break off his long-standing old relationship.

'I suppose it would make more sense if we were married,' Deans says he told her. It was a curious proposal.

'You better not be kidding,' he reports Judy replied.

'I'm not kidding,' Deans assured her, and on December 28, 1968, they left New York together on a London-bound flight not knowing exactly what they had to do to get married, since Deans was a Catholic and Judy was divorced from Luft and not sure of her marital status with Mark Herron. The only thing Judy was sure of was that she felt alive and loved and hopeful with Deans. He helped her to forget the bad things and remember the good. She clung desperately to his arm as they climbed aboard their flight. They traveled first-class, VIP. Deans had arranged it. He held her in his arms as the plane lifted off the ground. It was the first time in her life that she had not been afraid of flying.

Part Five

I've been around and seen the sights
And of this I'm sure
Yes, you're the one
I've waited for.
You'll be the one to last
I've had this feeling
Once on thin ice
But that's over, the past
Then was then
And Now is now
For you'll be the one to last
I've tried before
I'll try no more
No need to try again.
You were the one worth waiting for
I've found my where and when . . .

Unfinished lyrics
By Judy Garland
Written January 1969

CHAPTER THIRTY-EIGHT

THE plane nosed down through thick patches of fog, landing smoothly on a brightly lit runway at Heathrow Airport. A foggy London morning awaited them. More ominously, though, as Judy and Deans walked from the customs hall, they were greeted by Keith Cockerton, a private detective representing solicitors Lawford & Co. Mr. Cockerton handed Judy a writ claiming that Harper & Greenspan now owned exclusive use of her services and that an application for an injuction had been filed to restrain her from opening at The Talk of The Town two days later (Monday, December 30, 1968).

Judy, defying Luft and disregarding any contractual agreement with Group V, had signed two contracts – one with Raymond Nesbitt of Theatre Restaurants, Ltd., for her appearances at The Talk of The Town; the other with Blue Records, Inc., for an album that was to be cut in the spring of 1969 (for this she received a $1,000 advance payable directly to her) – using John Meyer's New York address as her mailing address. The vultures were now hovering for the feed.

The law firm of Lawford & Co., acting on behalf of Harper & Greenspan, had, in fact, delivered by hand to Nesbitt on the twenty-fourth of December a letter setting forth the legal situation between Group V and its client, closing the letter with the following paragraph:

We must ask you to undertake *not* to engage Miss Garland as arranged. Failing such an undertaking from you before 10 A.M., Friday, December 27th, we shall apply to the Vacation Judge for an injunction restraining you and

Miss Garland in the show 'Fine Feathers', or indeed in any other show without our clients' prior consent. To protect our clients' position we have already taken an appointment with the Vacation Judge (Mr. Justice Magarry) for 2:15 p.m. on Friday, 27th December. For the same reason we are immediately issuing a writ which we will endeavour to serve on you later today.

Yours faithfully,
LAWFORD & CO.

Nesbitt and his associate Bernard Delfont, having consulted their solicitors, Paisner & Co., and believing Harper & Greenspan had no legal case to restrain Judy from working in England, elected to reject Lawford & Co.'s warning and to back Judy against Harper & Greenspan in the court action – rescheduled for December 30 when it was made known that Judy would not arrive until December 28.

The writ was a shock to Judy. She should, of course, have sought out legal counsel in New York when she first found out about the Group V assignment. However, with the same kind of naiveté that guided almost all her actions, she had assumed that a legal document drawn in the United States would not be binding in England. The limousine ride with Deans to the Ritz, where they were to stay was, therefore, not the joyous experience she had hoped it would be. She had been looking forward to their arrival in London, wanting to share with Deans her great love of London, wanting him to see it through her eyes and fond experiences.

As Judy was awed by authority and greatly intimidated by her own deep sense of guilt, the thought of a court appearance terrified her more than it was possible to imagine. She felt 'on trial'; and the guilt she suffered from her addiction to the pills; the fact that Deans, not Joey and Lorna, sat next to her in the car; the fact that Ethel had died alone – one could travel far back into her past on her private guilts – all seemed to be evidence against her. She clung to Deans in the back seat of the luxurious car, begging him to reassure

her that everything would be all right – which he attempted
to do.

When they arrived at the cold, gray stone facade of the
grand old Ritz Hotel, the manager stood in the lobby await-
ing their arrival. When he saw her come through the re-
volving doors with Deans, he started down the lobby steps
to greet them. For a brief moment his English reserve
slipped, for he was unprepared for 'the incredibly tiny,
birdlike creature, huge floppy hat dwarfing her tiny face,
short skirt exposing toothpick legs'. Yet as she entered,
gripping her companion's arm as though unable to navigate
otherwise, he had known that it was, indeed, the legendary
Garland. She had thrown her head back to glance up at him
over the top of the massive staircase that rose from the entrance to the lobby. There had been a gesture, the wide eyes,
a familiar laugh. He rushed to greet her and welcome her
back to the Ritz. Then he led her up the staircase and across
the impressive expanse of the lobby, past the spectacular circular staircase that rises above the cavernous center well,
to the lifts, continuing up with them to the fourth floor,
where they were to occupy one of the two best suites in the
hotel.

Deans was outwardly impressed with the hotel, the suite,
the personal service, but to Judy it was another suite in still
another hotel, and after the manager had left, she complained that there was nothing more depressing than 'old
grandeur' – everything seeming shaded, tainted, much used,
and almost dingy to her. To compound the nervousness
caused by the impending court action, she confessed that she
could not control her feeling of 'shabbiness' when the manager had shown them into the suite, knowing they were unmarried and would be living there together.

However, the suite contained two bedrooms, a huge
white-tiled bathroom, and a commodious sitting room. The
large bedroom (Judy used the smaller one for a dressing
room) overlooked Piccadilly, as did the sitting room, and all
the sounds of midday London could be heard through the
sealed windows. If Judy had seemed overpowered in the

huge lobby of the hotel, she must have appeared to be a shrunken 'Alice Through the Looking Glass' in that bedroom. The room was fourteen feet tall, painted entirely in white, with great, ceiling-high mirrors lining one entire wall; a cavernous fireplace, unused for years, along another wall, over which hung a gargantuan gilt-framed mirror. The furniture was all antique white, and on the polished wide-planked floors was an antique, but once elegant, red Persian rug.

Those beds – they were the first thing that had caught Judy's eye as she entered the suite with the master-bedroom door standing open off the entranceway. They were the highest, largest beds she had ever seen, making it impossible for her to get into one without jumping up, as a child might do. The massive brass frames were cold to the touch, and the great rose satin quilt slippery.

Deans remembers Judy that day sitting rather stiffly on the sitting room's most elegant unyielding antiquity: a rigid well-preserved Regency sofa that faced still another bank of mirrors, still another open, unused fireplace; looking around her.

'We'll be married very soon?' he says she asked him.

'Monday, if British law permits,' he assured her.

That was December 30, the same day she was to go to court to answer the restraining writ. Deans got busy on the telephone. Plans were made first with Paisner & Co., who were representing Nesbitt, to represent her interests as well. She was asked to make a legal deposition in the presence of the Court Recorder, which she did.

His Lordship, Mr. Justice Magarry, was a well-seasoned and peppery man of few words and fast actions. As evidence he had the writ, Judy's deposition, The Group V Ltd. contract, the Group V Ltd. assignment and the promissory note Filliberti had given Harper & Greenspan. After listening to both sides and giving long consideration to the evidence he had in hand, His Lordship glanced down from the bench and in a voice edged with both amazement and disdain declared in no uncertain terms, 'This transaction is one which

266

I would not enjoin a dog,' caustically adding, 'Certainly, I would not enjoin Miss Garland.'

Then he dismissed the case, but not before publicly reprimanding all those in the action who had attempted 'to use the courts to implement their own base activities' and making Harper & Greenspan responsible for the sizable court costs of about £1,000 (approximately $2,600 at that time). The plaintiffs (Harper & Greenspan) had the right to appeal against the decision and, winning that, could seek an order for a speedy trial. But as Paisner & Co. explained to Judy, it was unlikely, owing to:

1. The time factor; all that would take more than the five weeks of her engagement with The Talk of The Town, allowing her to complete the appearance without interruption.

2. The question of costs; since the plaintiffs lived outside the jurisdiction of the English courts, the Court was entitled to ask for an order that they must lodge funds or provide security for the likely costs of the action. (Paisner & Co. immediately made application for such an order.)

3. The attitude of the British court; the fact that the judgment against the plaintiffs had been a very strong one based very much on matter of law, rather than on evidence, would make it a very difficult task for the plaintiffs to persuade a court of appeal to rule in their favor.

It seemed (and was) unlikely that Harper & Greenspan would proceed any further. Ridding herself of the Group V Ltd. contractual machinations was certainly one of Judy's most triumphant legal encounters, but the unsavory aspect of the episode, the loathing she now felt for Luft, the bitter feelings she harbored of the past were a high price for her to pay.

Before even leaving the court, Judy reminded Deans of his promise to see what he could do about obtaining a license to wed. She wanted to be married immediately; certainly she did care for Deans, but at least in her eyes, a new marriage would be closing of a door to the past. However, according to California law, where her divorce decree against Mark Herron had been filed, no divorce was absolute until the final papers had been picked up. Herron had, so far, neglected to do this. Added to this complication was an English law requiring a two-week waiting period before a foreigner could be legally wed.

Judy and Deans returned to their suit, and Deans called Herron in California. Herron promised he would pick up the papers. Still, there was little chance of their marrying for several weeks. The joyousness of the morning's victory was somehow dimmed, even though *The Evening News* came out with an early headline:

JUDGE TELLS JUDY:
CARRY ON SINGING!

adding the terse subheading:

AMERICANS' BID TO STOP SHOW
IS THROWN OUT OF COURT

and with the very conservative *Financial Times* commenting: 'For once the law has been anything but an ass.'

Judy and Deans ate a quiet dinner in their suite, and then Judy dressed for her opening night at The Talk of The Town.

The Talk of The Town might be called London's Copacabana. It is an immense restaurant-nightclub, holding well over a thousand people, serviced by massive kitchens and bars. There is a vast balcony as well as the huge main floor with its wide stage, full orchestra, and commodious dance floor. Every six weeks there is a new 'spectacular', with beautiful showgirls and elaborate costumes and sets, but, as well, impresario Delfont always manages to lure the crème de la crème of the entertainment world. Judy was following such greats as Lena Horne, Shirley Bassey, Tom Jones, Tony Bennett and her own daughter Liza Minnelli.

The lovers were met at the stage door by Glyn Jones who

was Delfont's 'ambassador'; his task was to assist Judy for the length of her run. They made their way past the mammoth backstage area, ascending the rear stairs to the first level, where the star's dressing room was situated to their left. On the right was a small sitting room with a bar where people could wait to see her. The two rooms formed a 'star suit'.

The club's resident makeup artist, Vivian Martyne, was waiting for Judy in the flower-packed dressing room. She offered to remove some of the bouquets, but Judy insisted they all be left. As Ed Baily had known, she loved flowers, adored receiving them. They were notes of love to her. Kidding she would say, 'When I die I want my casket to look like it's in a dressing room before an opening performance.'

With the exhaustion of the trip and the problems of the writ, Judy had only one rehearsal with Burt Rhodes, the musical director. Deans had met with him first, discussing with him the problem of the missing arrangements. Deans gave him the Carnegie Hall album and from that, and in forty-eight hours, Rhodes had rescored eight numbers. What was never taken into consideration was that Judy's physical condition had altered her stamina and her range since the Carnegie Hall concert. The numbers were arranged, therefore, in the keys she had sung in nearly a decade past. Some notes (especially the last in 'Over the Rainbow') were going to be almost impossible now for her to reach.

That evening (Saturday night) Rhodes went to the Ritz to meet Judy for the first time. He had seen her perform in '54 when she had been in one of her heavy periods, and he was staggered when he was led into her sitting room, unable to believe this tiny, frail figure was Judy Garland. He had thought he had covered his surprise and that they had hit it off very well. Early Monday afternoon there was a rehearsal at the club but Judy appeared unsteady on her feet and unable to sing at all, complaining she had a cold. Rhodes sat with her in the outer room of her suite and they talked about tempos as she watched workmen put up some red-flocked wallpaper. Judy was always putting personal touches into her dressing rooms. She loved the color red, even though she was not too fond of red roses, and often had red carpeting installed in her dressing rooms. In her *Valley of the Dolls* dressing room she had a pool table sent in, claiming pool was her current passion, but actually picking up a cue only once or twice.

Rhodes had been very concerned. He did not see how she could be expected to perform without benefit of rehearsal and under the conditions forced upon them (the lack of proper arrangements, etc.). But at eleven-fifteen Judy was dressed and walked onstage to an overwhelming ovation. At front tables sat Ginger Rogers (in London for *Mame*), Danny LaRue (England's greatest female impersonator), David Frost, and Johnnie Ray. Greeting them happily, Judy launched into her opening number 'I Belong In London', and proceeded to forget all the lyrics. Rhodes believing he was helping, prompted her. As Judy preferred confessing her lack of memory to an audience rather than covering it up, it irritated her that Rhodes interfered. A difficult relationship was thereupon begun and, unfortunately, was to continue throughout the run of the show. From that opening moment Judy seemed set on creating havoc in the programming, switching her numbers around at random, and bringing LaRue onstage to sing an unrehearsed song. The audience, assuming it was all part of the show, loved it, and when at the end she sat down at the edge of the stage to sing 'Over the Rainbow', confessing to her audience, 'We've been through a lot,' they gave her a tremendous ovation. The single spotlight was on her painfully thin and aging face. 'I may croak a bit,' she told them and then with some amazement added, 'You know, they tell me this is the twelve thousand three hundred and eightieth time I've sung this song!' Never had she sung it with more emotion, and never had it seemed to have more meaning. Derek Jewel in *The Sunday Times* had this to say about the performance:

Time has ravaged her singing voice. Within a certain

range of scale, tone, and volume it survives – most beautifully in a downbeat arrangement of 'Just In Time'; outside that range, the vibrato is wild and uncontrolled, the pitch uncertain. At times she needs to sing very artfully indeed to disguise the flaws.

But the singing is not so important as the tension and the compulsive gamble of the entertainment. For an hour she conducts a ritual whose contrasts would unhinge most performances. She moves around endlessly, with quick nervous gestures, darting uncertainly to her musical director or the glass on the piano. She bathes the ringside in schmaltz, kissing her admirers, dropping names, tempting applause to dry up. She mixes sharp cracks – 'I'm going to do something extraordinary. Not only am I going to appear . . .' (uproar) 'but I'm going to sing a new song' – with indistinct mumbling. Pert professionalism collides with urchin gaucherie.

That her first-night audience, even discounting its preponderantly showbiz nature, gave her so rapturous a reception is still not completely susceptible of explanation, but I will try.

She is a legend, and legends are revered. Yet her secret is partly that she makes fun of the legend, the songs, herself and her image, even the audience. Somehow, too, she has never grown up. Her body, slim and supple in a trouser suit of bronze, is frail and girlish. Yet when she sits in a spotlight to sing, 'Over The Rainbow' she is not only Dorothy on the way to Oz but also a woman in her middle forties whom life has pummelled. The pathos is terrifying.

Above all, she stands for the immaculate nostalgia of a whole generation – Andy Hardy, Odeons on steamy afternoons, records of Glenn Miller and early Sinatra, girls next door. They don't write life like that anymore, and Judy Garland evokes it for all those who wish that someone would.

How like a movie script of the Forties it is that half of her music was lost before the opening. But it was all right.

271

Bandleader Burt Rhodes listened to her records and produced sparkling orchestrations inside forty-eight hours. They don't make many musicians like that any more either.

She proved that she still had the star quality, the magnetism – that she could control an audience to the extent of bending all the rules to indulge herself; but in her heart she was scared. She could not be alone and insisted Deans be by her side as much as possible, bringing him onstage to introduce him (she would end the lyric of 'For Once in My Life' with 'For once in my life I have Mickey, who needs me'); had him tape her performances, which ensured he would be backstage when she came off; and before she would step out on stage she would say to him, 'Make me laugh.' To each interviewer she loudly proclaimed her love, her happiness. One interviewer indiscreetly asked her about her health. 'Listen, if my number comes up, I'll draw another' she retorted, as she clung to Deans.

Deans liked to think of himself as a swinger, and he thought it would be distracting and good for Judy to change her image. He took her to Carnaby Street, selecting mod clothes for both of them, buying everything in sight, unable to carry all the packages back to the hotel. She listened hungrily to his plans, his promises, his quick enthusiasms. He never seemed to be intimidated by the future. She liked that. He bossed her around. She liked that, too.

But the anguish and guilt at not being able to have Lorna and Joey with her was growing, her bitterness toward Luft intensifying with the knowledge that though he was unstable, he was the more qualified of the two to be a parent at this time. And try as she might (and she did), she could not crush her dependence upon the pills. When she did cut her intake (she was then taking between twenty and thirty Ritalin a day and about eight Seconals to sleep), the withdrawal pains and the depression were unbearable.

Several nights after the Talk of The Town opening, Deans found her in a withdrawal stage, pills gone, the show only hours away. He contacted Glyn Jones, who in turn contacted a doctor who came up to the Ritz Suite believing it was Deans in need of medical attention. It took only moments for the doctor to zoom in on the true picture, though he did not see Judy at all. She was in the large bedroom, lying concealed in the dark, and Deans led him straight past the door and into the sitting room. He issued Deans a prescription for a small supply, not refillable without his knowledge, and left. Several hours later, he was called back. Deans asked him if he would accompany them to the club; the doctor this time met Judy, who had not yet overcome her unsteadiness from the withdrawal. He agreed to go with them.

This physician might be termed a specialist in show-business personalities, having treated many of them over the years. He is himself quite a theatrical personality, charming, witty, able to dispense a good joke along with his diagnosis. Having treated pill-addicted stars for years, he took the familiar course of making the pills available to Judy, but in measured amounts.

He was quite talkative as they drove in the limousine toward the club, telling her about Tony Hancock, the famous English comedian, who had also been a patient of his. 'Tony was a great fan of yours,' he confided. 'It seems rather ironic that less than a year ago we were riding in a car on the way to an engagement of his and he told me that of all the entertainers in the world, someday he hoped to do a show with Judy Garland. And here I am in a car with you and Tony is dead. He died in Australia, you know, only eight months ago. Suicide. Such a waste.'

'He's not dead,' the physician says Judy replied. 'A great entertainer doesn't really die.'

Then he reports that he stared at the figure seated in the semidark beside him, thinking 'she looks like a wizened little old monkey.' She weighed under ninety pounds, her eyes were too big for her face, her bones protruded sharply wherever flesh was exposed, and though she was enveloped in perfume (she had recently switched from *Joy* to *Ma Griffe*), there was a strong underlying body odor. The doctor asserts that she was suffering from malnutrition and that she was having problems passing anything through her colon. He wondered about a colonic obstruction, but he didn't press the matter. Though he did openly discuss her addiction.

'Do you understand anything about the pills you are taking, Judy?' he claims he asked, going on to explain: 'Ritalin is an antidepressant, an "up" as you say, but it's not an amphetamine. There are many amphetamines with brand names like Dexedrine, Benzedrine, etcetera. I will never, ever prescribe those for you and I warn you severely, *never take them*. They will kill you.'

'Don't you know any good jokes?' she countered.

The doctor reached back in his repertory and found one.

It was a tragedy that Judy was always fearful that a doctor might report her to the authorities as an addict, and so did not discuss her physical problems. Still it remains a great enigma how all those close to her allowed her to ignore her appalling health problems. True, Judy was extremely strong-willed, but she could be influenced by each of the successive men she loved. Most of them encouraged her to perform, reminding her of her old nagging, childhood guilt that not to perform was the worst degree of misbehavior. There were many reasons why Judy felt she must perform: she needed her audience; she was fearful of not getting her pills if she did not perform; she felt she must be the one to pay the bills; and she desperately needed the approval and attention of those close to her, and only performing could bring her that. If it dawned on her that she had an equal right to expect a husband or lover to support her, she never gave it full consideration. That might have gone back to the relationship with her father; for Frank Gumm – though thoroughly capable of supporting his family – had not stopped Ethel from singling Judy out as the one child who was expected to work. In order to rationalize Frank Gumm's behavior, it was not unlikely that Judy might feel she had to excuse all the other men in her life.

She was leaning heavily upon religion, reading the Bible whenever she was in sound mind, and in the final analysis, looked to God as one would to a husband or father. 'Hasn't He always looked after me and the kids?' she would say, and quote passages at random. The fact that she had never been married in a church caused her great concern. There was a young clergyman in London whom she had known and consulted in the past. Prevailing upon Deans, she arranged for him to meet this young man, The Reverend Peter Delaney, to see if they could be married in his church.

The minister, whose church was the same one in which Elizabeth Barrett and Robert Browning had been wed, felt that if all the legal problems of the divorce from Herron could be settled, there would be no reason why the two could not be married at St. Marylebone Parish.

Taking the Reverend Delaney with him, Deans went down to file a marriage application at Caxton Hall and to establish residence for the two-week waiting period required. He had already called Judy's attorney in California, Godfrey Isaac, and knew that Herron had not picked up the final papers. He now was told Herron would sign a letter stating that he (Herron) was not responsible for any taxes accrued during their marriage, as he had, at the time, signed a joint income-tax return.

This meant more delays. Judy was frantic, apparently frightened that something would inevitably keep them from marrying. Her apprehension grew more unreasonable when Deans received a letter from Arthur informing him that he was fired. Interpreting this news as a possible impetus that might return Deans to New York to settle his affairs, Judy pressed for a blessing of their union in Peter Delaney's church, rationalizing that vows exchanged in a church would necessarily be binding even if they were not legal marital vows, Reverend Delaney agreed to bless them.

That night Judy appeared radiant onstage. The watchman at the club had a large brown-and-white Alsatian dog that Judy had mothered each night. He could see that Judy was in love with the animal and told Deans he would like Judy to have the dog. Deans accepted the offer that night. It seemed a very special omen to Judy. She named the dog (his name had been Rags) Brandy, and brought him into her dressing room. The dog was bigger than she was. She hugged him around the neck constantly as she dressed and left him backstage as she went on.

She was ecstatic, making it difficult for Rhodes, changing the program as she went along, inviting thirty to forty members of the audience to sit on the edge of the stage as she sang. She was wearing a glittering white pants suit with a red ruff about her neck and silver slippers on her feet, and shook hands with everyone near to her like a Presidential candidate. Borrowing drinks and handkerchiefs, she exchanged witticisms with Rhodes and members of the audience. At one point, as Rhodes valiantly struggled to follow a new music cue she had just given him, she said, 'Now I'd like to do *Aida*.' It brought down the house.

After the show, like a sixteen-year-old going out on her first date, she took tremendous pains in dressing, deciding upon a long, soft blue-gray dress, demurely high at the neck and tight at the wrists, and wearing a string of pearls and pearl earrings that Tony Bennett had given her the Christmas before – keeping on the silver slippers, and using very little makeup.

They knelt before the altar that Elizabeth Barrett and Robert Browning had knelt before. Judy had wanted Deans to give her a ring, but he had not brought one. Reverend Delaney gave him one that had belonged to his grandmother. It was immense for Judy, but she put it on her middle finger and held her fingers tightly together so that it would not slip off. By three A.M. the blessing had been concluded and Judy and Deans had exchanged vows.

For the next ten days the show went quite well. Judy, overflowing with happiness and yet frustrated that she had promised to keep the blessing secret, gave revealing interviews about her love for Deans, wanting the world to understand how sincere their feelings were. 'I love him,' she told columnist Arthur Helliwell, 'and loving him means I no longer have to love the lights and the applause.'

Her health now took a dramatic turn. She contracted the flu, and her frail and undernourished body had great trouble fighting it off. Then the medication the doctor prescribed for the flu conflicted with her other pills and a near-toxic condition arose. This was Thursday, January 23, and as luck would have it, she was scheduled to appear that Sunday night as the star on the television variety series *Sunday Night at the Palladium*.

Her performances Thursday, Friday, and Saturday nights were poor, Rhodes realized she was ill, but as he was conducting the orchestra for her for the Palladium, he still pressed her to work with him on the numbers she planned to sing (he did not even know which these were to be). She grew unreasonably angry at him. (There was a piece of business they did every night. She would come out onstage and take a drink from the piano and ask Rhodes to test it. 'Oh, it's fine,' he would reply 'you can drink that. It's Bitter Lemon.' And she would counter, 'Oh no! not Bitter Lemon again!' But that Friday night she turned to him and answered sharply, 'Himmler!')

Sunday night she stepped unsteadily from the car at the Palladium stage door with Deans on one side of her and the doctor on the other. Rhodes ran out to meet her and asked her legitimately and with concern, 'What numbers do you want to do?'

'Go play the overture,' Judy replied.

'You can't put a three-and-a-half-minute overture in the middle of a television program,' he warned her.

'You'll have to,' she told him tersely. 'Then I'll do "London" and "For Once in My Life".'

The Palladium show was live, and Judy's appearance was only minutes away. Rhodes consulted the two men, Alex Fine and Bill Ward, who were in charge of the show and asked what he should do. It was agreed that no one had a choice. Rhodes, therefore, after the half-time break, led the orchestra in the overture.

The head cameraman was confused. Assuming Judy would be stepping out onstage right away, he held the camera on the empty stage with only a backdrop which spelled J U D Y in neon lights, giving the fourteen million people in the television audience the impression that Judy might not show. As soon as the overture ended and 'London' began, Judy stumbled onto the stage, overly drugged, but appearing drunk and having trouble remembering lyrics. Somehow she got through the show.

That next afternoon, interviewer Pamela Foster-Williams came to see her at the Ritz and found her looking 'pathetically tiny, vulnerable, and sick'; but she noted that Judy's mind was sharp and her wit intact, and that there was a moment of radiance in her face when Deans entered the suite with Brandy, their dog. When Miss Foster-Williams asked about the 'forgotten' lyrics, Judy replied, 'Oh, that was part of the act.'

By that following Friday she was still ill but had managed (though some evenings disastrously) to get through all the performances but one – that night having to walk offstage after her fourth number. Friday night, she did not feel she could make it. She began crying when Vivian Martyne stepped in to help her dress, 'I can't go on,' she confessed miserably.

Deans insisted she go on. They had an argument about it. He forced the issue. 'Please, don't make me go on,' she begged. Deans kept insisting. Judy finally complied. She took extra medication. Tears had spoiled her makeup, and Miss Martyne repaired it. She was one hour and forty-five minutes late. The audience was hostile. She looked drunk, and they had been kept waiting a long time. She began to sing, but her voice failed her. She stood terrified not far from the piano. She began again, but halfway through the opener her voice faded. Members of the audience began to shout, and then someone at a ringside table hurled empty cigarette packets and rubbish from the ashtrays at her.

Judy, in a numbed state, near tears, and unable to account

for her actions, got down on her hands and knees and began to pick up the debris, muttering, 'Oh dear, Oh dear,' as she did. Before she could even get to her feet, a man had jumped onto the stage, demanding an apology as he grabbed the microphone from her, almost sending her, off balance to the floor. 'If you can't turn up on time, why turn up at all?' he sneered.

At that moment, someone from the same party threw some hard-lump sugar at her. It struck the glass of Bitter Lemon on the piano, and the glass shattered. Judy was shaking, but as she stood there facing that angry mob, no one at all coming to her assistance or stepping in to stop the show, she must have recalled the times Ethel and her sisters had suffered the same insults. She straightened, her head back, grasping the microphone tightly between both hands. 'I'm at least a lady,' she said with all the power she could muster, and then, putting the microphone back, she fought her tears and stumbled off the stage.

For two days she did not leave her bed at the Ritz. Brandy stood guard, refusing to leave his post at the foot of the massive bed. The doctor fought to get her to eat, fearing her worst danger to be malnutrition. Then, miraculously, she snapped back to life.

The last week of her engagement at The Talk of The Town, Burt Rhodes was quoted as saying, 'The lady was absolutely incredible.' She was in good humor, and most of the performances were excellent. One night she couldn't quite make the end note of 'Over The Rainbow', and a young girl in the audience with a soprano voice finished it for her. Judy laughed delightedly and applauded her. Her closing performance was on a Saturday night, February 1, 1969. It was a very emotional evening, and after a particularly good show there was a queue of people both at the stage door and up the stairs, waiting to see her. At two in the morning when she left, the queue was still there, jamming the sidewalk when she got into the car. Standing for a brief moment, she smiled and waved to them.

CHAPTER THIRTY-NINE

On February 11 shortly after her engagement at The Talk of The Town ended, Judy received the following telegram from Godfrey Isaac:

> FINAL JUDGEMENT HERRON VERSUS HERRON ENTERED
> FEBRUARY 11, 1969, IN JUDGEMENT BOOK 6308, PAGE 11
> AND SIGNED BY COURT JUDGE WILLIAM E. MACFADDEN.
> COURT WILL NOT SEND WIRE, BUT ENTRY MAY BE VERIFIED
> BY TELEPHONE DIRECTLY TO LOS ANGELES COUNTY
> SUPERIOR COURT CLERK.
> BEST REGARDS – GODFREY ISAAC.

Judy and Deans had just moved into a small mews house in Chelsea. Like most mews houses, it was built on two floors, one partially over a garage; it was located in a short cul-de-sac backing Sloane Square. (Mews 'houses' were originally built to accommodate the staffs of the mansion houses facing the main streets and were always in alleys or cul-de-sacs, where first carriages, then cars were kept. They have been especially attractive to Americans in London over the years.) It was, certainly, the most modest house Judy had lived in since childhood. Downstairs consisted of a living room that led directly off the cul-de-sac, a tiny kitchen, small dining room, and toilet. Upstairs, there were three small bedrooms and a bath. One of these Judy designated as her dressing room; one as a den for Deans to work in (having just been fired from Arthur, he was now functioning as her manager); the largest bedroom (still no more than ten by twelve feet), with the bathroom close at hand, becoming their 'suite'. Brandy's size presented something of a problem, as the staircase was so narrow that it was difficult for him to navigate. The house was furnished, but left a good deal to be desired. They had a small rehearsal piano, rented for them by The Talk of The Town when they were at the Ritz; a leased television set; and dozens of salt shakers and porcelain pieces that Judy collected.

Now that they were at last able to legally wed, Deans decided first to go to New York on business. His plans were to keep him away two weeks. Judy finally agreed to remain in London. They set the date of their wedding as March 15, giving them a three-day honeymoon before they were to leave on a preset Scandinavian concert tour. (She was to appear in concert with Johnnie Ray in Stockholm on March 19, Göteborg March 21, Malmö March 23, and Copenhagen March 25.)

Designer Beatrice ('Bumbles') Dawson was attentive. However, Judy had few other close friends. After Deans left, Judy would take walks with Brandy. At the corner of her cul-de-sac there was a beauty salon owned by two young men, Emil Abdelnour and John Francis. One day Abdelnour looked up and saw this very thin, pale face in an enormous hat, peering in his front window, eyes wide trying to see inside. The wind was ready to take her hat from her grasp, and she was holding a huge dog on a leash with her other hand. Abdelnour recognized her, opened the door, and asked her inside. Pleased, she sat down, telling him they were neighbors. They talked for a long time. She asked him back to the house for dinner that night. He insisted he bring the food. From that time on, Judy would see Abdelnour daily. Generally slow in revealing herself to people (covering by superficial conversation, either witty or wry), she found a kindred soul in Abdelnour. A large, soft-spoken young man, intelligent, very well read, he would discuss history, politics, and religion with her.

'Do you believe in God?' he asked her one day.

'Of course I believe in God. I'm very, very religious,' she replied.

'Do you read the Bible?' he pressed.

A game followed. Abdelnour would name a passage in the Bible and to his amazement, Judy would repeat it from memory. (She particularly loved the Psalms and Corinthians.)

They discussed the poets Shelley and Keats. Abdelnour, who had studied the poets at University, was surprised at her knowledge (which, of course, went back to her teen-age poetry writing). She had memorized many of Shelley's poems, favored 'The Skylark', and would repeat it often. She spoke a lot about the Kennedys, being greatly attracted by dynasties and by men and women of power. She was reading a book about Hearst and asked Abdelnour if he had ever read a book by Taylor Caldwell called *Dynasty of Death* (he had not).

The rest after the closing of the show at The Talk of The Town seemed to have done her much good. And she loved the feeling of being a 'housewife' that she had in the little mews cottage. Deans returned from New York to find her at peace with herself and very much excited about the impending marriage.

The plan was to have a civil service at the Chelsea Registry Office, then to go to the Reverend Delaney's St. Marylebone Parish Church for another blessing. Deans wanted a reception, and Judy turned the arrangements over to him and to her new English public relations office, Southcombe and West; but two days before the event, when she heard Deans and West discussing the guest list, reading off names like 'Diana Dors, James Mason, Ginger Rogers,' etc., she was beside herself.

'I don't know why they're inviting all those people,' she told Bumbles Dawson. 'I've been through too many weddings. I don't want a Hollywood premiere. I just want a marriage.'

Deans did not agree, feeling she should have a proper wedding befitting her 'star status'. By now it was too late to backtrack, as he had released the guest list to the press and sent out invitations by telegram.

Wearing a blue chiffon dress abounding in boa – too short and too sheer – and wearing as a hat a matching blue band with a pearl from the earrings Tony Bennett had given her dangling from it onto her forehead (John Francis having made it from her own design), she was a very unusual-looking bride. With Bumbles and Ray, both West and South-combe, the London doctor who had been treating Judy and a young invalid girl (a fan whom Judy had befriended), Deans and Judy were married by M. A. Laurence, a charming little man in Chelsea Registry. Judy seemed especially thin and frail, and the doctor was very much concerned about her; he felt she had never actually recovered from her illness during the Talk of The Town engagement. She was in a very nervous state, appearing feverish, and – unusual for Judy – she lost her temper at reporters outside the registry.

The grand ballroom at Quaglino's, the final choice for the reception, was a bizarre sight. Only fifty of the several hundred invited guests came, and the room selected was tremendous – large enough to comfortably accommodate several hundred guests; therefore, the fifty who came seemed lost in its vastness. One side of the room was completely lined with tables bearing large ice statues, huge floral displays and laden with food for an enormous crowd, at least thirty stiffly uniformed waiters standing close by. Of the fifty guests, half were from the press, and they unmercifully shot questions at the wedding couple, photographers' flashbulbs constantly exploding. Mounting the podium for the express purpose of giving the photographers a good shot of them, Judy and Deans posed to cut the cake.

Judy was now legally Mrs. Michael DeVinko. Clinging tightly to Deans, she beamed down at the army of press photographers. They asked her to kiss Deans. The lovers obliged. She laughed like a teen-ager when her short dress rode up a bit too indiscreetly. Deans helped her down off the bandstand. Her doctor remained close at one side of her, Johnnie Ray at the other as Deans mingled with the guests. There was a long line of reception chairs, and finally, she sat down. Having known Judy and being a neighbor, I had been invited to the reception, and Judy saw me standing a short distance from her and smiled. I went over to speak with her.

It will haunt me forever. Judy, with a desperate giggle like a distortion on a sound track of one of her old Rooney MGM films, grabbed my hand, her nails cutting into my flesh, not letting go long after she had said, 'I'm so grateful you came. Please stay long.' There was no wonder left in those wide brown eyes. 'Don't leave,' she said a short time later. 'Don't leave.' Again she grasped my hand.

We talked about writing. I told her about a Hollywood book I was working on dealing with the MacCarthy period and the blacklist, and how since it was so close to me, it was not an easy task. She spoke about writing the truth about herself. I advised her to do so and suggested she tape what she could if longhand was difficult.

My husband joined me then suggested that it was time for us to leave.

'It will be different now,' Judy said as she walked my husband and me toward the doors of the huge room. Deans was back at her side. 'I have Mickey now.' She leaned against him, smiling up at him. Mickey was grinning broadly. He spoke about the fantastic Scandinavian tour he had set up for her. He planned to take over her career as Ethel and Mayer and Luft had done.

CHAPTER FORTY

MARCH is a melancholy month in Copenhagen. The faces of the old, grand buildings appear haggard after a winter's long abuse. The glorious greens of summer, the burning autumn colors, the safe and sterile white of the winter snows have disappeared; the trees are bare and unprotected in the March rains, and lovers move inside for shelter. Night comes early, its dark hands violating the day before afternoon teatime. The people of Copenhagen, though, are a marvelously patient lot, secure in their knowledge that summer will eventually arrive as it always does, with week-ends filled with plush green, long sunlit days, country homes, and sailing on clear blue waters. But for Judy, who slept away most of the daytime hours and had been reared in the sun, Copenhagen was like a city besieged by the Ice Age.

With Johnnie Ray and Deans she had completed the Swedish part of the tour, being well received (in spite of one cancelled concert), but nonetheless ending the week in a state of nightmarish distraction. Deans, obviously believing he had done an astute thing, had contracted with a Swedish producer, Arne Stivell of Music Artists of Europe, for a documentary film to be shot of Judy while she was in Sweden. The film was to be called *A Day in the Life of Judy Garland*. There had been cameras installed everywhere – the dressing rooms, hotel suits, everywhere – and at all hours of the day. At first, unaware of them, Judy had dressed and undressed in her dressing-room. She then found out about the cameras, which had caught her in the nude. It would have been enough to make a perfectly well-adjusted woman upset. In Judy's case it sent her into a state that was on the narrow edge of paranoia, taking her back all those years to when she had been a girl at Metro and believed men looked through the windows of the bathroom at her; when she thought eyes peered out at her from the doors of the closets in her home.

There was an appreciable and noticeable difference in her appearance. She was nearly skeletal, and her eyes from time to time flashed a look that made one think of inmates at Dachau. Deans tried to soothe her, assuring her he would have the film confiscated if any objectionable footage was included. Stivell promised her everything would be all right. But the damage had been done. She was beginning to doubt all those close to her, harboring some frightening suspicions that Deans might have sold her out.

When she stepped off the boat that had taken her from Sweden to Denmark, Deans, Ray, Arne Stivell were still in her company. It was cold, raining; hotel reservations had been unsure, but a fortuitous circumstance brought them to the Kong Frederik Hotel. There had been no rooms available, the top floors, where the grand suites were located, being in the process of redecoration. But the hotel manager, Hans Jorgen Eriksen, had been a devoted Garland fan since childhood. Hearing it was his idol who was desperate for accommodations, Eriksen instantly agreed to find space and then had to move all incoming guests around to do so. He gave Judy Rooms 511 and 512 – a charming suite decorated with antiques and lovely porcelain. Under the eaves, the rooms slanted and shaped themselves cosily. The bedroom was wood-paneled; the bed, an oversized old four-poster; the bathroom fully tiled, the dressing room completely mirrored. Another bathroom off the living room connected to the bedroom of Room 510. Since Judy was travelling with a great quantity of baggage and wardrobe, it was decided that she occupy both rooms. Grand theatrical history was attached to these rooms. Sammy Davis Jr., and Marlene Dietrich had stayed in them before Judy.

The day was gray and showing very little promise as Eriksen stood waiting at the doors for Judy and Deans to arrive in their chauffeured car. He held in his arms a bright spring bouquet in the shape of a rainbow and presented it to Judy as she entered the hotel. He had written a card and read it to her: 'To the only performer who can carry us all over the rainbow. Judy, we love you.' The sight of this tall, spare, handsome Dane with his blond hair graying impeccably and his finely boned face open and revealing a pair of deep blue eyes, bending over her (for she was more than a foot shorter than he), reciting a sentimental greeting and handing her a sentimental bouquet, must have been too much for Judy. She accepted the flowers with some embarrassment and mumbled an almost inaudible 'Thank you.'

Mr. Telle Saaek, the reception manager, stood behind the dark mahogany desk. He had been assigned by Eriksen the job of personally seeing to Judy's needs while she was to be a guest of the hotel. The lobby, though quite elegant with its mahogany-paneled walls, its portraits of rather grand Danish

286

monarchs, and its antique furnishings, is narrow and small, with only a series of glass windows dividing it from its exclusive lobby restaurant. This area was filled with press and photographers, about forty-five strong. Telle Saaek could not help noticing how 'like a small broken bird' Judy looked as Eriksen and Deans guided her to the elevator, promising the press that she would greet them a short time later in her suite.

A little less than a half an hour had passed when a call came down to send the press up, along with a supply of liquor and food. The reporters were pleasantly surprised, having feared she might not meet them at all, but once they were upstairs, the suspicions gathered momentum. They had all heard rumors that her Swedish concert had been cancelled because she had been too drunk to appear. Actually she had been very ill and had appeared extremely confused, distracted because of the filming or perhaps because of the pills.

For three hours Judy remained secluded in the bedroom while the reporters packed into the living room of the suite. Deans made sure their glasses were kept full and came out from time to time to assure them that Mrs. Deans would join them as soon as possible.

When she finally appeared, she looked fresh, but incredibly fragile – thinner, weaker than anyone had expected. She hung on to Deans's arm and sat down on the one couch in the room – Deans on one side of her, Johnnie Ray on the other. She wore a glittering black jump suit and held a vodka and pineapple juice in her hand, sipping it slowly, absently, as she smiled radiantly and answered questions. Her sense of humor and wit kept the spirits in the room high. She constantly deferred to Deans or brought him into the conversation. She referred to herself throughout as Mrs. Deans.

The newspapers were kind to her, but there was no denying her delicate appearance and the cancelled performance in Sweden just before her coming to Copenhagen, so they were also expectantly pessimistic, and feared she might not be able to carry through on her commitment to appear at the Falkoner Centret Theatre on the twenty-fifth of March. Mr. Blicher-Hansen, general manager of the theater, was equally concerned, as eleven hundred seats had been sold for a record 125 kroner (about $18) a seat – a price only one other artist, Maria Callas, commanded, although many international stars had appeared at the theater in its short ten-year history. But he was a good deal more concerned about the star herself.

Mr. Blicher-Hansen arrived at the Kong Frederik to greet Judy just before the press left. The press conference had been too great an ordeal for her and she had faded quickly, looking to Mr. Blicher-Hansen, as she had to Telle Saaek, 'like a sick bird, broken and unable to fly.'

By now, Stivell had set up a film crew, which was in action photographing Judy in the suite. Deans was involved in the crew's activities, much to Mr. Blicher-Hansen's consternation, as he was immediately awed by the lack of protection and care being given Judy and the attention being extended to the film people.

By the next day, Judy had grown irritable and nervous. She was also more and more upset about Stivell and the filming. She was paranoid about it, certain the suite was bugged and that Stivell had installed secret cameras in the walls. Hans Eriksen had made arrangements for Telle Saaek to look after Judy and make sure she was not left alone too long, as Deans often went out with Stivell on various errands pertaining first to the concert, then to some interviews and recordings. One glance at Judy, and Eriksen knew she was in frail health. A conversation confirmed his fears that she was on a quantity of pills and at times not in control of her senses. It became a sixteen-hour-a-day job for Telle Saaek – and could have been around the clock if he could have taken the strain. Neither of the men minded ministering to Judy's needs. Both of them agreed that 'she was warm, intensely feminine, terrified of being alone and a very, very sick lady'. Neither of them felt she had long to live – in fact, could not see how she would even survive the rigors of the concert.

Telle Saaek called her room when he knew she was alone every hour or so and if she did not reply, sent a chambermaid to check the suite. Eriksen had food sent to her suite (she never ordered anything herself), but the trays were always left untouched. Twice alerted by Eriksen's concern, the hotel doctor was called to her suite, but Judy claimed all she needed was more Ritalin. The doctor refused to give it to her.

The concert was scheduled for the evening of March 25, a Saturday night just two days after Judy's arrival. One of Copenhagen's leading radio personalities, Hans Vangkilde, had been trying since Judy's arrival to obtain an interview with her for one of his programs, but had been unsuccessful. However, Hans had spent two years in New York City teaching in an American college and during that time had become friendly with Margaret Hamilton. Hans had an autographed picture of Miss Hamilton with a personal inscription that had been presented to his children; he sent this to Judy's room. That seemed to do the trick. With Judy desperate for an ally, a friend, no matter how remote, of the 'dear witch' seemed a likely candidate.

From that point in her Copenhagen stay, Judy was to turn to Hans Vangkilde whenever she was in need of friendship – or simply *in need*. It is not difficult to understand why, for the man has a much-lived, comfortable quality about him. He is a solidly built man, somewhat shaggy, who wears rough tweeds that have the newness off them. A broad face is lighted up by bright blue eyes. His English is fluent, but relaxed. There is a strong dash of Mr. Chips about him – but Chips when he was a young man. Judy agreed to tape the interview with Deans in their suite. She seemed happy as she asked Deans's opinion about everything, including him in all discussions. She held his hand, leaned against him, and kept referring to him as 'my man' or 'my husband' as he hovered close by, making flip side remarks. There was an immediate empathy between Judy and Vangkilde, and the interview became a very personal and honest discussion between the two.

'I've worked very hard, you know,' she confided to him, 'and I've planted some kind of – I've been lucky enough, I guess, to plant a star – and then people wanted to either get in the act or else they wanted to rob me emotionally or financially, whatever. And then walk away and it's always lonely.'

Her voice on the existing tape has an unfamiliar sound to it. The throb is there, but it is harder, more brittle, a dried branch that could crack very easily under the slightest pressure. 'You're either freezing at the top or lonely, or you're only surrounded by people who are not truthful and who are using you,' she continued. 'And if you're unaware as I am, and you're a woman, it could get pretty rough sometimes . . .'

She was silent for a few moments.

'You don't always keep on the top,' she began again. 'My life, my career has been like a roller coaster. I've either been an enormous success or just a down-and-out failure, which is silly because everybody always asks me, "How does it feel to make a comeback?" And I don't know where I've been! I haven't been away.' She paused, and Vangkilde waited. 'It's lonely and cold on the top . . . lonely and cold,' she said very quietly.

Stivell and his crew were much in evidence, and there was a constant flow of people in to and out of the suite. Judy grew increasingly paranoid about it, even though Deans assured her that it was all right and a necessary evil, and that the money they would make from the film distribution would do wonders for their empty pockets. There was a lot of noise in Suite 508–509, which was on the other side of Room 510, the room Judy was using for storage. She called Hans Jorgen Eriksen and told him they were filming her from that room and that they had hidden cameras. Eriksen attempted to reason with her, even telling her the names of the hotel guests who had that suite. Finally, when nothing else worked, he agreed to leave that suite empty and in her name when the current occupants left, which they were planning to do that same day – a promise he kept.

By that night, owing to an excessively heavy intake of Ritalin, she had prematurely exhausted her supply. Deans agreed to see what he could do about obtaining some. He spoke to some of the bellboys, finally hitting on one who knew where he could get the pills at that hour. The bellboy took him to a discotheque, the kind of place where the clientele are well aware of what is going on – who smokes grass, who takes pills, who takes ups and who takes downs. The bellboy made a connection and someone came up with a hundred pills, for which Deans paid $100. But when he got back to the hotel, Judy and he had a rather violent quarrel. Angered, Deans refused to give her the pills. The night was nearly over. It was to be a cold, gray day. The radio was playing softly by her bed. The light in the hallway was on. Deans sat by her side in the unfamiliar bedroom, and finally the sleeping pills she had taken, without the ups to counteract them, took effect.

The next day she increased the intake of her pills alarmingly and was drinking heavily, something she had not done for many years. She kept insisting Deans not leave her alone, but that was impossible in view of the fact that he was acting as her manager and arrangements had to be made for the concert. The night before her concert, Deans left her in the suite for several hours. Telle Saaek was on duty and Hans Jorgen Eriksen alerted. She called down to Telle several times in the first hour to ask him where her husband had gone. Saaek told her the truth: that Deans had left the hotel with an associate with word that he would return in a matter of three or four hours. A half hour later, Judy rang again from room 511 (the sitting room) and asked Saaek to ring 512. Saaek questioned this, explaining that 512 was her own bedroom. 'I just want to make sure the telephone will ring in there,' she insisted. Saaek did as she asked, and she picked up the receiver in her bedroom and began a long conversation with him. 'You don't think my husband has left me?' she asked. 'You do think he'll come back?' Saaek kept reassuring her that Deans would only be away a few hours, that he would return shortly. 'I don't know what I'll do,' she pleaded.

A half hour later she called again and said she had to speak to Hans Vangkilde. Vangkilde could not be reached, being away in the country. Saaek rang Eriksen, and Eriksen went up immediately to Judy's suite. He found her curled up in the corner of the settee, 'looking like a frail and excessively small child and crying'. She seemed thankful to see Eriksen. He talked to her quietly, assuring her, soothing her, offering to order her some food, sitting down on the settee beside her. A family man himself, he felt as if she were a small child who had had a bad nightmare and was afraid to stay alone, afraid of the dark. 'I think I'm going mad,' she cried, and put her head down on his lap, sobbing there. Eriksen was too frightened to move.

Finally, she appeared calmer, the sobs had stopped, and her body was still. She answered his questions with logic and promised to go into her bedroom and lie down. He called a chambermaid, who helped her into the bed, and then rang the doctor. Again she begged him for pills but he refused. She showed him an empty bottle of sleeping-tablets. That eased his mind, and Eriksen and the chambermaid left her alone, Eriksen remaining on duty in the lobby until Deans returned.

Before Deans left the hotel for a meeting the next day, he asked Saaek again to stay with Judy. According to Saaek, she was in better spirits and said she would like to go shopping for a piece of Royal Copenhagen china to give to Deans as a gift. Saaek agreed to go with her. He noticed with increasing fear that she was even weaker than the previous day, having to sit down in the lobby before being able to go out on the street (the porcelain shop was just down the road from the hotel). As she sat there, an American woman with a small child recognized Judy. 'There's Dorothy,' she announced. Judy was happy about this incident. She signed an autograph and then joined Saaek, leaning heavily on him as they left the hotel. Saaek reports she was 'frighteningly fragile'.

In the porcelain shop the weakness overcame her again, and she sat down as the salesgirl brought pieces over to her.

She finally selected a large plate that cost $200, charged it to her hotel bill, and left.

Saaek, Eriksen, Blicher-Hansen, Vangkilde – none of these men could see how 'this weak, frail lady could appear at the concert', much less give a professional performance. The concert was set up so that Johnnie Ray had the first half to himself. Then there would be an intermission, after which Judy was to appear, do a duet of 'Am I Blue?' with Ray, and then continue alone for the last half, or about sixty minutes.

By the end of the first half, Judy had not yet appeared at the theater. Blicher-Hansen rang her suite and spoke to Deans. He promised she would be there in the time it took to drive (about ten minutes); but in his own mind, Blicher-Hansen was already planning to cancel the performance. Ten minutes later, Judy appeared in a loose red chiffon dress with ostrich feathers at its hemline. The dress was a poor choice, having a sad, limp look and falling sharply over her scarecrow body, revealing her emaciated chest and arms and shoulders.

She stood center stage in that huge auditorium, Johnnie beside her for support, and smiled fondly at the audience. 'We love you, Judy?' they screamed at her. She and Johnnie sang 'Am I Blue?' both embarrassingly off-key. They cheered her on. A stool was placed center stage, Ray leaving her alone as she sat down, the spotlight framing only her face. She called Deans out on the stage, introducing him and kissing him – a rather awkward moment for the reserved Danes, who found this in poor taste. 'I may never go home,' she called out to the enthusiastic, loving audience, and sang her encores. People cried when she finally sat down at the edge of the stage, a small heap of bone and red chiffon, her great, warm, deep brown eyes seeing all, seeing nothing, seeming to still belong to Dorothy. If she had been off-key during her performance, her love, her personality, her very *giving* seemed enough to her audience. They stood up and cheered, cried, and screamed as Blicher-Hansen came on-stage and presented her with a bouquet once again in the shape and hue of a rainbow. He left her standing there alone.

'Good night,' she screamed back at them. 'I love you very much' – and then she was gone.

Except in one paper, the reviews were good, some of the best she had received in a long while. The *Politek* wrote: 'When Judy sang "Over the Rainbow", it was as if she sang it for the first time in her life, innocent and sweet. It was so beautiful. We cried. Everybody in the theater stood up and cheered.'

There was no doubting the concert had been a great victory.

Ray left the next morning, as did Arne Stivell, but the film unit remained. There were now great problems between Stivell and Deans. Deans made arrangements that day to hear the tapes from the concert. The technicians had goofed and had brought only monaural equipment from Radio Denmark. No one knew, of course, that this would be Judy's last concert ever, but Deans felt Judy should have been recorded in stereo.

The copy of the tape and the check from the concert had already been sent to Sweden and Stivell's company, Music Artists of Europe AB, at his request. Enraged, Deans managed to get Radio Denmark to stop the payment on the check until he could get things straightened out. He then came to the decision that he would have to go to Stockholm himself, as Stivell had already returned.

The problem was Judy. She could not go to Stockholm, nor could she return to London by herself. In the end, Deans sent most of their baggage back to London by train with the same young man he had been friendly with at the Kong Frederik and gave him the keys to open the house and get it ready for them; he arranged for Judy to remain in Copenhagen. Not alone, of course – that was impossible – so he called upon Hans Vangkilde, who, after speaking with his wife, offered to bring Judy to their home in the country. Accepting this generous offer, Deans then departed for Stockholm.

Vangkilde had planned to take his wife and Judy out for dinner, but just a glance at Judy and he knew this was inadvisable. Judy was on the brink. He had seen her sick and disturbed, stoned and confused – all in the short time they had known each other. This was different. She looked 'like a slender bough, snapped in two and ready to break', and 'she had the look of death camps, but her eyes – such beautiful eyes, warm and brown and childish, the whites clear and dazzling – almost feverish'. Hans had been a correspondent and had had to cover labor camps and concentration camps in his time, and also mental homes. He claims it was the image of these last inmates that haunted him now.

He drove Judy to his home in the country, where his wife, Grethe, their four children, and their huge collie dog, Eddie (who possessed the curiosity of one blue eye and one brown eye), waited. Grethe felt the same instinct as her husband had about Judy and before she prepared dinner called over a friend of hers to lighten the gathering and, at the same time, rang their doctor, who lived nearby, to make sure he would be home during the night in case they should need him.

Grethe's friend arrived and entertained Judy as Grethe prepared dinner. The four children, who speak English, having spent time in the States when Hans had taught there, gathered around Judy at her request, and the dog lay down at her feet. She was filled with instant empathy for Eddie, the collie, stroking and talking to him from time to time. As the children played a game on the floor, she watched them, and after a time, without any request – as though singing to herself – she began singing 'Over the Rainbow'. The voice was thin and small – the end, the very end of a distant echo.

Grethe served dinner, but Judy didn't touch her food. She was now drinking vodka and juice. They attempted to coax her to eat, but to no avail. She sat, curled up in the large armchair in the Vangkildes' new den, facing the fireplace, looking about ten years old.

'Everyone is trying to use me,' she told Grethe. 'There's no one I can trust. They are spying on me at the hotel. They

295

even have a hole in the bathroom wall and have a camera in it taking pictures of me when I take a bath.'

'Oh, I'm sure that can't be so,' Grethe assured her. 'The Kong Frederik is one of our best hotels and I understand the bathrooms are fully tiled.'

'Mickey left me only fifty dollars and the hotel bill's unpaid,' Grethe claims Judy complained.

'He'll be back, and you don't need any money here,' Grethe Vangkilde says she assured Judy.

'Please get Mickey for me. He's gone off and left me. He'll never come back. I can't live without him.' She began to cry.

Grethe went into the master bedroom and woke up her husband. They decided to try to reach Deans, but he had not informed them which hotel he would be staying at. Vangkilde went down the list of hotels in Stockholm alphabetically, calling each one of them, finally reaching Deans at the Strand. But he was incoherent, and Vangkilde was not sure he understood how serious Judy's condition appeared.

When Vangkilde returned to Judy, she asked for sleeping pills.

'We don't have any,' he states he told her.

'Any pills at all?' she asked him.

'Just for headaches,' he lied.

'I have one terrible headache,' Judy cried. He went to fetch her some aspirin. Grethe was alone with Judy.

'You don't look like a spy,' she says Judy told her incoherently.

'I'm not. I'm just an ordinary housewife,' Grethe replied.

'Have you kidnapped me?'

'No, we brought you here to wait for Mickey.'

Judy began crying again, saying she wanted to talk to Deans. 'I'd like to die,' she sighed, 'never wake up. There's no way out.'

Vangkilde returned with the aspirin and left the two women alone again at his wife's request. The Danish woman sat down beside Judy. They talked through most of the night. Grethe offered her food, but Judy wouldn't eat. She fell asleep, curled up, almost disappearing into the big chair by the fire with Eddie at her feet. Grethe went to cover her and she awoke.

'Will you stay here with me?' Judy begged.

'No, but I'll help you into the guest room. You can take Eddie with you.'

Judy could not walk, and Grethe (Hans now in an exhausted sleep) lifted her in her arms and carried her into the guest bedroom (Grethe claims Judy's weight was no more than that of one of her own children), helping her into one of the children's nightdresses. Judy sat on the bed holding on to Grethe, sobbing against her body. Finally the sobs subsided.

'Oh,' Judy sighed deeply, 'oh, I just want to go home.'

She rested on the bed but clung to Grethe's hand. 'Please don't leave me alone.'

'I'll leave the door open and the light in the hall on,' Grethe compromised.

'Just stay here until I fall asleep,' Judy asked.

Grethe stood by the side of the bed, Judy's small hand in hers. One moment she seemed to fall asleep, and then when Grethe tried to remove her hand, she awoke.

'You're sure this isn't a mental home?' she asked.

'Of course not. I'm Grethe Vangkilde, remember?' She patted Judy's hand and Judy fell back to sleep. Finally Grethe left her, the door open and a light on as she promised, Eddie remaining behind at his post. Less than an hour later, she heard sounds in the other part of the house and went to investigate. Judy was sitting by the dying fire in her small-girl's nightdress, her arms tight around Eddie's neck, pressing her face into his thick fur. 'You understand,' she was saying; '*you* understand'.

'You must try to sleep,' Grethe told her, and wrapped a robe around her bare shoulders.

'You know who I am?' Judy asked.

'Yes, of course. You're a great star – so great that in a

couple of moments you can give ordinary people something they will never forget.'

'Please, say that again,' Judy begged, as a child beseeches a mother to repeat a familiar story over and over again.

Judy and Deans left Copenhagen two days later. It was four o'clock, and the city was gray. It was cold. A limousine waited for them by the front door. They came down in the elevator and Judy said a personal goodbye to everyone there – Telle Saaek, Hans Jorgen Eriksen, and the telephone operators. She was gay. She wore one of her mad, funny hats that she herself had designed, and she held a vodka and pineapple juice in one hand – Deans holding his usual Scotch and Drambuie in one of his – as they got into the back seat of the car. Saaek and Eriksen stood on the curb watching the car pull away. They hoped she might look back, because they had confessed to each other that they were sure they would never see her alive again. She was so tiny, though, that even the back of her head was not visible in the car's rear window.

CHAPTER FORTY-ONE

A DRIVING rain greeted them upon their arrival in London. A limousine met them. Judy always felt protected in the back seat of a large car. Traffic frightened and overwhelmed her. Trucks and skyscrapers loomed over her. Speed terrified her; she would nervously call out to her chauffeurs and taxi drivers to slow down. Even as a young woman in California, where driving is supposedly necessary for survival, she preferred being driven.

The press was appalled at her appearance. Newspapers had called her 'thin' and 'frail' before the tour in Scandinavia; now with sickening heart they noted that 'she was nearly skeletal, looked like a small animal whose bones had been picked almost clean'.

It was night, and they drove directly to their small cottage at 4 Cadogan Lane. Deans was now aware that Judy was a very sick woman. He helped her to bed and then, at her request, sat on the edge of the bed, listening to her shallow breathing, somehow managing to rationalize that what she needed was the sun, deciding to leave immediately with her for a holiday in Spain. It seems irrational that his first move was not to get sound medical advice. But Deans had been married to Judy for only one month. He had a head filled with plans. He was going to franchise a string of Judy Garland miniaturized cinemas, would produce a film of her life, supervise new recordings. Blaming her failing health on money pressures, pills, and concerts, he believed he could make them both rich, stabilize the pills (after all, *he* was able to take them in moderation), and cut out the concerts if they made her unhappy. In pursuit of his own dreams, possessed by his own fantasies, he refused to face the reality of his situation.

Clearly, what Judy needed was a nurse-companion. A complete medical examination would have revealed that besides being tired, worn out, Judy had chronic and critical liver, kidney, colon, and rectal problems, along with all the side effects the drugs had created. But even more pressing was her mental health. Instead of a holiday in Spain that meant planes, hotels, changes in climate, foreign food, and doctors unfamiliar with her case, he should have considered taking her to a nursing home. So powerful was his own world of fantasy, however, that he was able to convince himself 'sunny' Spain would heal all wounds.

By morning, he was forced to delay the trip. The Swedish film had been sent to London for processing, since it required a special method not available in Sweden. The film was then nearly three hours running time and contained nude footage of Judy, shots of her stoned and drunk, and tracks of her singing not only badly, but embarrassingly so. Through his solicitor, George Eldridge, Deans, when notified, immediately slapped an injunction on the film.

The Swedish newspaper *Ekstabladet*, on April 12, 1969, carried the following article (English translation by its own offices).

JUDY GARLAND'S FILM OF HER SCANDINAVIAN TOUR IS CONFISCATED BECAUSE OF ITS NUDE SCENES

The showing of a Swedish documentary film of Judy Garland that would have undoubtedly caused a sensation has been prohibited by a London Court. The film is not to be delivered to its producer – Music Artists of Europe – from the London laboratory where it was sent for processing. It was Judy Garland's lawyer who had persuaded the court to issue the decision, which came as something of a shock to the producer.

'That is a fantastic complaint of which we are being accused,' says Arne Stivell, director of Music Artists of Europe. 'One agrees that the film contains pictures of Judy Garland in the nude and that the film shows her in an intoxicated condition, but she knew all along that she was being filmed according to the terms of the contract.

'The film is undeniably revealing,' states Stivell. 'It tells the story of a day in her life. It shows how she builds herself up to the time of her appearance on stage. She prepares in the same way that a boxer does before he goes into the ring. When my company organized her Scandinavian tour it received her permission to make the film. The whole thing is in the contract, and we agreed to share the world royalties fifty-fifty.'

The decision as to whether or not the film will be returned to the Swedish producer will be handed down on Wednesday by the London Court.

Even though Deans knew, therefore, that at least he would have to return to London by the following Wed-

nesday, he still was determined to take Judy to Spain, set-
tling on the seaside resort of Torremolinos.

Torremolinos was once a fishing village. Now, the hotels;
the concessions; the encroaching army of foreign artists, ex-
patriates, and tourists have enveloped it. The ocean, on a
sunny day, is still beautiful; the town curves picturesquely
and seductively around the neck of the Costa del Sol, red
clay-tile roofs dot the coastline – but it has been prostituted,
flagrantly abused. Elsewhere in Spain one can still hear the
distinguishing sounds of the country – a howling dog, fisher-
men singing as they pull in their nets, the squeak of donkeys,
rattles of old cars – but not in Torremolinos. When they
arrived, there was no sun and the town lay before them like
some jaded specter, old and bleached.

From the time of their arrival there were serious problems. Deans had not brought enough pills. The first night
was spent in a desperate search for a doctor who would give
him a prescription. Then the pills seemed to have a new and
adverse effect. Judy found it extremely hard to coordinate.
The first morning she took a very bad spill in the bathroom,
gashing her lip and knocking herself unconscious. The
doctor did not feel she had serious injuries (though he never
took her to the hospital for x-rays), but he did not think she
should be left alone. A search was then conducted for a
nurse who would stay with Judy. The next day, with Judy
still in an incoherent state, the doctor changed his mind and
recommended the hospital. Deans, conscious now of the
press and bad publicity, refused, deciding he would tend her
himself.

'I held her in my arms in a chair,' Deans says, 'and tried to
feed her some cold grapefruit juice, which she loved – her
mouth was all parched. I held her and rocked her. She was
like a little child, a small baby, and she would turn, eyes like
a little kid, and smile, the most innocent God-damned
loving smile. And I started to cry. "I promise I'll be good,"
she said. Then I put her back in the bed, but I held her and
rocked her and kissed her and just rocked her back and
forth. She was so frightened, so God-damned scared. She

301

didn't want the doctor to come. She was afraid she was going crazy.'

Nonetheless, he left her in the care of the nurse in Spain while he went to London for twenty-four hours to arrange the postponement of the Swedish matter. When he returned, he found her considerably worse. Nursing her for many days himself (they were in Spain a total of ten days), he finally became frightened when she began hallucinating. He managed to get her on a plane back to London, cabling Matthew West, the public relations man, to arrange for a car to meet them. As soon as they were back at Cadogan Lane, he put in an emergency call to her doctor, who came right over. The physician wasn't certain what the problem was, but feared possible brain damage, prescribing tranquilizers to quiet her. By the next morning, miraculously, Judy (again taking Ritalin) had snapped back. The medical diagnosis now was that she had suffered drug withdrawal. A nurse was employed to remain with her.

It was a great shock to both Judy and Deans that when the Swedish matter came up in court, they not only lost the case but had to pay court costs. Deans and Eldridge flew to Sweden in hot pursuit of Stivell and the film. On boarding, Deans says he noted a coffin being loaded into the baggage section. 'You know who's in that coffin, George?' he asked Eldridge, and then quipped, 'Arne Stivell, hanging on to the film and saying, "Mickey can't find us inside here"!'

In Sweden, with the help of a Swedish attorney, they managed to unearth an old but valid copyright law that made it a criminal offense to show any of the film footage in Sweden. Feeling victorious, they returned, to find Judy a bit improved. Deans took her for the weekend to the country house in Hazelmare belonging to West and Southcombe.

On April 22, the attorneys, following up the matter of the Swedish film and Arne Stivell, wrote her a letter informing her that her performances were covered by the Swedish law of copyright, and that Stivell could not legally exhibit the film or recording of her Scandinavian tour in Sweden with-

out her consent. There were other legal complications, but it
seemed fairly certain the film would not be exhibited.

CHAPTER FORTY-TWO

JUDY'S condition appeared to improve, so by the first of
June, Deans agreed that she could accompany him on a two-
week trip to New York. Deans was pressing on with the idea
of the Judy Garland Cinemas, and the 'money people' were
in New York, and Judy did not want to be left in London
alone. It was a disastrous trip. The minicinema project collapsed – and they were in New York with scant funds,
having to stay with friends. It was obvious something had to
be done about their financial situation. Deans discussed two
potentials with Judy – one, a film documentary to counteract the Scandinavian entry, to be called *A Day in the Life of
Judy Garland*; and two, a concert.

Before the plane that brought them back from New York
had landed at Heathrow, Judy had agreed to both plans and
had even jotted down ideas for the concert.

The following was written on a scrap of paper by her in a
difficult-to-read-scribble, her handwriting having become
very childish:

Orch[estra] Arrangements

Georgia Rose
Georgia On My Mind
Second Hand Rose
San Francisco Bay
You Came A Long Way From St. Louis
Before The Parade Passes By   (Segue)
Second Hand Rose

Into Orchestra and

I Love A Parade

Good new songs

Open 1. Someone Needs Me
2. Who Am I?

(segue into)
At Last I Have Someone Who Needs Me
(above—definite!)

Newley's This Dream

Get Lindsey's Orch [estration] of Here's To Us

Judy was reacting out of habit. Of course, when the chips were down, when her husband turned to her, there was no other recourse but to schedule still another concert – still another test of her endurance.

The next morning she was unable to get out of bed. The following days she was weak but managed to do household chores (which she had never done before). One evening she went to a party given by Jackie Trent and Tony Hatch (known in England as Mr. and Mrs. Music). It was a costume party, and she dressed in a brief cowgirl outfit reminiscent of her appearance with Rooney in *Babes on Broadway*. It proved to be too much of a strain, and Deans (also in cowboy attire) was forced to take her home early.

She was reading *Nicholas and Alexandra* and was caught up emotionally with it – concerned for the welfare of Anastasia if, in fact, she had been alive all those years. ('She must have been so alone. My God!' she confided her compassion to Deans.) And she also was thinking seriously of becoming a Catholic like Deans and Liza.

Four days after their return from New York was the Reverend Peter Delaney's birthday. He planned a small dinner celebration. Judy was looking forward to the evening, as she had not strayed far from the cottage except for the evening at the Hatches'. She decided to give him the Royal Copenhagen plate she had bought on the tour. Late in the day the minister called. He was concerned about her, he said, after reading the afternoon newspapers.

'Why?' Judy asked.

He read her the article stating that Luft had been arrested for passing a worthless check in the amount of approximately $3,000 (the Garden State Arts Center affair). She reacted in a very distraught manner, saying something quite harsh about Luft. Then she disconnected. Her old friend Roddy McDowall had recently given her as a gift a red leather book with gold tooling on the cover declaring it *Ye Olde Bitch Book*. Inside were blank pages – the idea being that when anything disturbed Judy to a rankling point, she would write it in the book in an attempt to exorcise it. Several hours later she made the entry:

> *Sid Luft Arrested! Hooray! Passed $3000 in bad checks, Freeport, New Jersey. Peter called to read the newspapers to me. Joe and Lorna!*

Later she called Lorna in California. It seemed to make her feel much better.

They went to the dinner, but left very soon after they arrived. Judy wasn't feeling well. That night she could not sleep even after an extremely heavy dosage of Nembutal. The next day she hardly left her bed.

For the six days since her return to London she had appeared remote, as though listening for distant drummers. Deans's mind was spinning with plans, his hours filled with conferences with Southcombe and West and with a neighbor, Richard Harris, a businessman who was advising him on film matters. He had formed a close friendship with a young associate of Southcombe & West, Phillip Arberge, who had come over this night to watch television. Deans's eyes were set on coming glory. Judy had said she would do a film and a concert. He went over and over the scribbled notes indicating the songs she might sing.

Upstairs, in that small bedroom – humbler than most hotel bedrooms she had lived in throughout her life – Judy took her pills and turned restlessly on her pillows, her small frame making very little impression on them at all.

Perhaps, in her drug-induced reveries, she was back in those childhood days of Ethel and herself – perhaps she was reliving the past.

Arberge left the house about midnight, and Deans went up to see how she was. That week in a last creative spurt she had begun a lyric. The verse began:

> When you've learned and you've grown
> Through the years of just living
> Then you've earned every right to be
> Proud of your years
> Not too old, not so young
> The quietness of age
> Well, then the young man comes along
> To smile, to take you up with him
> And hold you strong along a way to love ...

When he came and sat down on the edge of the bed, Deans claims she was propped up smiling. He had a sore throat. Nodding her head, laughing, she was proud she had one too. Her floppy slippers were askew on the floor; her ratty bathrobe at the end of the bed. She had not been smoking much, had eaten nothing. She asked him to stay with her, to lie down beside her on the bed. Many nights she had asked the same of him.

Even with the lights glaring, the radio blasting, he fell asleep. On the bedside table there was an open bottle of twenty-five Nembutals and an unopened new prescription of one hundred that Deans had just filled for her that day. She took pills from the opened bottle. Sometimes during the night she got up, taking a few more, and groped groggily around for her bathrobe and slippers. It was June 22 (she had celebrated her forty-seventh birthday just twelve days before in a stranger's New York apartment), but London was damp and the house cold. She had to go out of her bedroom and into the hallway to reach the bathroom. She locked the bathroom door. It was habit – one place she felt she must have privacy.

At ten-thirty the next morning Deans awoke with the insistent ringing of the downstairs telephone. Judy was not in the bed. Friends were calling from California.

The house seeming unnaturally quiet to him, he told the callers he'd ring them back, and started by instinct immediately for the upstairs bathroom. The door was locked. He pounded on it; then, fearing the worst, went outside the house, around the rear, and climbed up and onto a section of roof that allowed him to look into the bathroom window.

She was in a sitting position, her head collapsed onto her breast, like a small brown sparrow with a broken neck. She had been dead for several hours and rigor mortis had set in. He climbed into the room and unlocked the door from the inside and went downstairs to call an ambulance.

CHAPTER FORTY-THREE

THE plane with Judy Garland's body in the cargo section and Mickey Deans above it, in the first-class compartment, touched down at Kennedy Airport just past midnight on the twenty-sixth of June, 1969. Deans was wearing sunglasses and a dark suit. He looked tired and pale. He stood to the side with the Reverend Peter Delaney, who had accompanied him from London, and watched the cargo handlers slide the plain brown coffin, wrapped in burlap and tied with heavy cord, onto a cargo lift and into a waiting gray hearse.

Deans turned away and the two men strode across the field, making their way through the thirty or forty newsmen who had stood vigil during the humid New York summer night. Liza greeted them, wearing a floppy dark hat, much like the hats her mother had designed and worn, looking incredibly like her in it. She was accompanied by Kay Thompson.

'I think,' Liza told the army of newsmen, 'she [her mother] was just tired like a flower that blooms and gives joy to the world, then wilts away.'

Plans for the funeral were immediately set in motion. Calls went out to Gene Hills, Judy's old makeup man from MGM days, and to the young man from Kenneth's who did her hair whenever she was in New York. But Gene Hills was currently doing Eva Gabor's makeup for the television show *Green Acres*, and Eva said she could not spare his services; and the stylist from Kenneth's refused the assignment. A white coffin had been ordered, but the funeral home said it didn't have one.

'Well,' Kay Thompson told the funeral director, 'MGM would grab a can of white paint and paint it.' The man looked at her with a bit of shock, but he agreed, and a mahogany coffin was brought in and spray-painted white.

Campbell's Funeral Home, on Madison Avenue at Eighty-first Street, had been selected and a private one P.M. service for personal friends already arranged. The gathering would be stellar: Mickey Rooney, Ray Bolger, Lauren Bacall, Jack Benny, Sammy Davis, Jr., Cary Grant, Katharine Hepburn, Burt Lancaster, Dean Martin, Lana Turner Freddie Bartholomew, Alan King, Otto Preminger, Mayor Lindsay, and Spyros Skouras, among others.

The funeral accouterments were to be in yellow and white, so that everything would be as cheerful as possible, and Liza had requested that those invited for the private service not wear black. A blanket of yellow roses was ordered to drape the coffin, and there was to be a backdrop of yellow and white mums.

By the time the first mourners were allowed in, Judy was dressed in the dark gray crepe gown she had worn just six months before, at her first and secret wedding ceremony to Deans in January. Her small hands were sheathed in immaculate white gloves and rested on a white Bible. She wore silver slippers and a silver brocaded belt decorated with pearls. She rested on light blue velvet, and the sprayed-white coffin now had a glass top.

More than twenty-two thousand persons filed past her coffin. Outside, thousands more stood behind barriers, cheering each star who arrived. The fans were grouped together around portable tape recorders and phonographs. 'Over the Rainbow' segued from one group to the next. As Alan King arrived, he saw an emotionally distracted Mickey Rooney running up the street, away from the funeral home. The guests had been told to be there promptly by one. At one sharp the doors closed. King leaned forward to say something to Liza, who sat two rows in front of him, wearing a blue wool suit and a black velvet cardinal's hat in spite of the broiling heat.

'This is the first time that your mom was ever on time for a performance,' he quipped.

Liza managed a broken smile.

Loudspeakers had been set up outside the chapel, and the easily recognizable, deep-timbred voice of James Mason, who had flown in from Geneva for the funeral, filled the area from Eightieth to Eighty-second Street and from Fifth Avenue to Park Avenue.

'The thing about Judy Garland was that she was so alive. You close your eyes and you see a small vivid woman, sometimes fat, sometimes thin, but vivid. Vitality ... that's what our Judy had.'

And then he quoted Liza: 'It was her love of life that carried her through everything. The middle of the road was never for her. It bored her. She wanted the pinnacle of excitement. If she was happy, she wasn't just happy. She was ecstatic. And when she was sad she was sadder than anyone.'

The Reverend Peter Delaney read from I Corinthians, Chapter 13, Verses 1–13, which began:

'If I speak with the tongues of men and of angels, but have not love, I am become sounding brass, or a clanging cymbal. And if I have the gift of prophecy, and I know all mystery and all knowledge, and if I have all faith, so as to remove mountains, but have not love . . .' It was, according to Deans, Judy's favorite verse.

Then one of her former accompanists played 'Here's to Us' – an innocuous Cy Coleman–Carolyn Leigh song that Deans said had been *their* song.

Luft – none of the other ex-husbands attended – sat flanked by Lorna and Joey, all three joining the singing as the congregation concluded the service with a rising chorus of 'The Battle Hymn of the Republic.'

A hush fell over the thousands of fans outside as the coffin was carried to the waiting maroon hearse. A flower truck filled with more than one hundred floral remembrances idled behind it.

Judy was on her way to Ferncliff Cemetery, in Westchester County, for burial.

The previous day, Deans had gone out to Ferncliff. He had been the pivotal force in selecting a New York site. (Luft had wanted her buried on the West Coast, where he and the younger children lived.) Deans had had no sleep that night and was looking distraught. Frank Angerole, Ferncliff's director, was impressed by the grief he displayed.

All of Ferncliff is dominated by a massive white building – the Mausoleum, which also houses the main offices. Entering the building is like entering a giant crypt. It has an Egyptian-tomb quality. Over the massive doors is one ugly, neorealistic pastoral scene in stained glass. The walls are white imported marble; the crypts, constructed like drawers in a police morgue, labeled like files for the dead.

The director's office has no windows. It is wood-paneled, and the desk is very impressive. On the walls, hunting dogs are poised in stark frames and a tape of funereal music, in a constant major key, is repeated over and over again.

'Your wife,' Angerole assured Deans, 'will be the star of Ferncliff. Jerome Kern rests here, and Moss Hart, Basil Rathbone, and Elsa Maxwell; but your wife will be our only star.'

Angerole had shown Deans a special prototype niche, the most expensive accommodation at Ferncliff. Crypts were

310

$2,500, the niche $37,500. Deans agreed to the latter. It seemed to him the only possible reservation one could make for a star.

A niche would not be ready until the new wing was completed in six months' time. That gave Deans time to raise the money. Personally insolvent, he felt friends, family, and fans would rally to such a 'cause'. In the meantime, it was agreed that Judy would be held in a temporary crypt until final arrangements – the payment of $37,500 to Ferncliff – were concluded.

Only a small group and the flower truck accompanied Judy there. They were taken directly to the Chapel of the Lilies. The room is simple and stark. A grape-carved altar in sweet-smelling wood dominates the room. There are no windows in this room either.

Judy was placed in the temporary crypt – a file drawer, really – its label not yet in place. She remained there over a year, from June 28, 1969, until November 4, 1970, when she was moved to her final resting place. Liza, taking over the arrangements from Deans, had seen to it that her mother was buried in dignity and without seeking aid from strangers.

The crypt selected was in the new wing, the one truly lovely section of the mausoleum building dominated by a huge glass window with trees beyond. It almost turns your heart when you come upon it, for it is like leaving a dead theater and entering a world of the light and the living.

Appendices

FILMS OF JUDY GARLAND

DIRECTOR	FILM	YEAR	STUDIO	CO-STARS
	La Fiesta de Santa Barbara	1934/5	MGM	All-Star
Felix Feist	*Every Sunday*	1936	MGM	Deanna Durbin
David Butler	*Pigskin Parade*	1936	20th	Stuart Erwin
Roy del Ruth	*Broadway Melody of 1938*	1937	MGM	Robert Taylor Sophie Tucker
Alfred E. Green	*Thoroughbreds Don't Cry*	1937	MGM	Mickey Rooney Sophie Tucker
Edwin L. Marin	*Listen, Darling*	1938	MGM	Freddie Bartholomew Mary Astor
Edwin L. Marin	*Everybody Sing*	1938	MGM	Fanny Brice Allan Jones
George B. Seitz	*Love Finds Andy Hardy*	1938	MGM	Mickey Rooney Lana Turner
Victor Fleming	*The Wizard of Oz*	1939	MGM	Frank Morgan Ray Bolger Bert Lahr Jack Haley
Busby Berkeley	*Babes in Arms*	1939	MGM	Mickey Rooney Charles Winninger
George B. Seitz	*Andy Hardy Meets a Debutante*	1940	MGM	Mickey Rooney Lewis Stone
Busby Berkeley	*Strike Up the Band*	1940	MGM	Mickey Rooney Paul Whiteman
Norman Taurog	*Little Nellie Kelly*	1940	MGM	George Murphy Charles Winninger
Robert Z. Leonard	*Zeigfeld Girl*	1941	MGM	Hedy Lamarr Lana Turner
George B. Seitz	*Life Begins for Andy Hardy*	1941	MGM	Mickey Rooney Lewis Stone
Busby Berkeley	*Babes on Broadway*	1941	MGM	Mickey Rooney

Robert Z. Leonard	*We Must Have Music*	1942	MGM	Short Documentary Excerpt – *Ziegfeld Girl* Music Dept.
Busby Berkeley	*For Me and My Gal*	1942	MGM	George Murphy Gene Kelly
Norman Taurog	*Presenting Lily Mars*	1943	MGM	Van Heflin
Norman Taurog	*Girl Crazy*	1943	MGM	Mickey Rooney June Allyson
George Sidney	*As Thousands Cheer*	1943	MGM	All-Star Gene Kelly Mickey Rooney
Vincente Minnelli	*Meet Me in St. Louis*	1944	MGM	Margaret O'Brien Tom Drake
Vincente Minnelli	*The Clock*	1945	MGM	Robert Walker
George Sidney	*The Harvey Girls*	1946	MGM	John Hodiak Angela Lansbury
Vincente Minnelli	*Ziegfeld Follies of 1946*	1946	MGM	All-Star Fred Astaire Gene Kelly
Richard Whorf	*Till the Clouds Roll By*	1946	MGM	All-Star Frank Sinatra Robert Walker
Vincente Minnelli	*The Pirate*	1948	MGM	Gene Kelly
Charles Walters	*Easter Parade*	1948	MGM	Fred Astaire
Norman Taurog	*Words and Music*	1948	MGM	All-Star Tom Drake Gene Kelly Mickey Rooney
Robert Z. Leonard	*In the Good Old Summertime*	1948	MGM	Van Johnson
Charles Walters	*Summer Stock* (British title: *If You Feel Like Singing*)	1950	MGM	Gene Kelly
George Cukor	*A Star Is Born*	1954	Warner Bros.	James Mason
George Sidney	*Pepe*	1960	Columbia	All-Star (Judy sang but was not seen)
Stanley Kramer	*Judgment at Nuremberg*	1961	UA	All-Star Spencer Tracy Marlene Dietrich Burt Lancaster

Abe Leviton	*Gay Purr-ee*	1962	Warner Bros.	Animated (Judy was voice of 'Mewsette,' the cat)
John Cassavetes	*A Child Is Waiting*	1962	UA	Burt Lancaster
Ronald Neames	*I Could Go On Singing* (Also called *The Lonely Stage*)	1962	UA	Dirk Bogarde

RECORDS OF JUDY GARLAND

SINGLES

Swing Mr. Charlie/Stomping at the Savoy	Decca 848 (78)	1936
Everybody Sing	Decca 1332 (78)	1937
All God's Chillun Got Rhythm/ Everybody Sing	Decca 1432 (78)	1937
(Dear Mr. Gable) You Made Me Love You/You Can't Have Everything	Decca 1463 (78)	1937
Cry, Baby, Cry/Sleep, My Baby, Sleep	Decca 1796 (78)	1938
It Never Rains But It Pours/Ten Pins in the Sky	Decca 2017 (78)	1938
	Brunswick 02656 (78)	1938
Over the Rainbow/The Jitterbug	Decca 2672 (78)	1939
Over the Rainbow/Dear Mr Gable	MGM-KGC 166 (45)	1939
	Decca 2-3962 (78)	1939
	Decca 9-23961 (45)	1939
Embraceable You/Swanee	Decca 2881 (78)	1939
Zing! Went the Strings of My Heart/ Fascinatin' Rhythm	Decca 18543 (78)	1939
In Between/ Sweet Sixteen	Decca 15045 (78)	1939
	Decca 29233 (78)	1939
	Decca 9-40219 (45)	1939
Oceans Apart/Figaro	Brunswick 2953 (78) (U.K.)	1939
Friendship (w/Johnny Mercer)/ Wearing of the Green	Decca 3/65 (78)	1940
Buds Won't Bud /I'm Nobody's Baby	Decca 3174 (78)	1940
The End of the Rainbow	Decca 3231 (78)	1940
Our Love Affair/I'm Always Chasing Rainbows	Decca 3593 (78)	1940
It's a Great Day for the Irish/ A Pretty Girl	Decca 3604 (78)	1940
	Decca 25043 (78)	1940
	Decca 9-25043 (45)	1940
The Birthday of a King/Star of the East	Decca 4050 (78)	1940
	Decca 23658 (78)	1940
	Decca 9-2368 (45)	1940
How About You?/F.D.R. Jones	Decca 4072 (78)	1941
Blues in the Night	Decca 4081 (78)	1941
Poor You/Last Call for Love	Decca 18320 (78)	1941
For Me and My Gal/When You Wore a Tulip (w/Gene Kelly)	Decca 18480 (78)	1942
	Decca 9-25115 (45)	1942
	Decca 25115 (78)	1942

I Never Knew/On the Sunny Side of the Street	Decca 18524 (78)	1942
That Old Black Magic /Poor Little Rich Girl	Decca 18540 (78)	1942
Embraceable You/Could You Use Me?	Decca 23303 (78)	1943
But Not for Me	Decca 23309 (78)	1943
Over the Rainbow/I May Be Wrong	V-Disc 335A (78)	1943
Bidin' My Time/I've Got Rhythm	Decca 23310 (78)	1943
No Love, No Nothin'/A Journey to a Star	Decca 18484 (78)	1943
Meet Me in St. Louis/Skip to My Lou	Decca 23360 (78)	1944
The Trolley Song/Boys and Girls Like You and Me	Decca 23361 (78)	1944
Have Yourself a Merry Little Christmas/ The Boy Next Door	Decca 23362 (78)	1944
The Trolley Song/Meet Me in St. Louis	Decca 25494 (78)	1944
	Decca 9-25494 (45)	1944
Yah-ta-ta/You've Got Me Where You Want Me (w/Bing Crosby)	Decca 23410 (78)	1945
Connecticut/Mine (w/Bing Crosby)	Decca 23804 (78)	1945
If I Had You/On the Atchison, Topeka and the Sante Fe (w/The Merry Macs)	Decca 23436 (78)	1945
Have Yourself a Merry Little Christmas/ You'll Never Walk Alone	Decca 9-29295 (45)	1945
The Boy Next Door/Smilin' Through	Decca 9-29296 (45)	1945
This Heart of Mine/Love	Decca 18660 (78)	1945
Smilin' Through/You'll Never Walk Alone	Decca 23539 (78)	1945
	Decca 9-23539 (45)	1945
In the Valley/When the Evening Sun Comes Down	Decca 23438 (78)	1945
Round and Round	Decca 23459 (78)	1945
It's a Great Big World (w/Virginia O'Brien)	Decca 23460 (78)	1945
For You, For Me, Forevermore/Aren't You Kinda' Glad We Did? (w/Dick Haymes)	Decca 23687 (78)	1946
Changing My Tune	Decca 23688 (78)	1946
There Is No Breeze/Don't Tell Me That Story	Decca 23746 (78)	1946
I Wish I Were in Love Again/Nothing But You	Decca 24469 (78)	1946
Look for the Silver Lining	MGM 30002 (78)	1946
Who?	MGM 30003 (78)	1946
Look for the Silver Lining	MGM 30431 (78)	1946
	MGM (X-45) 30212	1946
Be a Clown	MGM 30097 (78)	1948
Love of My Life/You Can Do No Wrong	MGM 30098 (78)	1948
Mack the Black	MGM 30099 (78)	1948
Johnny One Note/I Wish I Were in Love Again	MGM 30172 (78)	1948
Easter Parade/A Fella with an Umbrella (w/Peter Lawford)	MGM 30185 (78)	1948
A Couple of Swells/Medley (w/Fred Astaire)	MGM 30186 (78)	1948

Better Luck Next Time	MGM 30187 (78)	1948
Put Your Arms Around Me, Honey/ Meet Me Tonight in Dreamland	MGM 50025 (78)	1949
Play That Barbershop Chord/I Don't Care	MGM 50026 (78)	1949
Merry Christmas	MGM 30212 (78)	1949
Happy Harvest/If You Feel Like Singing	MGM 3025 (78)	1950
Friendly Star/Get Happy	MGM 30254 (78)	1950
	MGM (X-45) 30254	1950
Send My Baby Back to Me/Without a Memory	Columbia 40010 (78)	1954
Go Home, Joe/Heartbroken	Columbia 40023 (78)	1954
The Man That Got Away/Here's What I'm Here For	Columbia 40270 (78)	1954
Maybe I'll Come Back/Over the Rainbow	Capitol 6128 (45)	1955–56
It's Lovely to Be Back Again in London/ By Myself	EMI-CL 14791 (45) (U.K.)	1957
Zing! Went the Strings of My Heart/ Rockabye My Baby	Capitol 4624 (45)	1961
San Francisco/Chicago	Capitol 6125 (45)	1961
The Man That Got Away	Capitol 6126 (45)	1961
Swanee/That's Entertainment	Capitol 6129 (45)	1961
Come Rain or Come Shine/Rockabye My Baby	Capitol 6127 (45)	1961
Little Drops of Rain/Paris Is a Lovely Town	Warner Bros. 5310 (45)	1962
Comes Once in a Lifetime/Sweet Danger	Capitol 4656 (45)	1962
Hello Bluebird/I Could Go On Singing	Capitol 4938 (45)	1962
Hello, Dolly/He's Got the Whole World in His Hands (w/Liza Minnelli)	Capitol 5497 (45)	1964

ALBUMS

Miss Show Business	Capitol EDM 676 (45)
	Capitol w/DW 676 (33⅓)
Judy	Capitol EAP 374 (45)
	Capitol EAP 734-1 (45)
	Capitol EAP 734-2 (45)
	Capitol EAP 734-3 (45)
	Capitol T/DT 734 (33⅓)
	Capitol LCT 6121 (33⅓) (U.K.)
Alone	Capitol EAP 835 (45)
	Capitol EAP 834-1 (45)
	Capitol EAP 834-2 (45)
	Capitol EAP 834-3 (45)
	Capitol T/DT 835 (33⅓)
Judy in Love	Capitol EAP 1636 (45)
	Capitol EAP 1636-1 (45)
	Capitol EAP 1636-2 (45)
	Capitol EAP 1636-3 (45)
	Capitol T/ST 1036 (33⅓)
Judy at Carnegie Hall	Capitol EAP 1569 (45)
	Capitol WBO/SWBO 1569 (33⅓)

Garland At the Grove	Capitol T/ST 1118 (33⅓)
The Letter	Capitol TAO 1188 (33⅓)
	Capitol T/ST 1188 (33⅓) (U.K.)
Judy, That's Entertainment	Capitol T/ST 1467 (33⅓)
	Capitol SLER 6528
The Garland Touch	Capitol w/WS 1710 (33⅓)
You'll Never Walk Alone	World Record Club T/ST 675
(Same album as above)	(33⅓) (U.K.)
The Hits of Judy Garland	Capitol T/ST 1999 (33⅓)
I Could Go On Singing	Capitol W/WS 1861 (33⅓)
Just for Openers	Capitol W/WD 2062 (33⅓)
Judy Garland and Liza Minnelli, Live at the Palladium	Capitol EWBO/SWBO 2295 (33⅓)
The Judy Garland Deluxe Set	Capitol STCL 2988 (33⅓)
I Feel a Song Coming On	Pickwick PC 3053 (33⅓)
By Myself	Sears Roebuck SP 430 (33⅓)
(as above)	
Judy Garland Over the Rainbow	Pickwick PC 3078 (33⅓)
Judy Garland – Her Greatest Hits	Pickwick PC 2010 (33⅓)
Judy in London	Capitol 94407 (33⅓)
Judy Garland – Liza Minnelli: Live at the London Palladium	Capitol ST 11191 (33⅓) (an abbreviated re-recording of Capitol WBO/SWBO 2295)
Our Love Letter	Capitol T/ST 1941
Judy Garland	Capitol LSY 5217
Los Hitos Del Hit Parade, Vol. 8	Capitol ST 20994
Greatest Hits of the 30's & 40's	Capitol ST 23032/49
World's Best Love Songs	Capitol ST 23090
Collector's Best – Ten Legendary Song Stylists	Capitol SL 6706
The Greatest Hits of the 30's	Capitol SL 6716
Greatest Artists of our Time – Dinah Shore /Judy Garland	Capitol SL 6752
The Stereo Collector's Set, Vol. 7	Capitol SL 6603
The Best of the Great Song Stylists	Capitol 4XL 6617
The Stereo Collector's Set, Vol. 2 – Broadway & Hollywood Show Stoppers	Capitol 4XL 6612
Showstoppers	Capitol SL 6524
Broadway & Hollywood Show-stoppers	Capitol 4XL 6591
Popular Gold Album	Capitol T 972
More Stars in Stereo	Capitol SW 1162
Hits of Judy Garland	Capitol SY/8XY 4605
A Star Is Born	Columbia BM 1201 (78)
	Columbia BA 1201 (45)
Judy Garland	Columbia B 2598 (45)
A Star Is Born/House Party	Columbia CL 6299 (33⅓)
A Star Is Born	Columbia BL 1201 (33⅓)
	Phillips BBL 7007 (33⅓) (U.K.)
	CBS Realm RM/RMS 5206 (33⅓) (U.K.)

	Hallmark SHM 654 (33⅓)
	Columbia CL 1101/CS 8740 (33⅓)
	Columbia Harmony HS 11366 (33⅓)
Pepe	Colpix CP/CPS 507 (33⅓)
	Pye International NPL 28015 (U.K.) (33⅓)
The Wizard of Oz	Decca A 74 (78)
The Judy Garland Souvenir Album	Decca A 76 (78)
George Gershwin Songs, Vol. II	Decca A 97 (78)
The Judy Garland Second Souvenir Album	Decca A 349 (78)
Girl Crazy (w/Mickey Rooney)	Decca A 362 (78)
Meet Me in St. Louis	Decca A 380 (78)
The Harvey Girls	Decca A 388 (78)
The Judy Garland Third Souvenir Album	Decca A 671 (78)
Judy Garland Sings (w/Dick Haymes & Gene Kelly)	Decca A 682 (78)
Judy at the Palace	Decca A 899 (78)
	Decca 9-287 (45)
	Decca ED 620 (45)
Girl Crazy	Decca ED 2020 (45)
Judy Garland, Vol. II	Decca ED 2050 (45)
The Magic of Judy Garland	Decca DL 4199 (33⅓)
	Ace of Hearts AH 128 (33⅓) (U.K.)
Girl Crazy (w/Mickey Rooney)	Decca DL 5412 (33⅓)
Judy at the Palace	Decca DL 6020 (33⅓)
Judy Garland – Greatest Performances	Decca DL 8190 (33⅓)
	Ace of Hearts 121 (33⅓) (U.K.)
Selections from The Harvey Girls/ Meet Me in St. Louis	Decca DL 8498 (33⅓)
The Best of Judy Garland	Decca ×B 172/D ×SB 7172 (33⅓)
	MCA 24003 (33⅓)
Judy Garland's Greatest Hits	Decca 75150 (33⅓)
Collector's Items (1936–45)	Decca DEA 7 5 (33⅓)
	Coral CP 53 & CP 54 (33⅓) (U.K.)
Miss Show Biz	Brunswick AH 48 (33⅓) (U.K.)
A Garland for Judy	Capitol EAP 20051 (45)
Maggie May	Capitol CL 14791 (45)
Judy. London 1969	Juno S 1000 (33⅓)
	Sunset Records 50196 (33⅓) (U.K.)
The Immortal Judy Garland	Longines SY 5217, 218, 219, 220, 221 (33⅓)
I Could Go On Singing Forever	Longines SY 5222 (33⅓)
Judy Garland in Concert – San Francisco	Mark 56 Records 632 (33⅓)
Frances Ethel Gumm-Harry Lillis Crosby	Legend WM 1973 (33⅓)
Judy Garland – 'Drive In' (drama)	Command Performances Record

Till the Clouds Roll By	MGM-MI (78)
	MGM-XI (45)
	MGM E 501 (33⅓)
The Pirate	MGM M 21 (78)
	MGM-X21 (45)
	MGM E 21 (33⅓)
Words and Music	MGM M 37 (78)
	MGM X 37 (45)
	MGM E 505 (33⅓)
Easter Parade	MGM M 40 (78)
	MGM X 40 (45)
	MGM E 502 (33⅓)
In the Good Old Summertime	MGM L 11 (78)
Summer Stock	MGM M 54 (78)
	MGM X 56 (45)
	MGM E 519 (33⅓)
Merry Christmas	MGM M 169 (78)
	MGM M 169 (33⅓)
Judy Garland	MGM X 268 (45)
Get Happy	MGM X 1038 (45)
Look for the Silver Lining	MGM X 1116 (45)
The Wizard of Oz	MGM X 3464 ST (45)
Judy Garland Sings	MGM E 82 (33⅓)
Till the Clouds Roll By/Gentlemen Prefer Blondes	MGM E 3231 (33⅓)
The Pirate/Summer Stock	MGM E 3234 (33⅓)
The Pirate/Les Girls	MGM C 763 (33⅓) (U.K.)
Easter Parade/Annie Get Your Gun	MGM E 3227 (33⅓)
In the Good Old Summertime/An American in Paris	MGM E 3232 (33⅓)
Judy Garland	MGM 3149 (33⅓)
The Wizard of Oz	MGM E 3464ST (33⅓)
The Judy Garland Story – The Star Years	MGM E 3989 P (33⅓)
	MGM C 886 (33⅓) (U.K.)
The Judy Garland Story, Vol. II – *The Hollywood Years*	MGM E 4005 P (33⅓)
	MGM C 887 (33⅓)
Magnificent Moments from MGM Movies	MGM E 4017 (33⅓)
The Very Best of Motion Picture Musicals	MGM E/SE 4171 (33⅓)
The Very Best of Judy Garland	MGM E/SE 4204 (33⅓)
The Wizard of Oz	MGM E 3996 (33⅓)
Judy Garland	MGM M/MS 505 (33⅓)
Judy Garland in Song	MGM M/MS 581 (33⅓)
Judy Garland – The Golden Archive Series	MGM GAS 113 (33⅓)
Judy Garland – The Golden Years at MGM	MGM SYPL 2 (33⅓)
Forever Judy	MGM PX 102 (33⅓)
The Wizard of Oz	MGM PX 104 (33⅓)
Easter Parade/Singing in the Rain	MGM 2 SES 40 (33⅓)
The Pirate/Hit the Deck/Pagan Love Song	MGM 2 SES 43 (33⅓)
Born to Sing	MGM D 134 (33⅓) (U.K.)
The Wizard of Oz	MGM 2353044 (33⅓) (U.K.)
The Pirate/Easter Parade	MGM 23530 (33⅓) (U.K.)

Judy Garland – The Hollywood Years	MGM 2683005 (33⅓) (U.K.)
Judy Garland – The Star Years	Music for Pleasure MFP 1003 (33⅓) (U.K.)
Over the Rainbow with Judy Garland	Music for Pleasure MFP 1237 (33⅓)
Judy Garland at Home at the Palace	Paramount-ABC/ABCS 620 (33⅓)
Judy	Radiant 711-0101 (33⅓)
Judy in Hollywood	Radiant 711-0102 (33⅓)
Judy – The Legend	Radiant 711-0103 (33⅓)
Judy's Portrait in Song	Radiant 711-0104 (33⅓)
The Unforgettable Judy Garland	Radiant 711-0105 (33⅓)
Hollywood on the Air	Radiola 3 and 4 (33⅓)
Judy Garland (1935–1959)	Hartone ST 201 (33⅓)
The Judy Garland Musical Scrapbook (1935–1949)	Hartone ST 208 (33⅓)
Judy Garland in Annie Get Your Gun	Sound/Stage 2302 (33⅓)
Judy: All Alone	Tucker TLP 201 (33⅓)
Three Billion Millionaires	United Artists Y & S 54 YXL4 (33⅓)
Gay Purr-ee	Warner Bros. B/BS 1479 (33⅓)
	Warner Bros. W/WS 802 (33⅓) (U.K.)

TELEVISION APPEARANCES

DIRECTOR	SHOW	DATE	CO-STARS
Norman Jewison	*The Ford Star Jubilee*	1955	
Norman Jewison	*The Judy Garland Show*	2/25/62	Frank Sinatra
			Dean Martin
Bill Hobin	*The Judy Garland Show*	9/29/63	Donald O'Connor
(Series Director)	(Premiere)	10/6/63	Smothers Bros.
			Barbra Streisand
			Ethel Merman
		10/13/63	Terry Thomas
			Lena Horne
		10/20/63	George Maharis
			Jack Carter
		10/27/63	June Allyson
			Steve Lawrence
		11/3/63	Vic Damone
			George Jessel
		11/10/63	Count Basie
			Mel Tormé
		11/17/63	Liza Minnelli

(11/24/63 was preempted because of the assassination of President Kennedy)

		DATE	CO-STARS
		12/1/63	Peggy Lee
		12/8/63	Mickey Rooney
		12/15/63	Tony Bennett
			Steve Allen
		12/22/63	Jack Jones
			Lorna,
			Joey Luft
		12/29/63	Bobby Darin
			Bob Newhart
		1/5/64	Steve Allen
			Jayne Meadows
		1/12/64	Ethel Merman
			Shelley Berman
		1/19/64	Vic Damone
			Ken Murray
		1/26/64	Martha Raye
			Peter Lawford
		2/2/64	Louis Jourdan
			Ken Murray

		2/9/64	Judy in Concert
		2/16/64	Diahann Carroll
			Mel Tormé
		2/23/64	Jack Jones
			Ken Murray
		3/1/64	Ray Bolger
			Jane Powell
		3/8/64	Judy in Concert
		3/15/64	Vic Damone
		3/22/64	Bobby Cole
		3/29/64	Judy in Concert
Stan Harris	*On Broadway Tonight*	2/5/65	Rudy Vallee
			Christopher and
			Peter Allen
	The Jack Paar Show	1968	
	The Johnny Carson Show	1968	
	The Mero Griffin Show	1968	
	Sunday Night at the Palladium	1969 (London)	

RADIO APPEARANCES

The Bob Hope Show   3/7/39
      5/9/39
      9/26/39–5/14/40 (Judy was a weekly guest
                           during these weeks)
      12/24/40
      1/30/51

Silver Theatre   1939–1942 (exact dates unknown)

Lux Radio Theatre

Strike Up the Band	10/28/40
Merton of the Movies	11/17/41
Morning Glory	10/12/42
A Star Is Born	12/28/42
The Clock	1/28/46
Meet Me in St. Louis	12/2/46
The Wizard of Oz	12/25/50
Lady in the Dark	2/16/53

(The Lux Radio Theatre programs have been transcribed on tape and donated to the Academy of Motion Picture Arts and Sciences)

THE MAIN CONCERTS

(There were well over 100 concerts; the following are among Miss Garland's
most famous)

The Palladium   4/14–5/12/51
                                                 6/25/51
                                                 11/18/54
                                                 8/28/60
                                                 9/4/60
                                                 12/1/60
                                                 7/23/64
                                                 11/8/64
                                                 11/16/64
The Palace (first appearance) 10/16/51
The Los Angeles Philharmonic 4/26/52
The Curran (San Francisco) 6/4/52
The Palace (second appearance) 9/26/56
The Metropolitan Opera House 5/11/59
Carnegie Hall 4/23/61
At Home at the Palace (third appearance) 8/18/67
Garden State Arts Center 6/25–6/29/68

EARLY VAUDEVILLE

The Meglin Kiddies Circuit (West Coast)

The Chicago World's Fair

Keith-Orpheum Circuit (West Coast)

ACKNOWLEDGMENTS

This book would never have been written without the co-operation and assistance of many individuals. Over a time span of several years I have, in the book's behalf, corresponded with well over a hundred such individuals and conducted probably as many interviews. My gratitude to all, but especially I would like to thank (in no particular order of contribution): John Milne, Sr. (Judy's uncle); Dr. James Milne, Jr. (Judy's cousin); Frank Milne (Judy's uncle); Mrs. F. Hessevick (Judy's aunt); Mrs. Irene Mathias (Judy's cousin); Al Rosen; Joe Pasternak; Fred Astaire; Gene Kelly; Tom Drake; Mrs. Etta Berkeley; Busby Berkeley; Abe Lastfogel; Barron Polan; Bobby Cole; Dirk Bogarde; Burt Rhodes; Vivian Martyne; Tony Hatch; Jackie Trent; Bryan Southcombe and Matthew West; Judith Heard; Phillip Roberge; I. Blicher-Hansen; Hans Vangkilde; Mrs. Grethe Vangkilde; Hans Jorgen Eriksen; Telle Saaek; Mickey Deans; Robert Jorgen; Leonard Gershe; Victor Angerole; Ed Baily; William Prendergrast; Noel Coward (who was helpful when I was his neighbor in Switzerland); Geoffrey Johnson (Mr. Coward's secretary); Mrs. Beatrice 'Bumbles' Dawson; Lloyd F. Hawe (Capitol Records); Alan King; Norman Mailer; Gerald Griffin (Curator of Museum of City of New York); Ms. Mary MacDonald (once head of the MGM school); Ms. Lorna Smith; E. Schwenter (former manager of the Ritz); Dr. Richard Grundy (of the Carson City Medical Group); Ms. Margaret Hamilton; Frank Bromber (former manager of the Stanhope Hotel); Charlotte Mayerson; Emil Abdelnour; G. A. Grahame (General Manager of the Ritz); John Francis; William Ludwig; Joseph Ruttenberg; Jerome Londin; George Eldridge;

Joseph Dempsey; Glyn Jones; Jens Lyngby Jepsen; Mary McCarthy; Robert Blake; Harry Fredericks (Westinghouse Group W); Mrs. Bonnie Boyer (Superior Health Dept.); Ms. Leonore Terry (ASCAP); the staffs of the Academy of Motion Picture Arts and Sciences, the Lincoln Center Library of Performing Arts, the Stockbridge Library, the New York Public Library, the Bettmann Archive, the Palace Theatre, Time-Life; Ms. Anne Abel Smith of A. P. Watt, Ltd.; Ms. Susan Scott of the BBC; expert researchers Joan Saunders in London, Jay Schlein in Hollywood, and Eleanor Wolquitt in New York; Mrs. Martha Winston; Leon Becker; Harold Schiff; Walter Scott; Howard Shultsinger; Vivian Bell (William Morris Agency); Mrs. Helen Prince (Time-Life); Rachel Fleischman; Gene Callahan; Ms. Nina Digangi; John Behrendt (B.C.S.); Arthur Klur (souvenir book publishers); and Mr. Richard Twarog.

Special appreciation goes to Ms. Monica McCall; Ms. Jo. Stewart; Hilary Rubinstein; and William Ewald; my fine editor, Ms. Freya Manston, and to my two secretaries, Mrs. Marion Thompson and Mrs. Jessie F. Nielson; typist, Mrs. Lorna Sheldon, and my daughter, Catherine Edwards, who helped me with research.

But two people receive my greatest debt of gratitude: Mr. Steve Citron, whose love, encouragement and patience never flagged during one solid year of the book's writing; and – in deepest humility – Miss Judy Garland, perhaps the greatest entertainer in my generation, or any generation before me.

ANNE EDWARDS

Stockbridge, Massachusetts
1974

Index

INDEX

336

341

342

☐ **Audrey: Her Real Story** £6.99
ALEXANDER WALKER
1 85797 352 6

☐ **The Big Yin: The Life and Times of Billy Connolly** £6.99
JONATHAN MARGOLIS
0 75281 722 1

☐ **Callas** £8.99
ANNE EDWARDS
0 75284 844 5

☐ **Confessions of an Actor** £5.99
LAURENCE OLIVIER
1 85797 493 X

☐ **The Cult of Violence** £6.99
JOHN PEARSON
0 75284 794 5

☐ **Doris Day** £7.99
ERIC BRAUN
0 75281 715 9

☐ **Elizabeth** £7.99
ALEXANDER WALKER
0 75280 579 7

☐ **Himoff!** £6.99
RICHARD WHITELEY
0 75284 345 1

☐ **Ian Fleming** £8.99
ANDREW LYCETT
1 85799 783 2

☐ **Judi Dench: With a Crack in Her Voice** £8.99
JOHN MILLER
0 75284 894 1

☐ **Judy Garland** £6.99
ANNE EDWARDS
0 75280 404 9

☐ **Katharine Hepburn** £6.99
BARBARA LEAMING
1 85799 440 X

☐ **Kurt Cobain** £6.99
CHRISTOPHER SANDFORD
0 75284 456 3

☐ **Marilyn** £6.99
GLORIA STEINEM
0 75284 372 9

☐ **Mrs Kennedy** £8.99
BARBARA LEAMING
0 75284 929 8

☐ **Orson Welles** £8.99
BARBARA LEAMING
1 85799 092 7

☐ **Streisand** £7.99
ANNE EDWARDS
0 75281 104 5

☐ **True: An Autobiography** £6.99
MARTIN KEMP
0 75283 769 9

☐ **The Unruly Life of Woody Allen** £8.99
MARION MEADE
0 75381 117 0

☐ **Up in the Clouds, Gentlemen Please** £7.99
JOHN MILLS
0 75284 449 0

☐ **Vivien** £6.99
ALEXANDER WALKER
1 85797 927 3

All Orion/Phoenix titles are available at your local bookshop or from the following address:

Mail Order Department
Littlehampton Book Services
FREEPOST BR535
Worthing, West Sussex, BN13 3BR
telephone 01903 828503, *facsimile* 01903 828802
e-mail MailOrders@lbsltd.co.uk
(Please ensure that you include full postal address details)

Payment can be made either by credit/debit card (Visa, Mastercard, Access and Switch accepted) or by sending a £ Sterling cheque or postal order made payable to *Littlehampton Book Services*.
DO NOT SEND CASH OR CURRENCY.

Please add the following to cover postage and packing

UK and BFPO:
£1.50 for the first book, and 50p for each additional book to a maximum of £3.50

Overseas and Eire:
£2.50 for the first book plus £1.00 for the second book and 50p for each additional book ordered

---

BLOCK CAPITALS PLEASE

name of cardholder ....

address of cardholder ....

....

postcode ....

delivery address
(if different from cardholder)

....

....

....

postcode ....

☐ I enclose my remittance for £ ....

☐ please debit my Mastercard/Visa/Access/Switch (delete as appropriate)

card number ☐☐☐☐ ☐☐☐☐ ☐☐☐☐ ☐☐☐☐

expiry date ☐☐☐☐   Switch issue no. ☐☐

signature ....

prices and availability are subject to change without notice